CONTENTS

PREFACE

This book covers the material that is typically included in an introductory course on social statistics for sociology students. We have used it both as the basis of a course for first- and second-year undergraduates and, at a much faster pace, for a one-semester course for masters' students in social research.

Why another book on social statistics? Partly because statistics is an ever advancing discipline. Social statisticians find new ways of understanding data and new ways of explaining statistical concepts. Partly because, although there are some excellent general social statistics texts, we felt that none of them had quite the right tone or coverage for sociology students.

In this book, we start from the assumption that most students will have done little or no previous work in statistics and that many will not have done any formal mathematics of any kind for several years. This is not to say that students come entirely ignorant of the kinds of analysis we cover in this book: many of the techniques that we describe in the early chapters are used in newspapers, in TV programmes and in other sociology textbooks. Nevertheless, most readers will find this the first time that they have had to consider statistics in a systematic way.

Both the authors are sociologists and not surprisingly, therefore, the focus of the book is on statistical tools that are valuable for sociologists, especially when dealing with the large amounts of data that are typically collected in social surveys. To provide a sociological theme, most of the examples have been chosen to relate in some way to the position of women in UK society. There are many illustrations and examples of analyses because we believe that it is only through examples that students will find that the ideas and methods of statistics come alive.

Nearly all the analyses we demonstrate are based on data from either a subset of the General Household Survey or a set of national indicators of development collected by the World Bank (see Chapter 1 for more information about these data sets). We are grateful to the Office for National Statistics, the World Bank and the Essex Data Archive for enabling us to make these data sets available over the World Wide Web (see Appendix A), so that students and teachers can repeat the examples for themselves using the original data. Each chapter is followed by additional exercises for students, also based on these data sets.

Learning how to use a data analysis computer program is nowadays an integral part of learning social statistics. We have selected SPSS because it is the most widely available statistical analysis package in universities. The text is liberally illustrated with screen shots from version 9 of the Windows edition of SPSS, and we are grateful to SPSS Inc. for granting permission to reproduce them. The advantage of this approach is that students can see immediately what they need to do in order to perform SPSS analyses. One of the disadvantages is

SAGE Publications
London • Thousand Oaks • New Delhi

SAGE Publications Ltd
6 Bonhill Street
London EC2A 4PU

SAGE Publications Inc
2455 Teller Road
Thousand Oaks, California 91320

SAGE Publications India Pvt Ltd
32, M-Block Market
Greater Kailash - 1
New Delhi 110 048

British Library Cataloguing in Publication data

A catalogue record for this book is available from the British
Library
ISBN 0 8039 7982 7
ISBN 0 8039 7983 5 (pbk)

Library of Congress catalog card number 99 075722

Typeset by Keytec Typesetting Ltd, Bridport, Dorset
Printed in Great Britain by The Cromwell Press Ltd, Trowbridge,
Wiltshire

that SPSS itself is constantly changing: when we started writing the book, the current version was version 6.1. Nevertheless, even if the details of what appears on the screen may alter as newer versions appear, we are confident that the principles behind the analyses we describe will remain the same.

The book begins with an introduction to the nature of quantitative data. In Chapter 2, we consider the use of computers to analyse social science data and introduce SPSS. The next chapter considers basic univariate distributions and how SPSS can be used to examine them. Some graphical devices for displaying variables are described in Chapter 4. Chapter 5 introduces the first descriptive statistics: the mean, standard deviation and other measures of central tendency and dispersion. We return to graphical display in Chapter 6, which explains some of the tools of exploratory data analysis.

Chapter 7 prepares the reader for the more complex techniques to come, describing the central role of the normal curve in statistics. This is also the place to consider methods for the transformation of data to yield distributions closer to the normal. Chapter 8 considers correlations between two continuous variables using regression and explains the importance of looking at residuals. Tabular methods for examining bivariate relationships between categorical variables are the subject of Chapter 9. Chapters 10 and 11 are concerned with sampling, inference and testing hypotheses, extending the previous discussion to situations where one wants to draw conclusions about a population from the characteristics of a random sample. Finally, Chapter 12 develops the idea of statistical modelling through introductions to multiple regression and loglinear analysis. A glossary has been included to explain important terms. Appendices list the variables available in the two data sets used in the book and provide the standard tables for the normal, chi square and t distributions.

The book reflects more years of experience teaching social statistics to Surrey sociology students than we care to remember. We are grateful to many cohorts of first-year BSc sociology and MSc social research methods students who unwittingly played guinea pig as our ideas about presenting the material in the book were developed. We are also grateful for the extraordinary patience of Karen Phillips at Sage, who expected a manuscript a year after commissioning it and eventually received it five years later. We also owe a considerable debt of gratitude to our colleagues, both for their direct help and advice (especially Mike Procter and Roger Tarling), and for their contributions to the stimulating and friendly environment of the Department of Sociology at Surrey.

Jane Fielding
Nigel Gilbert
April 1999

PART I

PRELIMINARIES

NUMBERS, DATA AND ANALYSIS   1

CONTENTS

'More women go out to work … Then do chores too', said a *Daily Mirror* headline.[1] To back up the point, it quoted a report from the Office for National Statistics (ONS), a branch of the Civil Service, which showed that 72 per cent of women have jobs (up from 57 per cent in 1971), and that women with full-time jobs spend about two hours a day doing housework, compared with an average of 32 minutes for men. Nevertheless, 62 per cent of couples think that household tasks should be shared equally.

Being at ease with figures and charts is an essential part of becoming a good social scientist. This book is about how to calculate and interpret percentages and other similar statistics. In this introductory chapter, we shall consider where quantitative data come from, how they differ from qualitative data and how quantitative data can be organized and compared.

---

[1] *Daily Mirror*, 22 October, 1998, p. 6.

Throughout the book, we shall be using examples from two social surveys. The General Household Survey (GHS) is run by the ONS and questions a large sample of British households every year. The Social Indicators of Development (SID) data set is collected by the World Bank and consists of data about 171 countries of the world. In this chapter, we shall also briefly introduce these two data sets.

COLLECTING DATA

Most social science data is collected by interviewing people. Sociologists either ask a set of pre-set questions (a structured interview) or conduct an interview which is more like a conversation, often recording the answers on a tape-recorder for later transcription and analysis. In the former case, every respondent is asked essentially the same set of questions and the answers can be quantified relatively easily. A large number of interviews can be carried out quickly. In the latter case, the interviews often last much longer and are much harder to compare with one another. Nevertheless, the insights these qualitative interviews give can be much deeper than those offered by standardized quantitative interviews.

There are other ways of gathering data. You have probably filled out and returned questionnaires which arrived through the post, where you tick boxes according to how you want to answer (a 'mail survey'). This type of data is also easy to quantify. Other social scientists gather data through observation of social settings, or through examining administrative records or documents. In each of these cases, there is a choice about whether to quantify the data – that is, express them in terms of numbers – or leave them in qualitative form, using terms such as 'larger', 'more frequent' and so on, without putting a numerical value on them. Often, a sociologist will want to express some data quantitatively and some qualitatively, because this is best for the topic at hand. Neither quantitative nor qualitative data are intrinsically 'best'. It all depends on what you are trying to achieve. And often a mixture is better than either alone.

Not all sociologists find that they need to collect data themselves. Often it is quicker, cheaper and better to analyse data which have already been collected. For example, if you wanted to find out about the proportion of women who are now working full-time, it would be a waste of time and money to undertake a survey yourself. The job has already been done by the General Household Survey (and by other large government surveys) at considerable expense and with great attention to the accuracy of the data collected. Fortunately, the data can be obtained at little or no cost from a data archive, a type of library which holds data from previous surveys.

Analysing data that were collected for some other reason or by some other organization is called **secondary analysis**, as contrasted with the **primary analysis** which you carry out on data you collect yourself. Secondary analysis as a form of research is increasingly popular as more and more high-quality data sets covering a very wide range of topics become available.

This book is only about the analysis of quantitative data. Analysing qualitative data requires somewhat different techniques and tools and is therefore left to other texts (e.g. Burgess, 1984; Fielding and Lee, 1993; Mason, 1966). It also focuses specifically on the analysis of the data, saying little about how to collect it. Again, other texts will help you with data collection (e.g. de Vaus, 1996; Robson, 1993). Guidance on the overall process of research, of which statistical analysis is but one part, can be found in Gilbert (1993a).

ANALYSIS

The numbers collected from a survey tell you very little by themselves. Sociologists are much more interested in patterns and regularities: the features which are common to groups of people in different contexts and situations. To find these patterns, you need to engage in analysis. For example, the government survey which the *Daily Mirror* quoted from and which we summarized at the beginning of this chapter asked several thousand people throughout Britain about how much time they spent doing domestic tasks. Their actual answers, taken one by one, are not of much interest to a sociologist. But put the answers from all the men and all the women together and it becomes plain that women say that they still do many more of the household chores than men.

Analysis consist partly of constructing generalizations: for example, the generalization that women do more household work than men. Another important element of analysis is explanation. As sociologists, we not only want to know about the social world, but also about why it is like it is. So, for example, we might come to the data believing that UK society remains patriarchal, that is, with men still dominating women. We might therefore not be surprised to find that women are still doing the majority of the housework. Alternatively, we might think that as the proportion of women in employment increases, the distribution of housework in dual-earner couples would tend to equalize and therefore be surprised that it is still so unequal. In either case, we would be approaching the data with a prior theory and then testing that theory against generalizations derived from the data. The data either support or cast doubt on the theory.

INDUCTION AND DEDUCTION

Where does such theory come from? There are two sources: theory can be generated from comparing lots of examples and finding where they have features in common, a process called **induction**. Or theory can come from deriving consequences from a more wide-ranging, 'grander' theory, a process called **deduction**.

For example, suppose that you noticed that among couples you knew, the women were doing a lot more of the cooking and cleaning and men much more of the repairs and decorating, even though the men said that they were in favour of equality in doing domestic chores. You might wonder about this disparity between what your friends say and what they actually do. In a small way you are building a theory by induction. You have made an observation and generalized it. The next step would be to see whether what you observed among your friends is true within a wider circle of people. One of the government social surveys might provide data for this purpose. A national survey could give you information about a cross-section of couples, without the danger that your generalization would be checked only on your own friends.

If you had access to national data you could also **elaborate** your theory to take account of other factors that might affect the division of domestic labour. For example, you could see whether it was as true for young couples as for old, for the rich as well as the poor and for the well educated as well as those with only basic educational qualifications. In this way you could enrich the theory to take account of different factors.

Clearly the theory about the division of domestic labour we have been developing here is not the same kind of thing as the grand theories of classical sociologists such as Marx and Weber. More modest theories which describe small parts of social life are often called **middle-range** theories. Many middle-range theories have been deduced from grander theories. For example, Talcott Parsons (Parsons and Bales, 1956) argued that the family has the function of socialization, educating children in the ways of the society in which they live. In order to carry out this function, the family needs to have the roles of mother and father clearly differentiated, with the mother maintaining the home and the father providing an income. From this grand theoretical statement, we could derive a middle-range theory about the differentiation of household tasks within families. Of course, Parsons's functionalist theory has been much criticized (see, for example, Skidmore, 1979, for a summary) and other theories have emphasized the very unequal division of labour between the sexes and the power relations which help to maintain this (Charles, 1993). Feminist theories of the family can also be used to deduce generalizations that can then be compared with data from surveys.

Deduction and induction are therefore opposite sides of a coin: in carrying out induction, we start with some examples and develop a theory which covers them all. Deduction involves explaining a theory, a generalization, or particular cases with reference to a more overarching theory. Thus, induction is a method for generating theories and deduction for applying them. However, in practice, the two tend to get intertwined: one first develops a theory through induction, then tests it against some data using deduction, finds that the theory is not quite right and amends the theory, tests it again and so on.

Neither induction nor deduction is foolproof as a method of doing social science. A survey sample might not be exactly typical of the wider population and so theories based on it could be misleading. With luck, checking the theories using additional and more representative data sets should reveal this and prevent you from drawing invalid conclusions. It is wise always to be aware a theory could be wrong, even if it seems to be backed by a wide range of data. A good strategy when testing theories is to aim at **falsification**, that is, try to find data which might show the theory to be false. For example, if the domestic division of labour tends to be particularly egalitarian among those who have university-level education, the way to test the theory that men and women have unequal loads within the household is to seek out data about those who are well educated. If the theory is true even for university students, it may be true for all; if it fails for university students then we know at once it cannot be a valid theory for the population as a whole. Falsification can be summed up as a strategy for testing theories which goes for the most difficult cases first.

VARIABLES

VARIABLES AND CASES

A survey consists of the same set of questions asked of a large number of respondents. When the pile of completed questionnaires returns to the survey office, the data need to be put into the computer for analysis. For ease of calculation, survey analysis programs generally assume that the data are numerical. This means that the survey questionnaires (which will show the answers as ticks in boxes, or as written verbatim responses) need to be **coded** to convert the answers into numerical form.

Often, questionnaires are **pre-coded**, with every possible answer to a question assigned a number which is printed on the survey form. An example is the question reproduced in Exhibit 1.1 from the General Household Survey. If there is no answer at all, for example if the question is not relevant to a respondent or no answer was given, there still needs to be a numeric code provided. In this case, a special code is assigned, often 9 or −9, to indicate **missing data**. Chapter 3 describes coding procedures in more detail.

Once coding has been completed, the data can be entered into the computer. To help with keeping the data organized, the numbers are arranged in a regular form called a **data matrix** (or data array). Imagine a grid of rows and columns

```
4.  During the 2 weeks ending              Yes..   1
    yesterday, apart from any visits to
    a hospital, did you talk to a
    doctor for any reason at all,
    either in person or by telephone?
    EXCLUDE CONSULTATIONS MADE ON           No ...   2
    BEHALF OF CHILDREN UNDER 16 AND
    PERSONS OUTSIDE THE HOUSEHOLD
```

Exhibit 1.1   *Question showing pre-coding from the GHS*
Source: ONS, 1995

– one row for each respondent, and one column for each question in the survey. The numeric codes for every answer can be entered in the body of the grid. The grid is like a map: to find the answer code for a particular respondent on a particular question, look along the row for that respondent until you find the column corresponding to that question. Every cell in the grid will have a number in it, although some, where no answer was given, will contain the missing-data code.

There will be one row for every respondent (or, as it is sometimes called, **case**). The order of cases in the grid does not matter, although often the rows will be arranged in order of the identification numbers assigned to respondents. Each column contains the coded answers for one survey question, that is, for one **variable**. For example, one of the columns of the GHS data matrix will hold data about the variable 'whether the respondent has consulted a doctor in the last two weeks', derived from answers to the question shown in Exhibit 1.1. Generally speaking, there will be one variable for every question in the survey, although some complicated questions including sub-questions may generate more than one variable.

Thus the raw material of quantitative data analysis is a rectangular data matrix of rows, one per respondent or case, and columns, one per variable. The main job of the survey analysis program is to store this matrix of numbers, so permitting statistics about the variables to be calculated.

Variable-centred analysis

Almost all statistical analysis in the social sciences is focused on finding relationships between the columns (variables) of the matrix and is therefore called **variable-centred** analysis. Suppose we take two variables such as sex and occupation from a data matrix constructed from a survey of the general population. We might be interested in whether there is some link between the two variables: do women tend to have different occupations from men? Another way of expressing the question is to ask whether there is a **bivariate** relationship between the two variables (bivariate meaning about two variables). We shall be examining the idea of bivariate relationships and how they can be assessed in much more detail in later chapters. For the moment, let us assume that we can detect a relationship between sex and occupation in the data. We can use this conclusion in two ways. We might make a **prediction**: for example, that women graduating from university are likely to go into a different range of jobs than men. Having made this prediction, we might go on to make policy recommendations about how inequalities in occupational selection might be reduced. Alternatively, we might use the finding as the basis for an **explanation**. Suppose we had found that on average women in full-time jobs earn less than men. One explanation could be that women are paid less than men for doing the same job, but another explanation might rely on the relationship between gender and occupation to suggest that women earn less than men on average because they tend to be in lower-paid occupations. (Of course, both these explanations might be true at the same time).

Variable-centred analysis dominates sociological research using quantitative data, but it is not the only possible approach. One alternative is to use data to contribute to a history or narrative account of events. In this approach, generalization tends to be downplayed in favour of understanding the particularities of the event under study (Abell, 1987). Another possibility is to build computer models which reproduce some of the patterns in the data, an approach now coming to be called social simulation (Gilbert and Troitzsch, 1999).

THE DATA SETS

Throughout this book, we shall be illustrating the use of statistical methods and tools by using data from two data sets: data assembled by the World Bank about conditions in most countries of the world; and data from the General Household Survey, a survey of households in Great Britain that gathers factual data about household members and the homes they live in. These data sets are commonly used by social scientists for secondary analysis. In the examples in the following chapters, we have focused on aspects of women's position from a number of points of view, using the two data sets in complimentary ways. In doing this, however, we have only scratched the surface of the information available in the data sets. There are many more variables in each of them than we have mentioned in this book and many other important issues that can be explored using them.

THE GHS DATA SET

The General Household Survey is carried out by the ONS, to provide background information for policy-making. It was started in 1971 and runs continuously – data are sought throughout the year and then collected together and distributed annually. The respondents are people who live in private households in Great Britain. They are approached by ONS interviewers in their own homes to take part in the survey. Interviews are sought with all the household members aged 16 and over.

The proportion of those approached who respond averages around 82 per cent, very high for a survey as complex as the GHS. Of those who do not respond, around 13 per cent decline to participate and 3 per cent cannot be contacted (these percentages vary slightly from year to year).

There is a set of core questions which are always asked, and in addition new sections are introduced each year and others dropped, while others are repeated every few years. The core questions include those on housing, employment, education, health and household membership. Other topics covered in some years include informal caring for other members of the household, burglary, dental health, pension schemes, drinking alcohol, fertility, long-distance travel, smoking, voluntary work and many others. The GHS consists almost entirely of factual questions about the household and its members; there are very few questions asking for statements of attitude or belief. Full details about the GHS can be found in the annual reports (e.g. ONS, 1995).

In this book, we have mainly used a subset of the data collected by the GHS during 1995. The same subset may be accessed on the World Wide Web if you would like to repeat these analyses or do your own (see Appendix A). We have also used some data collected in 1991. The data in computer-readable form for all recent years of the survey are available for academic research from the Data Archive at the University of Essex. The Archive also holds many other data sets of interest to sociologists.

THE SID DATA SET

The Social Indicators of Development data set was put together by the World Bank from a wide range of variables, called social indicators, which were themselves developed and measured by other international agencies such as the World Health Organization (WHO), the United Nations Children's Fund (UNI-CEF), Unesco and so on. The indicators measure such matters as health, education, nutrition and economic activity in most countries of the world.

For this data set, therefore, the rows of the data matrix represent countries, rather than individuals, and the columns are the social indicators. The indicators are published in a book of tables (World Bank, 1992) and also as a data file on disk. Having them as a data file means that all manner of comparisons and summaries can be done on them by social scientists. This data set is also available on the World Wide Web (see Appendix A).

In contrast with the GHS, the SID data set does not record information about individuals, but about countries. Collecting data about countries can be even more difficult than getting data from individuals. The World Bank relies on statistical information published by others, often by the countries themselves. There are three major difficulties with this which need to be borne in mind when using the data. First, the countries' definitions of terms may differ. For example, if one is interested in the proportion of the population that has completed secondary education in different countries, one has first to define exactly what is meant by 'secondary education' in a way which makes sense when applied to the education systems of all the countries involved. With some indicators, including education, this can sometimes be hard or impossible to achieve. Secondly, when a suitable definition of the indicator has been agreed, one has to find data which have been measured according to that definition in all the countries. Sometimes this may mean making estimates from other, more easily available data; sometimes the data are simply not available in the form required (in which case the data will be coded and recorded as 'missing' for that country and that variable). Thirdly, ideally the indicators should be measured at the same time − or at least in the same year − for all countries. Again, in practice, this is hard to achieve. Most of the data set used in this book relates to measurements made in the mid-1980s, but sometimes even earlier measurements have had to be used because nothing later is available.

CONCEPTS AND INDICATORS

The problem of finding good indicators for the SID data is an example of a general problem in sociological research: the relationships between indicators and the concepts that they are intended to measure. **Concepts** are the building blocks of theory: ideas such as occupation, gender, education, status, and income are all concepts. Most quantitative theories express some relationship between concepts, for example, that income is related to level of education. However, concepts themselves are not measurable directly. Instead, for each concept in the theory there must be a corresponding **indicator**. An indicator is a method of measurement that aims to measure the concept accurately. For example, an indicator for income might be the sum of money that respondents report when asked about their total weekly earnings. An indicator for education might be the highest educational qualification obtained by the respondent. There are often a variety of possible indicators for a given concept, some of which are more accurate and others more easily measured (for example, the indicator of income could be improved, but made more onerous for the respondent, by including interest from savings accounts and dividends from shares; the sums reported may need to be averaged over a number of weeks; and the respondent may need to be asked to produce pay-slips, rather than relying on memory). One of the skills of a good researcher is to devise good indicators for the theories being investigated.

How good an indicator is, is a question about its validity and reliability. **Validity** concerns the extent to which an indicator accurately measures the concept. **Reliability** concerns the consistency of the measurement. For example, an indicator that asked respondents how much they earned last week in order to assess their income will probably not be very valid: the answer will depend on the respondent's memory and is likely to omit some components of income. It is also likely to be rather unreliable: if the respondent is paid weekly and sometimes does overtime, the answer will depend on which week of the year the question happened to have been asked. A degree of measurement error is likely to creep in, however valid and reliable the indicators we choose to use are, and this needs to be remembered when analysing sociological data.

KINDS OF DATA

There are a number of kinds of quantitative data. It is important to distinguish between them because the kind of data affects the types of analysis that can be done. For example, while it is perfectly acceptable to find the average age of a group of people, it would not be sensible to calculate their average religious affiliation because the result would be meaningless. Unfortunately, finding the average of a set of numerical codes representing respondents' religions is just as easy as finding the average of their ages: in either case, one simply has a batch of numbers to average. Thus, when doing statistical analysis it is important to keep your wits about you, so that you do not unreflectively apply statistical procedures to obtain meaningless results.

There are three ways in which data can be classified that have consequences for the way in which they should be analysed: whether the data are about individuals or aggregates; whether the data are measuring a continuous or discrete variable; and the level of measurement of the variable. Let us consider each of these in turn.

INDIVIDUAL AND AGGREGATE DATA

Every individual person is different. It is therefore hard to predict with any accuracy how a particular individual will behave. Even if we have quite detailed knowledge about a person, we can still be surprised by what they do. For example, while, as we saw earlier, women with full-time jobs do an average of two hours of housework a day, some full-time working women do much less than this, and some do more. The actual number of hours per day is quite unpredictable, however much data you have about individuals, and is quite likely to vary from one day to the next.

In contrast, if we have data about aggregates, we expect to be able to make much more accurate predictions. For example, if the aggregate amount of housework per day in the UK among full-time working women was two hours in 1998, we can be reasonably confident that it is not going to be different by more than a few minutes in 1999. This is because the figure has been obtained by averaging over very many people: individual idiosyncrasies tend to be smoothed out in the process.

Another example of data for an aggregate variable is shown in Exhibit 1.2. The data concern the rates of infant mortality (number of deaths per annum of infants under one year of age per 1000 live births). The variable describes the aggregate infant mortality rate in each of the 171 countries covered by the SID data set. Exhibit 1.2 shows how many countries have infant mortality rates in each of the given bands. Less than one-third (52) of the 171 countries have rates of infant mortality of 20 deaths per 1000 or lower. About the same number (51) have rates exceeding 80 deaths per 1000. Not surprisingly, it is the less developed countries that have the higher infant mortality rates. Later in the book, we shall be examining some of the factors that influence countries' rates of infant mortality, such as the number of doctors, the level of literacy and the rate of population growth.

In general, statistical analyses tend to give more reliable results when they depend on aggregate data than when they use individual data. You will find that

Range of infant mortality rate*	Number of countries
0–20	52
21–40	30
41–60	20
61–80	17
81–100	15
101–120	15
121–140	16
141–160	3
161–180	2
No data	1
Total	171**

*Number of deaths per annum of infants under one year of age per 1000 live births.
**There are no data for French Guiana.

Exhibit 1.2   *The variation in infant mortality around the world*
               Source: World Bank, 1992

the analyses in this book based on the SID data set – which consists of variables aggregated over whole countries – often give 'better' results than those based on the GHS, which consists of data about individuals. Of course, this is not a reason for using only aggregate data. The unit of analysis (e.g. the individual or the country) needs to be chosen with a view to the problem or topic that you want to study.

CONTINUOUS AND DISCRETE

The second way in which data vary is according to whether what is being measured comes naturally in 'lumps' or not. For example, children come in units of one child. There is no such thing as 0.5 of a child. We call a variable measuring the number of children in a family a **discrete** variable. On the other hand, the distance of someone's home from their place of work could be any number of miles; for example, we would have no difficulty with the idea that the distance is 1.237 miles. Variables measuring such quantities are known as **continuous** variables.

The importance of the distinction between discrete and continuous variables is that different kinds of statistical methods are appropriate for each. In addition, the distinction can sometimes be a source of confusion. For example, in 1995 the average size of a household in Great Britain was 2.4 people. Obviously, this does not mean that there are households with 2.4 people in them, because people only come in units of a whole person. An average is a measure which is continuous, taking any value, while the variable on which this average has been based, the number of people in households, is discrete.

Another example of potential confusion arises from the practice of grouping categories for the purpose of collecting data. While age is in principle a continuous variable, a survey question will certainly not ask for age in terms of so many years, months, weeks, days, hours, minutes and seconds. Instead you might be asked how old you are, expecting an answer in years, or just in which age group you fall, given a list of five or six groups from which to choose. Once the data from this question have been processed, the result will look to the analyst as though the age variable is discrete even though the underlying variable is continuous.

An example is shown in Exhibit 1.3, which shows age divided into age groups (observe that although most of the age groups cover five years, the first two only include two years each). The right-hand column shows the percentage of women who use the contraceptive pill in each age group. The proportion in the youngest age group, ages 16 and 17, is a quarter (25 per cent). It rises to nearly half (49 per cent) in the 20–24 age group and then falls again to only 3 per cent among those aged 45–49. Dividing the sample into age groups in this way is convenient because it shows at a glance the trends in contraceptive use by age. If the table had one row for each different age, 16, 17, 18, 19 and so on, it would become a much larger table and harder to make sense of.

LEVELS OF MEASUREMENT

Earlier in this chapter, we remarked that the quantitative data with which this book is concerned are often obtained from respondents' answers to survey questions. Usually the answers themselves are not numerical, but to include them in a data set such as the GHS and to analyse them statistically, we need to convert them into numbers using a coding procedure. In doing this, we are converting from qualitatively different answers (for example, 'disagree', 'neutral' or 'agree' in reply to a question about building out-of-town supermarkets) to quantitatively different codes (e.g. 1, 2 or 3). While this is an acceptable procedure, it can give rise to difficulties because the numbers have different properties from the original answers provided by the respondent. For example, if we had just the numerical codes, we might be misled into assuming that we could calculate the average view about out-of-town supermarkets from these

Age	% using pill
16–17	25
18–19	37
20–24	49
25–29	41
30–34	29
35–39	20
40–44	9
45–49	3

Exhibit 1.3   *Use of the pill as the usual method of contraception by age, among women aged 16–49, Great Britain, 1995*
Source: ONS, 1995

codes. But this would be incorrect: since we do not know how strongly individual respondents agreed or disagreed with the idea, we cannot pool all the responses to find a meaningful average.

The problem stems from the **level of measurement** of the variable. Conventionally, social scientists distinguish four levels of measurement, although in practice they only use three of them.

If a variable measures only differences between cases, it is measuring at the **nominal** level. For instance, a variable measuring political preference is measured at the nominal level. If one person is recorded as voting Labour and another Conservative, this means only that they vote differently. This remains true even if, for the purpose of analysis, Labour voters are coded as 1 and Conservative voters as 2. Although the Tory voters are coded 2, one cannot conclude that they are twice as political as Labour voters coded 1. The numbers must be used only as indications that the respondents are in different categories.

In some questions the answers are clearly ordered in terms of bigger and smaller, or better and worse. For example, we might ask respondents about their level of education by finding out about their highest educational qualification, suggesting categories such as GCSE exam passes only, A levels and a degree, coded as 1, 2 and 3 respectively. Someone who has a degree is clearly better educated than someone who only has GCSEs. However, it would not be right to say that someone who has a degree is three times as well educated as someone with GCSEs, even though the numeric code for a degree is 3 and that for GCSEs is 1. The categories for the respondents' answers are different, as with the nominal level of measurement, but in this case they are also ordered from low to high educational achievement. We therefore say that this variable is measured at the **ordinal** level of measurement. While the categories of an ordinal variable can be ordered (or 'ranked'), the amount of difference between categories is not available. Variables measured at the nominal and ordinal levels are sometimes referred to as **categorical** variables.

The third level of measurement is the **interval** level. Variables measured at this level have ordered categories, where we can calculate the relative difference between any two categories. There are very few examples of interval-level variables in social science.

The fourth level is the **ratio** level. These are variables for which there is a meaningful concept of a zero amount. It follows that it is possible to calculate ratios (such as two to one) for variables measured at the ratio level. For example, income is a ratio-level variable: there is no problem about the meaning of zero income, and we can say that one person's income is twice as much as someone else's. Like all ratio-level variables, income also has the interval property: the difference between someone who earns £10,000 and someone who earns £20,000 is simple to calculate. In fact, social scientists commonly speak of interval-level variables when they ought to be referring to ratio-level variables. The difference between the two levels of measurement is usually not important for statistical analyses.

These levels of measurement can be arranged in order. Variables at all the levels of measurement share the feature of having distinguishable categories. Ratio, interval and ordinal variables have categories that are ordered. Ratio and interval variables have meaningful differences between their categories. And only ratio variables have a true zero. We shall see in later chapters how the level of measurement of a variable affects the types of statistical analysis that can be performed. In general, ratio and interval variables allow more complex and more informative analyses to be carried out because variables measured at these levels contain more information (e.g. about the numerical difference between categories) than variables measured at the ordinal or categorical levels.

OVERVIEW OF THIS BOOK

Most sociological research involves more data than can conveniently and easily be analysed by hand. Computers are therefore now an integral part of the process of analysis. In the next chapter, we introduce the best-known computer program for managing sociological data. Throughout the book there are examples of and instructions on how to use this package. In the following four chapters (Chapters 3–6), we consider how to calculate, analyse and display variables from a data matrix. Chapter 7 considers the importance of the normal distribution. This leads us on to considering bivariate relationships between two variables in Chapters 8 and 9. Chapters 10 and 11 discuss the idea of sampling from large populations and the accuracy of the conclusions that you can derive from samples. Finally, in Chapter 12, we consider forms of analysis that examine the relationship between more than two variables.

SUMMARY

This book is about how to analyse quantitative data, collected either by the researcher specifically for the purpose (primary analysis) or by others, possibly for other purposes (secondary analysis). Analysis consists of constructing and testing theories. Theories are usually composed of concepts linked by relationships. They are developed through a process of induction from data, and tested by means of deriving consequences and then comparing the expected consequences with data – a process of deduction. In order to subject theories to the most stretching test, one tries to find situations where the theory is at risk of being falsified, rather than collecting confirming instances.

Quantitative data consist of measurements made on a number of variables about a set of respondents or cases. The data (e.g. ticks on a postal questionnaire or answers to an interviewer's questions) have to be coded in numerical form before they can be analysed. The numbers can most easily be analysed if they are arranged in a data matrix of variables by cases. Variables are measured using indicators, whose accuracy is assessed in terms of their validity and reliability.

Depending on the topic and the source of the data, quantitative data may be collected about individuals or aggregates such as countries. What is measured may come in discrete units, such as children, or may take on any value, as with age and income. Data may be measured at any one of four levels of measurement – categorical, ordinal, interval and ratio – each successive level representing additional information that has been built into the variable. Arithmetic operations can be carried out on interval and ratio variables, but not on categorical and ordinal ones.

EXERCISES

1. For each of concepts (a)–(d) listed below:
   - describe an indicator for that concept;
   - suggest the level at which the concept is being measured nominal, ordinal or interval/ratio);
   - list one or more problems which might threaten the validity of the indicator's measurement of the concept;
   - assess the likely reliability of the indicator.
     - (a) Level of education
     - (b) Alcohol consumption
     - (c) Opinion about recycling domestic waste for environmental reasons
     - (d) Actual behaviour in recycling domestic waste
2. Construct a plausible hypothesis involving at least two of the four concepts listed in Exercise 1.
3. Locate an article in a recent issue of an academic journal (e.g. *Sociology, Sociological Research Online, British Journal of Sociology, American Journal of Sociology*) that uses quantitative data. See whether you can find examples within the article of:

   - Hypothesis
   - Concept
   - Indicator
   - Variable
   - Case

Did the research follow a deductive or inductive research strategy? Is it based on primary or secondary analysis?

USING COMPUTERS IN STATISTICS 2

CONTENTS

A book on introductory statistics nowadays also has to include an introduction to using computers. You may feel that this is an added complication to an already complicated subject, but we will show that computers are there to take the grind out of statistics. It is important that you understand what a computer can do and what it cannot do for you.

In this chapter, we shall review the important features of a computer and introduce one of the most often used and most powerful computer programs for analysing sociological data, SPSS. Formerly, this acronym stood for the 'Statistical Package for the Social Sciences', but now it represents 'Statistical Products and Service Solutions'. To show how SPSS is used, we will work through two examples: first using the program to examine the marks obtained by some sociology students, and then using it to explore variations in the average life expectancy in countries around the world. In the first example, although there are less than a couple of dozen marks to analyse in all, so that the work could have been done by hand, the computer helps to organize the marks neatly and avoid arithmetic slips. The second example is much more typical of sociological research. There are data from 171 countries, which is far more than one would want to deal with using pencil and paper. As we shall see, however, a computer makes short work of it. Later in the book we shall encounter data sets with thousands of cases which would be impossible to manage without a computer to help.

WHAT KIND OF COMPUTER?

Computers, like cars, come in many different shapes and sizes, with corresponding differences in performance. In most academic institutions there will be a mainframe computer. This is usually a very powerful machine capable of performing many different tasks at once. If you are interested in analysing very large data sets, like the General Household Survey mentioned in Chapter 1, then you will probably need to use a mainframe computer. However, if you are just learning statistics and the data sets you want to use are relatively small, a desktop computer will be adequate for your needs. There are two main ranges of desktop computer: the IBM-compatible personal computer (PC), and the Apple Macintosh. This book will concentrate on the IBM-compatible PC.

When you buy a computer you need to consider three questions. How powerful is it, and how much memory and how much hard disk space does it have?

HOW POWERFUL IS IT?

This question concerns the processing power of the computer, that is, what kind of chip it contains. Today, the most powerful PCs have Pentium chips, but many older machines use 486 or 386 chips. The difference between them is in how fast a particular process is carried out. For instance, you may be using word-processing software and want to go from the first page to the last of a very large document. This would be a comparatively quick task using a Pentium but would be infuriatingly slow with a 386. A computer's speed of processing is measured in megahertz (MHz). At the time of writing an entry-level computer runs at about 350 MHz.

HOW MUCH MEMORY DOES IT HAVE?

This refers to the random access memory (RAM), used to store data for processing by the chip. These days the minimum for most new software is 16 MB (megabytes). A megabyte is enough to store about 1 million characters. The more RAM you have, the faster and more easily the software runs.

HOW MUCH HARD DISK SPACE DOES IT HAVE?

The hard disk is the physical storage area of the computer. Here all the files, including the software, are kept. The size of the hard disk can affect the speed of the computer, but only when it starts to fill up. Typically, new computers have hard disk capacities between 2 and 4 GB (gigabytes). A gigabyte is 1000 million bytes. As with RAM, software will usually specify a minimum amount of hard disk needed to install the program.

Many students will not own their own computer and therefore rely upon the machines provided by their institution. Their main concern is therefore not the hard disk capacity, but the floppy disk capacity. Since they will generally be using shared computers, they must ensure that any work they do is saved on to a portable 'floppy' disk. The floppy disk in use today is the $3\frac{1}{2}$ inch high-density floppy disk which has a storage capacity of 1.44 MB. However, newer hardware is available which will allow you to store much greater capacities of information. If you have a Zip drive attached or fitted to your computer you can store up to 250 MB on portable zip disks. To put these numbers into perspective, a page of A4 double-spaced typed text occupies approximately 2 KB kilobytes – (1024 kilobytes is 1 MB).

However, having a computer is only half the equation. It would be like having an oven but with nothing to cook. In order to get the computer to perform a task you need to tell it what to do; you need to **program** it. Depending on your programming expertise, you could create a program from scratch or you could use a program written by someone else. Of course, it is far easier to use someone else's program. With this book and some statistical software, we will to show you that it is possible to use the computer yourself to explore data.

PROGRAMS

A program is also often referred to as software, to distinguish it from the hardware, the computer itself. Most PCs come with some basic software installed. The most likely to be included is the Microsoft Disk Operating System or MSDOS. However, using MSDOS involves learning commands and typing them in for the machine to execute. As a simple example, if you want to look at the contents of a floppy disk in the **a:** drive, you have to type the MSDOS command:

DIR A:

to get the computer to give you a list of all the files on the disk.

To make using PCs easier, a more visual approach was developed in the early 1980s. A pointer on the screen can be moved around with the mouse to select icons (or pictures) representing programs and files. The computer screen is arranged like a desktop on which you have placed icons representing everyday tasks. The operating system, Windows, is one of several which have adopted this desktop metaphor.

When you buy a new computer it usually comes with Windows as well as MSDOS software. Both MSDOS and Windows (versions 3.1, 95/98 and NT) will perform basic routine functions such as file copying, printing and deleting. However, the computer is usually required to do more than that, and then further software is needed. Dedicated software has been written to help create written documents, add up lists of figures and keep addresses, to name just a few tasks a computer can help with. Initially, all software was written to run under MSDOS, then with the growth of interest in Windows, software was rewritten for this interface. Software designed for Windows has a common mode of operation, so that once you have mastered one Windows program, you are half-way to mastering any Windows software.

STATISTICAL PROGRAMS

Although there are many statistical programs on the market, in this book we will concentrate on one of the market leaders, SPSS. Other programs include Minitab, Stata, Statview, Genstat and SAS; the *SocInfo Software Catalogue* (CTI, 1997) lists many more.

SPSS – A SHORT HISTORY

Not so long ago (during the early 1960s) social scientists wishing to calculate statistics from large data sets would have needed either to create their own recipe (statistical routine or algorithm) or find someone else who had already done so. Clearly the former required some programming capability and the latter a good network of statistical friends. Even if the appropriate recipe could be found, it was often the case that it would not work with the computer. There was a lack of standardization. To be a quantitative social scientist you had to have a good knowledge of computers and programming. This problem was identified by Norman H. Nie, Dale Bent and C. Hadlai Hull, three Stanford University graduate students, who gathered together all the most popular statistical recipes, rewrote them in the same language (Fortran) and released them into the academic community as a 'statistical package'. And so in 1968 the first version of SPSS became available for two types of large computer, the IBM 360 and the CDC 6000.

In those early days, these packages required the user to specify what they wanted using computer cards, each card containing a line of characters. Even a simple procedure required a stack of cards, all in the correct order for processing. This stack was read into the computer using a card-reader. Since each institution generally only had one mainframe computer, this meant that the results might take several hours or days to complete, depending on how many people were before you in the queue. However, even this represented a great saving in time compared with hand calculation.

It was not until 1981 that the first interactive version of SPSS, SPSS-X version 2, became available. With this, you could ask for a statistic to be calculated and then wait while the computer performed the task for you. This was like a while-you-wait service compared with one which needed to be booked in advance. You might have to wait a long time, but you could at least hope to go away the same day with the goods.

With the spread of personal computers during the early 1980s, a version for the PC was released in 1984. This meant you did not need to rely on the vagaries of central computing services, and could even work at home. The development of the Windows interface and the intuitive 'point and click' operation with a mouse during the late 1980s led to the development in 1992 of the first Windows version, followed by a version for the Macintosh. At the time of writing, the latest version for Windows 3.1 is SPSS for Windows version 6.1 and SPSS for Windows version 9.0 is available for Windows 95/98/NT. The latest version for the Macintosh is version 6. Despite all these developments for personal computers, the mainframe version continues and is still the best for handling very large data sets. This book will illustrate statistical procedures using SPSS for Windows version 9.0.

SPSS FOR DATA MANAGEMENT AND DATA ANALYSIS

It was noticed long ago that social scientists using statistical routines to analyse their data spent more time on data management than on data analysis. This was not because data management was more complicated, but because the statistical routines available did not provide management facilities for this important preparatory work. For instance, it is often necessary to merge more than one data file to increase the number of cases or change the coding scheme for certain variables. **Coding** is the process of assigning numerical values to the responses of a variable in order to create a data file for computer analysis. For example, the variable sex has two possible categories, male and female, to which we might decide to assign values of 1 and 2 respectively. There will be more about coding in Chapter 3.

From the very beginning SPSS was designed to facilitate data management. We can divide statistical packages like SPSS into two parts, the data management and the data analysis procedures. Exhibit 2.1 gives a few examples of each type.

STARTING SPSS VERSION 9.0

The following assumes that you have some familiarity with Windows 95/98/NT and have a mouse attached to your computer to enable you to select areas on the screen.

Data management	
Recode:	to change the coding scheme of certain variables
Compute:	to create new variables using the values of existing variables
Select if:	to select a subset of cases to analyse

Data analysis	
Frequencies:	counting occurrences of categories of a variable (see Chapter 3)
Crosstabulation:	counting occurrences of the categories of a variable depending on the categories of another variable (see Chapter 8)
Regression:	a statistical technique concerned with predicting the values of one variable, knowing the values of another (see Chapter 7)

Exhibit 2.1   *Data management and data analysis in SPSS*

The SPSS program is started by selecting the SPSS program from the **Start** menu, usually stored under Program Files.

The opening screen should look like Exhibit 2.2, although there may be a prompt screen asking you what you want to do. If this prompt screen appears, click on **Cancel** to remove it.

Menu items can be selected with the mouse as with any other Windows program. A drop-down list will appear offering further selections. For instance, under **File** you can save, open or print files. Most statistical procedures are accessed via the **Analyze** menu. Under the **Edit** menu you can set **Options** for how you would like SPSS to behave.

When you start SPSS you begin in the **Data Editor** window. After SPSS has performed any tasks, another window will appear, the **Viewer** window. There are other windows within SPSS, most notably the **Syntax** window and the **Chart Editor**, which appear when appropriate.

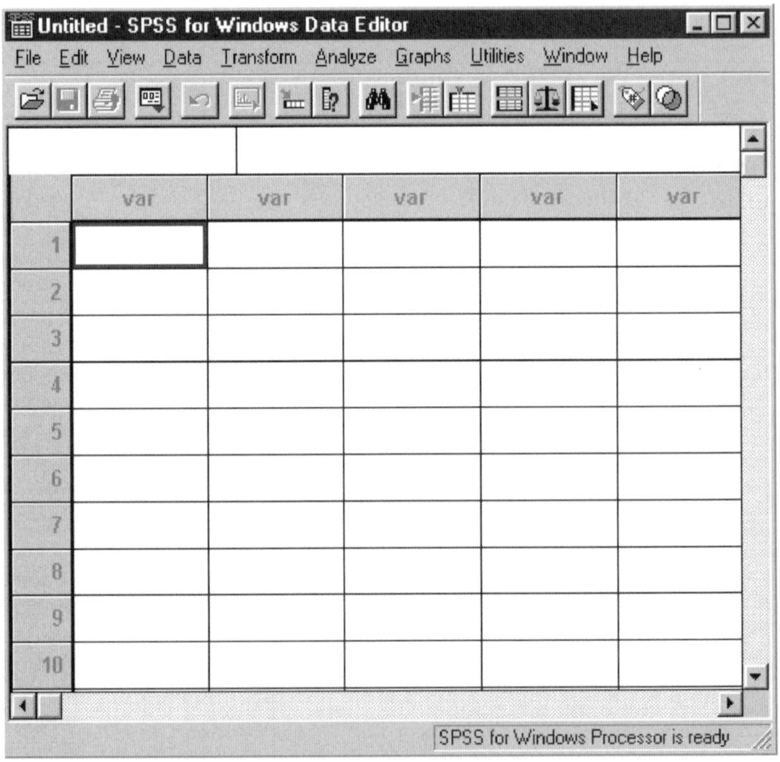

Exhibit 2.2   *The **Data Editor** in SPSS version 9.0*

THE DATA EDITOR WINDOW

When you start SPSS this window appears on top of the others and has the title **Untitled**. This is where you create or edit data. SPSS data files usually have the suffix .SAV. It is a good idea to follow this and other file-naming conventions in SPSS. This is because SPSS will try to find files with the data file suffix when you next want to open it, unless you tell it otherwise.

THE VIEWER WINDOW

This is the window in which your results appear. When you start SPSS, this window appears with the default title **Output1.** The contents of this window can be saved as a file called an output file, also known as a listing file. Output or viewer files usually have the suffix .SPO.

THE SYNTAX WINDOW

This window may or may not appear on starting the program, depending on how SPSS has been set up (see the section below on 'setting options in SPSS'). If it is present it will have the name **Syntax1** in the title bar. The **Syntax** window is where you type SPSS commands for execution. This is useful if you wish to repeat your analysis by saving the commands in a syntax file and reusing those commands. Syntax files usually have the suffix .SPS. This book will not be using SPSS syntax, but it is useful to know that underlying *every* menu selection there is accompanying syntax code that could have been written and saved in a file. Using syntax is useful not only when you want to repeat an analysis but also as a record of your investigation.

As you use SPSS you will see messages regarding the processing status of SPSS in the status bar. In Exhibit 2.2, the message *SPSS Processor is Ready* in the status bar indicates that SPSS is currently inactive and awaiting instructions. When SPSS is processing a file you will see a case count in this bar as SPSS works through the data.

The toolbar in SPSS (Exhibit 2.3) provides several shortcuts to procedures that can also be accessed via the menu bar. As you place the pointer over the icons in the toolbar you should see a message in the status bar telling you the

Exhibit 2.3   *The toolbar in SPSS version 9.0*

purpose of that icon. For instance, the first button on the left is the tool to open a file.

SOME PRELIMINARY TERMS IN SPSS

It is useful before we start using SPSS to clarify some of the common terms used by the program.

VARIABLE NAME

Each variable must be given a unique variable name of no more than eight characters. This variable name *must* start with a letter and cannot contain any spaces. There are some words, reserved keywords, that you cannot use as variable names in SPSS – for instance ALL, ANY, IF, TO. See the *SPSS Base 8.0 User's Guide* (SPSS, 1998) for a full list. Although it is perfectly valid to use variable names such as v1, v2, ..., v100, it is far more useful to create mnemonic names for your variable. So marital status could be given the variable name MARSTAT. Note that, although we will be using a particular font for SPSS variable names throughout this book, SPSS is case-insensitive. So marstat, Marstat and MARSTAT all refer to the same variable in SPSS.

VARIABLE LABEL

Although you may have supplied mnemonic names (e.g. AGE, SEX, MARSTAT) to all your variables, it may be difficult to remember exactly what each variable is about, especially if there are hundreds of variables. For this reason SPSS allows you to create variable labels longer than the eight character limit for variable names. In fact variable labels can be up to 256 characters long, but you usually create much shorter labels. So MARSTAT may have the variable label 'Respondent's marital status'.

VALUE LABELS

We briefly mentioned coding in Chapter 1 and we return to it in Chapter 3, but coding is the practice of giving a number or code to responses to questions in a survey. This enables the computer to analyse the responses. However, it is also very useful to give each value (code) a value label so you can remember what it means. So people responding to a question about marital status may be given code or value 1 if they are married and code or value 2 if they are single. To enable you to remember what each code means you can add this information to your data file as value labels. Value labels have a limit of 60 characters, but it is best to create very much shorter labels. This is because SPSS may truncate your labels, sometimes to as few as 11 characters, when it gives you your results.

Both variable labels and value labels are optional. SPSS will still carry on with your analysis even if you do not create them. See Exhibit 2.4 for a summary of the difference between variable names, variable labels and value labels.

SETTING OPTIONS IN SPSS

It is best to work with SPSS using the default preferences at first. If at a later stage you need to change them, you should refer back to this section.

There are many ways of customizing SPSS to your personal preferences. Only two changes to the default program have been made to make SPSS appear as it does in this book. These changes, in our opinion, make SPSS easier to use and understand. First, variables have been made to appear in alphabetical name order rather than by file order using variable labels. This enables you to find your variables more easily. Secondly, output labels have all been changed to include the variable name and values where appropriate. To carry out these changes, select **Edit|Options** to see the dialog box in Exhibit 2.5.

To make variables appear in name order, proceed as follows. Make sure the **General** tab is selected. Then in the **Variable Lists** section of the dialog box, select **Display names** rather than the default **Display labels**. In addition, change the order to **Alphabetical** rather than **File**.

Then, to make our second change, select the **Output Labels** tab in the **Options** dialog box to see Exhibit 2.6. Then change each section so that **Names and Labels** and **Values and Labels** are selected as shown in Exhibit 2.6.

	Limit	Example	
Variable name (compulsory)	up to 8 characters must start with a letter no spaces unique in any one data file	MARSTAT	
Variable label (optional)	256 characters	Respondent's marital status	
Value label (optional)	60 characters	**Value**	**Value label**
		1	Married
		2	Single

Exhibit 2.4   *Variable names, variable labels and value labels in SPSS*

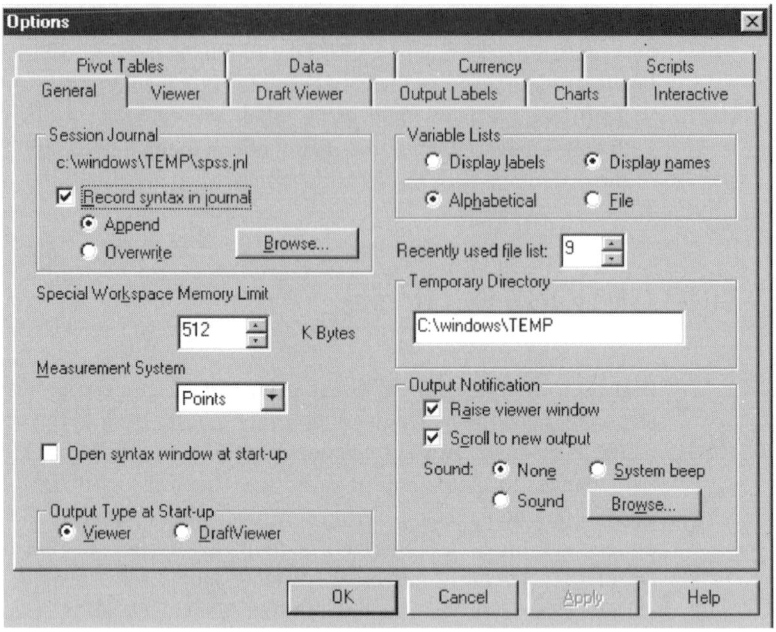

Exhibit 2.5   *Changing options in SPSS*

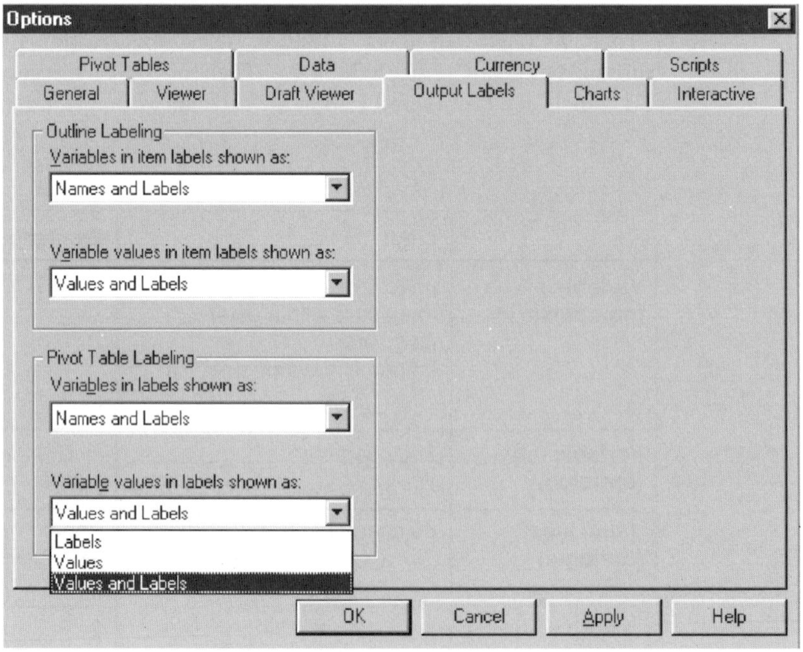

Exhibit 2.6   *Changing output label options in SPSS*

WHERE DO THE DATA COME FROM?

For most of the examples in this book you can access the data files on the **Understanding Social Statistics Web pages** (see Appendix A for details). These files have already been 'prepared' for SPSS and are ready to use. Chapter 1 describes these data sets.

You may also like to try creating your own data file. For instance, the following instructions create the marks data that are used in Chapter 5. These data are a set of sociology and psychology exam marks for a group of ten students on a joint honours course (see Exhibit 2.7).

First, start SPSS to see the **Data Editor** window. The top left-hand cell has a bold border around it – this is the current data cell. If you type 55 on the keyboard, the number 55 will appear above the cells of the spreadsheet and will be transferred to the spreadsheet when you press the **Enter** key on the keyboard. As you press the **Enter** key, the column heading VAR changes to VAR00001 and the second cell down becomes the active cell with a heavy border around it. Exhibit 2.8 shows the **Data Editor** window when the next number, 45, is about to be entered. When all the sociology marks have been typed in, use the cursor keys on the keyboard to make the first line in the second column active and enter the psychology marks.

When all the marks have been input you are ready for analysis. However, a further refinement would be to change the default variable names, VAR00001 and VAR00002, to something more meaningful. To do this, place the mouse

Student	Sociology mark	Psychology mark
1	55	49
2	45	55
3	66	56
4	34	45
5	67	73
6	53	37
7	78	85
8	45	12
9	57	58
10	60	63

Exhibit 2.7   *Marks data for ten students*

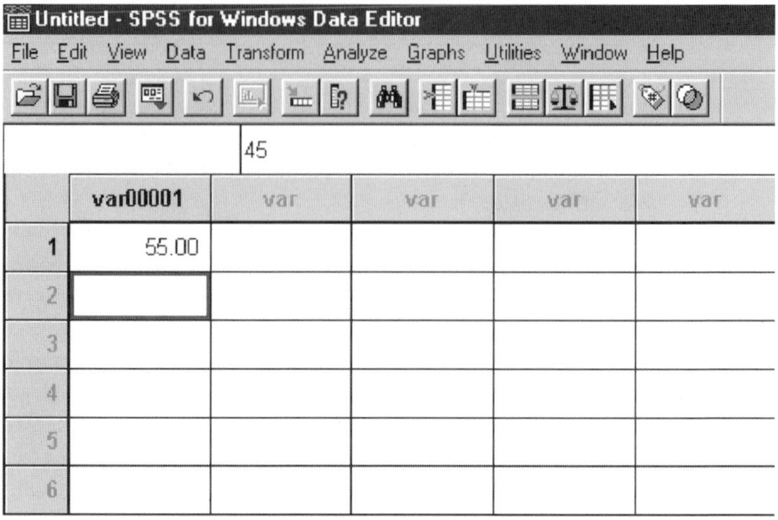

Exhibit 2.8   *Entering data in the **Data Editor** in SPSS*

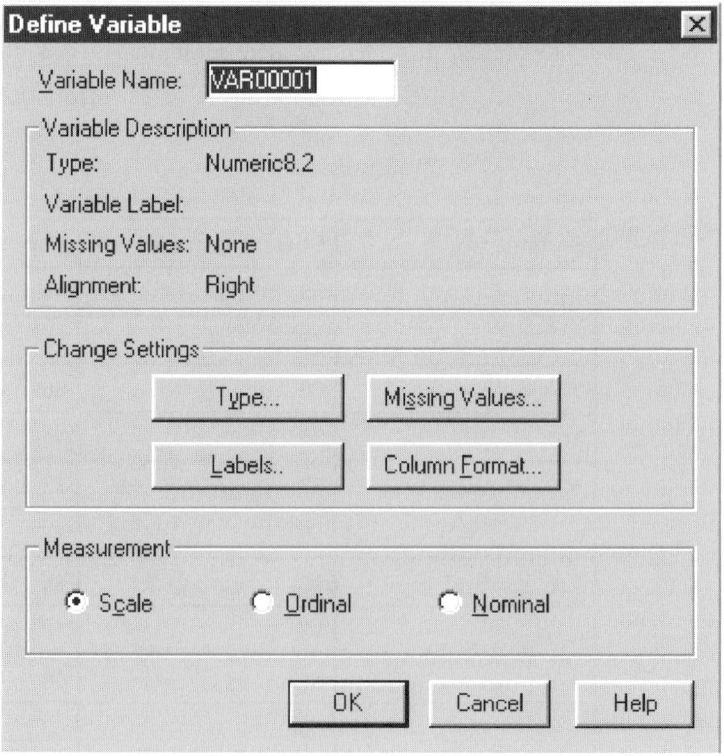

Exhibit 2.9   *Defining variable names in SPSS*

cursor over the grey column heading marked VAR00001 and double-click. The dialog box shown in Exhibit 2.9 will appear.

If you now type SOCIOLOGY on the keyboard, you will find that it overwrites VAR00001 in the variable name box. However, you will find that you can only type SOCIOLOG because SPSS will only allow a maximum of eight characters in a variable name. Click on **OK** or press the **Enter** key to return to the **Data Editor** window. The psychology marks can also be named, replacing VAR00002, but you will only be able to call them PSYCHOLO.

When you have named the variables the **Data Editor** window should look like Exhibit 2.10.

SAVING YOUR DATA FILE

Having created the data file in the **Data Editor** window and named the variables, you can save the file to a floppy disk if you share the computer with others or to the hard disk if you are its sole user.

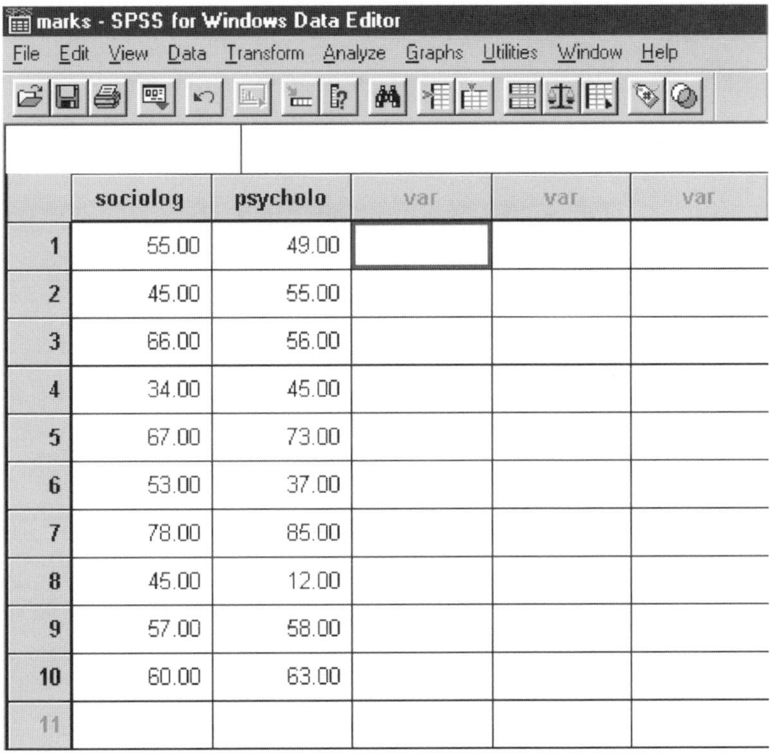

	sociolog	psycholo	var	var	var
1	55.00	49.00			
2	45.00	55.00			
3	66.00	56.00			
4	34.00	45.00			
5	67.00	73.00			
6	53.00	37.00			
7	78.00	85.00			
8	45.00	12.00			
9	57.00	58.00			
10	60.00	63.00			
11					

Exhibit 2.10 *Data for sociology and psychology marks in the* **Data Editor** *in SPSS*

To save the data file, make sure that the **Data Editor** window is the active window and click on **File|Save** ... to see the dialog box in Exhibit 2.11. If you are saving the data file to a floppy disk, change the default drive from **c:** to **a:** in the **Save in:** box. Leave it as **c:** if you are saving to the hard disk. In the **File name** box, type the name of the file, for example, **MARKS.SAV**. The suffix .SAV is recognized by SPSS as indicating an SPSS data file. It is a good idea to give all your SPSS data files this suffix. Then click on **Save**.

USING SPSS FOR DATA MANAGEMENT

Usually more time is spent on data management than on data analysis. Data management is the process of putting your data into the right shape for the chosen analysis. This might involve regrouping some of the categories of a variable, for instance regrouping age into those under and over 40, or selecting a subsample, for instance only women, from your sample. Clearly you need to know what analysis you want to do *before* you embark on data management. This section will explain how to regroup a variable and select a subsample of cases.

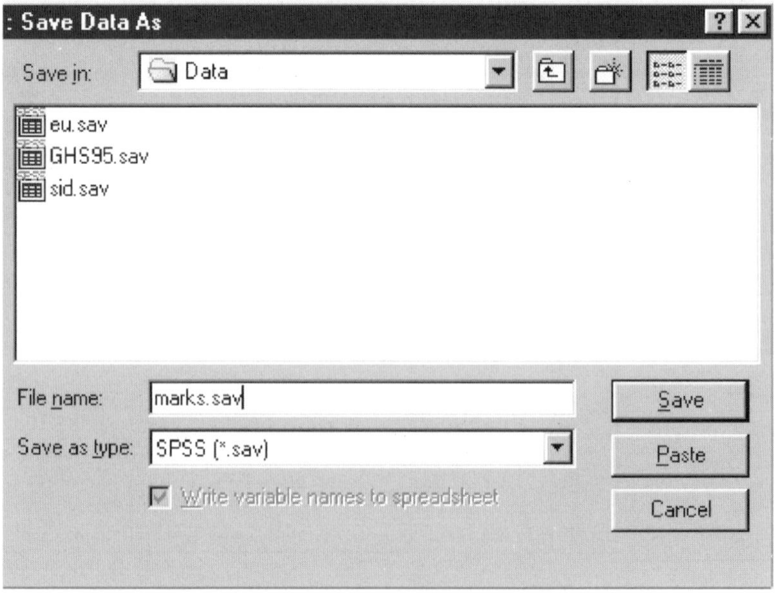

Exhibit 2.11   *Saving the* MARKS.SAV *data file in SPSS*

REGROUPING A VARIABLE

Suppose we wish to group the students into those who failed sociology and those who passed. We shall consider all those with marks of 49 and below as having failed and those with 50 and above as having passed. We shall assign the numerical code zero to a fail and one to a pass.

Because we still want to keep the original sociology marks, we shall give this pass/fail classification a new variable name, SOCPASS. We therefore want to recode SOCIOLOG into SOCPASS where codes 0 through 49 are recoded into the new code 0, and codes 50 to 100 into 1.

From the menu bar, select **Transform|Recode ▶|Into Different variables** .... The variable SOCIOLOG is selected from the variable list by double-clicking it. This transfers the variable name to the **Numeric Variable → Output Variable** box. Then the name of the new variable, SOCPASS, is typed into the **Output Variable** box. Clicking on the **Change** button causes the **Numeric Variable → Output Variable** box to read sociolog → socpass (see Exhibit 2.12).

To specify the new codes, click on the **Old and New Values** ... button. Exhibit 2.13 shows the **Old and New Values** dialog screen. This dialog box is split into two areas, the whole of the left-hand side where you describe the old values you want to change and the top right-hand side where you describe the corresponding new values. All recodes follow the same basic pattern:

... one or many old values = only one new value.

There are several ways to specify the recoding at this stage: the following instructions take you through just one.

1.   Click on **Range** in the old value box.
2.   Type in **0** in the first box and **49** in the second box, after **through**.

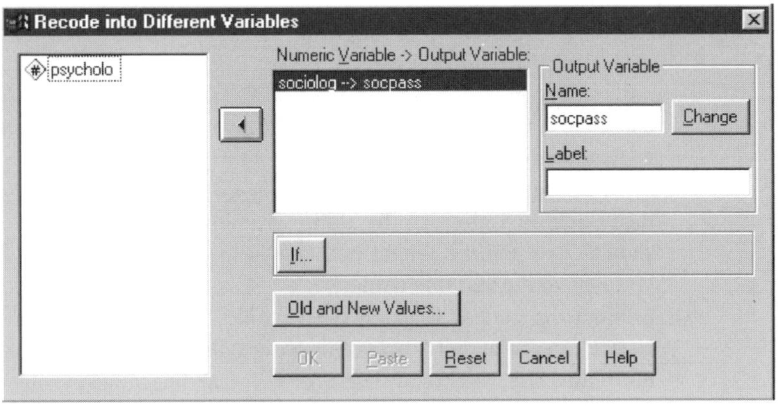

Exhibit 2.12   *Recoding into different variables in SPSS*

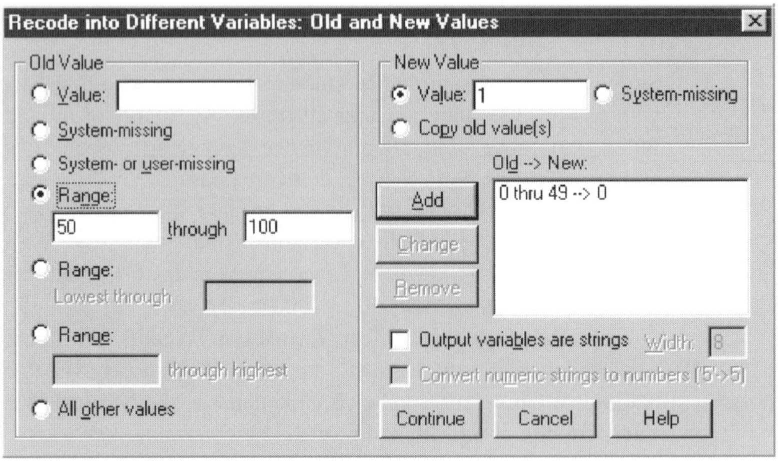

Exhibit 2.13   *Recoding values in SPSS*

3.   Then click on **Value** in the new value box and type **0** in the box.
4.   Click on **Add**.

Repeat steps 1–4 to recode **50 through 100** (old values) into code **1** (new value). Notice that whenever you click on **Add**, a record of the recoding so far appears in the **Old → New**: box. When you have finished recoding all old values to new values, click on **Continue**. This returns you to the **Recode into Different Variables** dialog box. Then click on **OK**. You will return to the Data Editor window, where there are now three variables, SOCIOLOG, PSYCHOLO and SOCPASS (Exhibit 2.14).

CHANGING THE VALUE LABELS

Although *you* may remember that the variable SOCPASS is coded 0 for a fail and code 1 for a pass, we can get SPSS to attach labels to these codes so that it is clear for others.

To do this, double-click on the grey column heading marked SOCPASS and then click on **Labels** in the **Define Variable** dialog box (see Exhibit 2.9). This should give you the dialog box shown in Exhibit 2.15. This dialog box allows you to give the variable name SOCPASS a more meaningful description and also to label the codes. To label the variable, type a description into the **Variable Label** box. To attach labels to the codes, use the mouse to position the cursor in the **Value** box, click and then type a **0**. Use the mouse to position the cursor in the **Value Label** box, click and type the label **fail**. After entering each value and its accompanying label, click on **Add** and it will appear in the larger labels box.

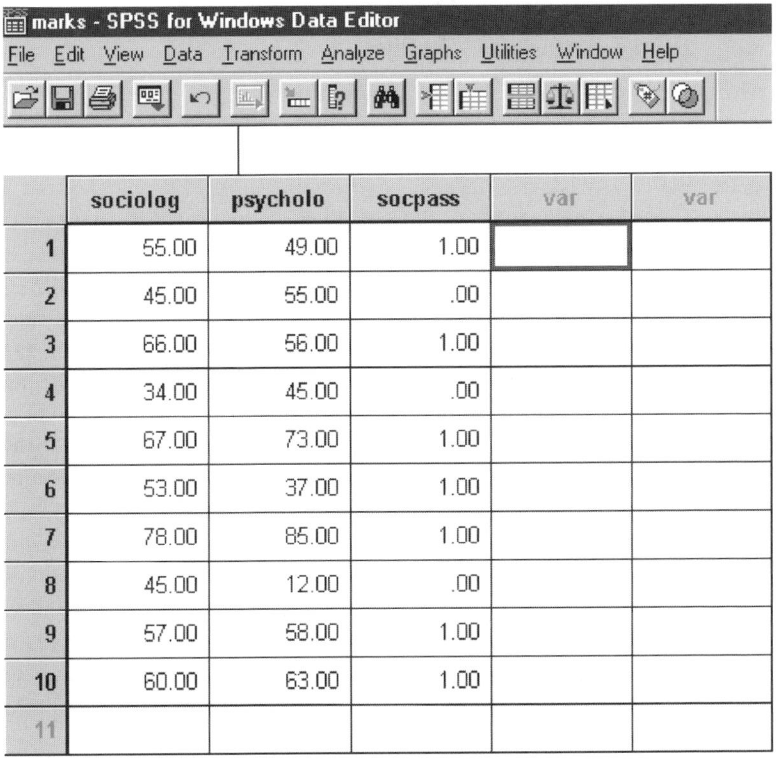

	sociolog	psycholo	socpass	var	var
1	55.00	49.00	1.00		
2	45.00	55.00	.00		
3	66.00	56.00	1.00		
4	34.00	45.00	.00		
5	67.00	73.00	1.00		
6	53.00	37.00	1.00		
7	78.00	85.00	1.00		
8	45.00	12.00	.00		
9	57.00	58.00	1.00		
10	60.00	63.00	1.00		
11					

Exhibit 2.14   **Data Editor** *window showing the new variable* SOCPASS

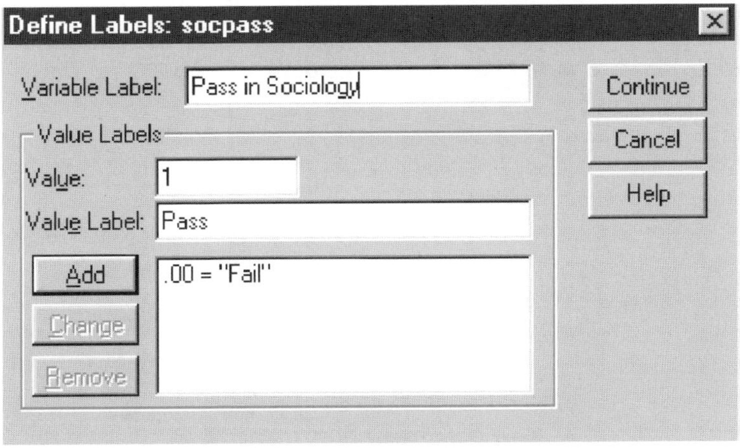

Define Labels: socpass

Variable Label: Pass in Sociology

Value Labels
Value: 1
Value Label: Pass

Add   .00 = "Fail"
Change
Remove

Continue
Cancel
Help

Exhibit 2.15   *Labelling variables in SPSS*

When all the labels have been entered, click on **Continue** and then on **OK** in the **Define Variable** dialog box.

A SIMPLE ANALYSIS

What we would now like to know is how many people passed their sociology assessment. To find out, we select **Analyze|Descriptive Statistics ▶|Frequencies** ... to display the **Frequencies** dialog box (Exhibit 2.16). By clicking first on socpass in the left-hand variable list (Exhibit 2.17) and then on ▶, that variable is transferred to the **Variable(s)** box. Click on **OK** to get SPSS to provide a frequency listing of the number of passes and the number of fails.

Note that in previous versions of SPSS for Windows (version 8.0 and below) a frequencies analysis was carried out by selecting **Statistics|Summarize ▶|Frequencies** .... Otherwise all other operations are the same.

LOOKING AT YOUR RESULTS

The **Output Viewer** is divided into two panes (Exhibit 2.17). The left-hand pane contains an outline view of the output: the log file (a record of SPSS syntax commands – see Exhibit 2.18), the title, notes (including information about the data file the analysis is using and the time of analysis – see Exhibit 2.19), and the frequency table itself (Exhibit 2.20). Note that the log file (Exhibit 2.18) is only included in your output if you requested that option in the **Options** screen.

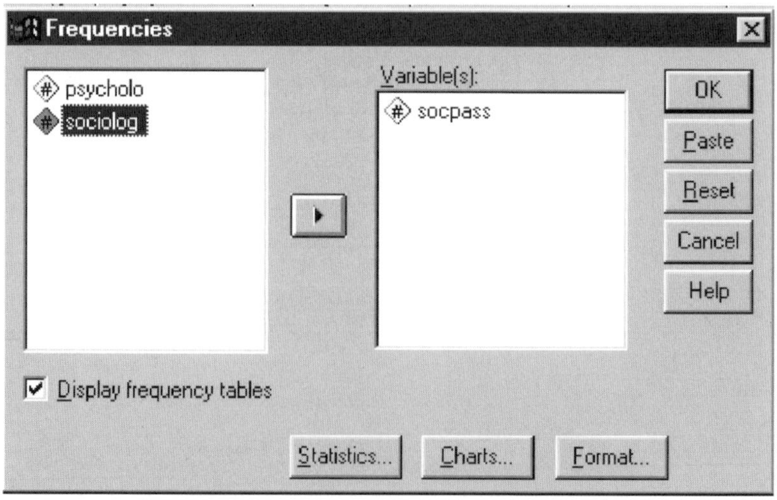

Exhibit 2.16   *Selecting a variable for a frequency table in SPSS*

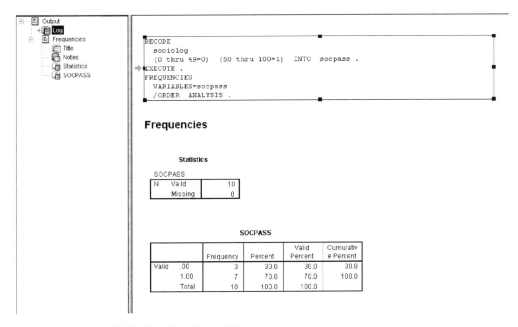

Exhibit 2.17   *The **Output Viewer***

```
RECODE
   sociolog
   (0 thru 49=0)    (50 thru 100=1)    INTO    socpass .
EXECUTE .
FREQUENCIES
   VARIABLES=socpass
   /ORDER   ANALYSIS .
```

Exhibit 2.18   *SPSS Log in the **Output Viewer***

You can do that by selecting **Edit|Options**, clicking the **Viewer** tab, and then ticking **Display commands in log**.

If you look closely in the outline view you will notice that each component of the output is represented by an open or closed book. If the book is open the output is visible in the right-hand pane. If the book is closed, it is hidden. To display a hidden item, you can double-click the icon in the outline pane. Doing the same to an item on display hides it. In Exhibit 2.21, notice that all the book icons are open, except the **Notes** icon.

If we look at the frequency table for SOCPASS we see under the column

Notes

Output Created		27 Jan 99 17:24:41
Comments		
Input	Filter	<none>
	Weight	<none>
	Split File	<none>
	N of Rows in Working Data File	10
Missing Value Handling	Definition of Missing	User-defined missing values are treated as missing.
	Cases Used	Statistics are based on all cases with valid data.
Syntax		FREQUENCIES VARIABLES=socpass /ORDER ANALYSIS.
Resources	Total Values Allowed	18724
	Elapsed Time	0:00:00.50

Exhibit 2.19   *Notes in the **Output Viewer***

SOCPASS Passes in Sociology

		Frequency	Percent	Valid Percent	Cumulative Percent
Valid	.00 Fail	3	30.0	30.0	30.0
	1.00 Pass	7	70.0	70.0	100.0
	Total	10	100.0	100.0	

Exhibit 2.20   *A frequency table of the new variable* SOCPASS

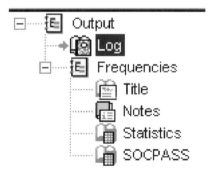

Exhibit 2.21   *The Outline view in the SPSS Viewer*

headed **Frequency** that there are 3 fails and 7 passes (Exhibit 2.20). Chapter 3 discusses the calculation of percentages and cumulative percentages.

SELECTING CASES FOR ANALYSIS

Suppose we are interested in knowing what psychology mark was obtained by those who passed sociology. One way of doing this would be to **select** only those cases who passed sociology and then list their psychology marks. This section shows how to do this.

To select cases with passes in sociology we first select **Data|Select Cases** … (see Exhibit 2.22). The default selection is **All cases**, so first click on **If condition is satisfied**. Then click on the box marked **If** … in order to make a condition for selection (see Exhibit 2.23). The condition to type in the large box is socpass=1 – in other words, those who have passed sociology. Then click on **Continue** and **OK**.

Having selected those students who passed sociology, we now need to list their psychology marks. This can be done using the frequencies procedure described above under simple analysis. Exhibit 2.24 shows the results from the frequencies procedure. Notice that only seven cases are displayed, the seven

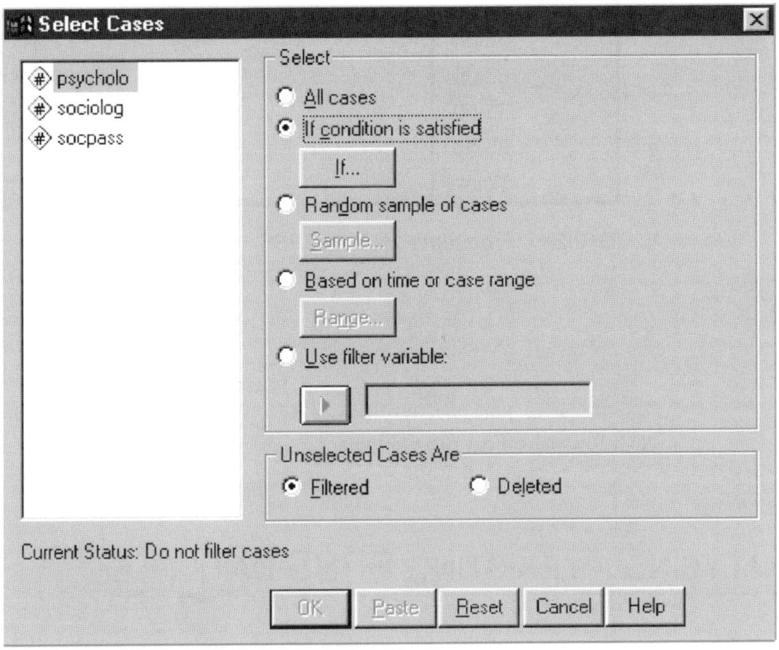

Exhibit 2.22   *Selecting cases in SPSS*

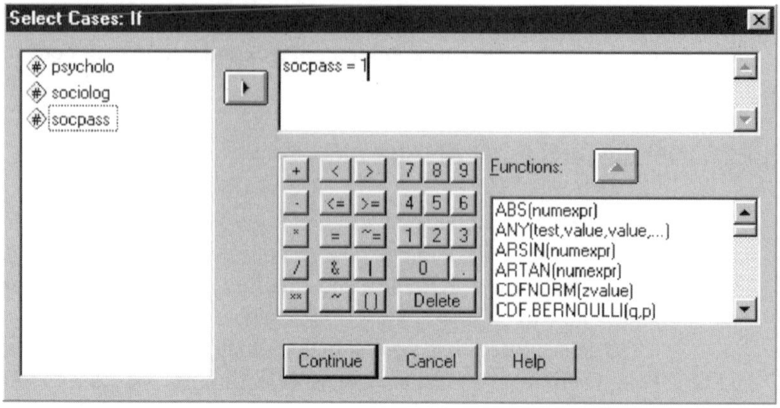

Exhibit 2.23   *Defining the criteria for selecting cases in SPSS*

PSYCHOLO

		Frequency	Percent	Valid Percent	Cumulative Percent
Valid	37.00	1	14.3	14.3	14.3
	49.00	1	14.3	14.3	28.6
	56.00	1	14.3	14.3	42.9
	58.00	1	14.3	14.3	57.1
	63.00	1	14.3	14.3	71.4
	73.00	1	14.3	14.3	85.7
	85.00	1	14.3	14.3	100.0
	Total	7	100.0	100.0	

Exhibit 2.24   *Frequency table in SPSS*

students who passed sociology. The remaining three failed and have therefore been filtered out of the analysis.

ANALYSING AN EXISTING SPSS DATA FILE

An SPSS data file is a file created by SPSS which includes both the data and other information (such as variable labels and value labels). Aside from SPSS

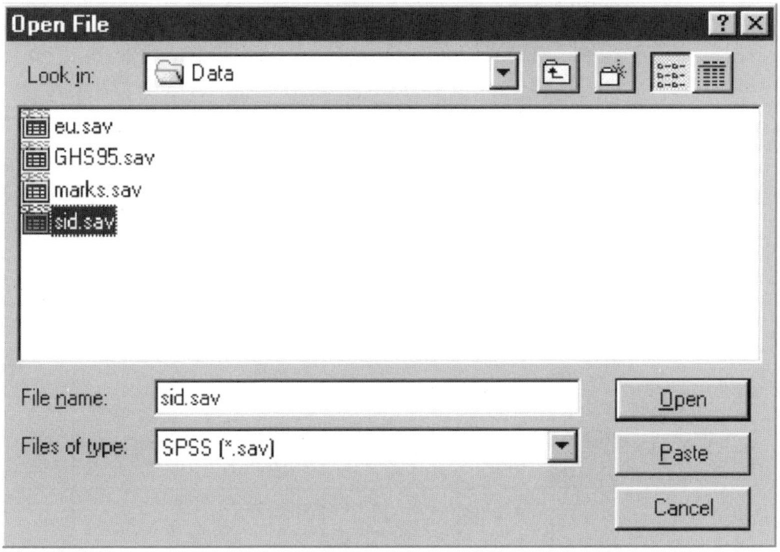

Exhibit 2.25   *Opening the SID data in SPSS*

itself, only a few programs, mainly other statistics packages, are able to read SPSS data files. You cannot print an SPSS data file except from within SPSS and you cannot edit or look at an SPSS data file with an ordinary editor or word-processor program.

To open an SPSS data file, select **File|Open** .... The **Open File** dialog box appears (Exhibit 2.25). Here you can select a file for analysis. The example shows the SID.SAV data file selected for opening. This file consists of data from the 1992 World Bank Social Indicators of Development including 97 variables for 171 countries (see Chapter 1).

After opening this file, the data window should be filled with data and the name in the title bar should have changed from **Untitled** to **SID**. The variables are named along the top in grey boxes. The cases are numbered sequentially down the side. In the lower right-hand corner are the scroll arrows, ▶ and ▼. Click on these to see more variables and/or cases (see Exhibit 2.26).

Notice that the third column is the name of the country in alphabetical order. Although SPSS expects all your variables to be numeric, it is possible to input **alphanumeric** or **string** variables into SPSS. This is done in the **Define Variable** dialog screen (which appears when you double-click on the grey variable name in the column heading) by selecting **Type** .... Exhibit 2.27 shows the **Define Variable** dialog box for the variable COUNTRY with the **Define Variable Type** dialog box superimposed. Typing **20** in the **Characters:** box limits the number of characters for each country to just 20 characters. The maximum number of characters we could define is 255. This can be useful if we

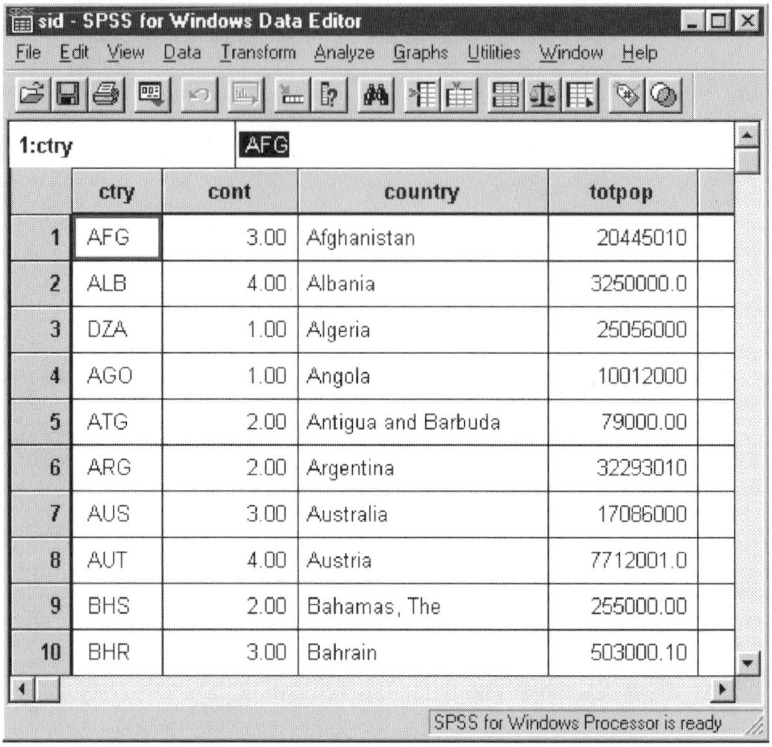

Exhibit 2.26   **Data Editor** *window with the SID data*

wish to record verbatim responses to open-ended questions from a survey questionnaire.

LISTING DATA

We have seen that the countries have been entered in the data alphabetically but if we want to look at a list of countries listed by continent we could do that by grouping the listing by the variable CONT. CONT, for continent, has been coded so that code 1 has been given to countries in the African continent, 2 for those in the American, 3 for those in Austral/Asia and 4 for those in Europe. We can get SPSS to list the countries by each continent by using the **Case Summaries** procedure as follows. Select **Analyze|Reports ►|Case Summaries** ... to see Exhibit 2.28.

Select country for the **Variables** box and cont as the **Grouping Variable**. Deselect **Limit cases to first** so that all 171 countries can be listed. Then click on **OK**. Your results should look like those in Exhibit 2.29, although only the first few countries in Africa are listed here. To see all the results you can double-

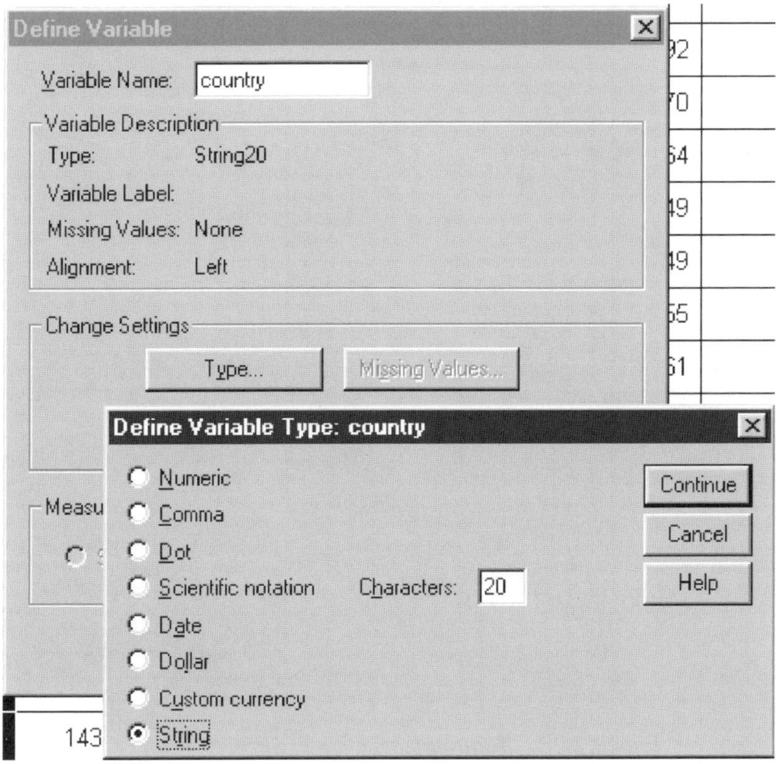

Exhibit 2.27   *Defining the character length of a string variable*

click on the table to open the **Pivot Table Editor** and use the scroll buttons to see all your results.

COPYING YOUR RESULTS INTO A WORD PROCESSOR

It is very easy to copy your results from SPSS into your favourite word processor. Simply select the results in SPSS and then a right click of the mouse will allow you to select **Copy**. You can then open your word processor, or switch to it if it is already open, to **Paste** the results in. Incidentally, cutting and pasting this way will transfer a frequencies table into your word processor as a table. If you want it transferred as a picture, then you will have to select **Paste Special** and select **Picture**. Exhibits 2.30 and 2.31 demonstrate the difference between these two ways of transferring tables from SPSS by copying the **Case Processing Summary**. Although the information is the same in each of these exhibits,

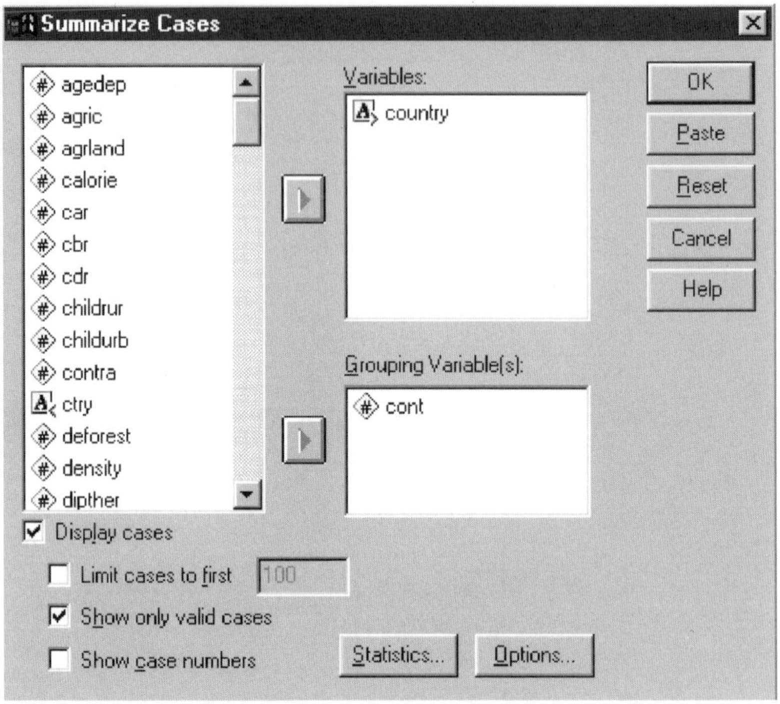

Exhibit 2.28   **Summarize Cases** *in SPSS*

that in Exhibit 2.30 can be edited using your word processor while that in Exhibit 2.31 cannot.

GETTING HELP IN SPSS

SPSS has an extensive help facility invoked by selecting **Help** from the main menu bar (see Exhibit 2.32). Apart from help with any procedure you are not sure about, SPSS also provides a tutorial and even a statistics coach which asks you a set of questions about your proposed analysis and then suggests a statistical procedure for you to follow.

SUMMARY

This chapter has introduced SPSS for Windows. Emphasis has been placed on the dual roles of statistical software. In the first place SPSS is useful for data

Case Summaries

			COUNTRY
CONT	1.00 Africa	1	Algeria
Continent		2	Angola
		3	Benin
		4	Botswana
		5	Burkina Faso
		6	Burundi
		7	Cameroon
		8	Cape Verde
		9	Central African Rep
		10	Chad
		11	Comoros
		12	Congo
		13	Cote d'Ivoire
		14	Egypt, Arab Republi
		15	Equatorial Guinea
		16	Ethiopia
		17	Gabon
		18	Gambia, The
		19	Ghana

Exhibit 2.29   *Case Summaries of country by continent*

Case Processing Summary

	Cases					
	Included		Excluded		Total	
	N	Percent	N	Percent	N	Percent
COUNTRY* CONT Continent	171	100.0%	0	.0%	171	100.0%

Exhibit 2.30   *Using **Copy** in SPSS and **Paste** in WordPerfect*

Case Processing Summary

	Cases					
	Included		Excluded		Total	
	N	Percent	N	Percent	N	Percent
COUNTRY * CONT Continent	171	100.0%	0	.0%	171	100.0%

Exhibit 2.31   *Using **Copy** in SPSS and **Paste Special**, **Picture** in WordPerfect*

Exhibit 2.32   *The **Help** menu in SPSS*

management tasks, such as recoding values and case selection to create subsets of data. In the second place, SPSS will perform data analysis, demonstrated using the **Frequencies** and **Case Summary** procedures.

EXERCISES

1. Create and save the MARKS.SAV SPSS data file using the data in Exhibit 2.7. As described in the text, create a new variable called SOCPASS by recoding the sociology marks so that all those who failed (i.e. got a mark of 49 and below) are given the code 0 and all those who scored 50 or more get the code 1. Create a frequency listing of the new variable SOCPASS. Do your results match those seen in Exhibit 2.20?
2. Using the marks data set created in Exercise 1, select those students who passed psychology and list their sociology mark.

PART II

UNIVARIATE ANALYSIS

FREQUENCIES, PROPORTIONS AND PERCENTAGES

3

CONTENTS

The first step on the path to understanding a data set is to look at each variable, one at a time, using **univariate statistics**. Even if you plan to take your analysis further to explore the linkages, or relationships, between two or more of your variables you initially need to look very carefully at the distribution of each variable on its own.

FREQUENCY DISTRIBUTIONS

One of the first things you might want to do with data is to count the number of occurrences that fall into each category of each variable. This provides you with **frequency distributions**, allowing you to compare information between groups of individuals. They allow you to answer questions like 'how many married people are there in the data' and to calculate 'what percentage of people think that nuclear testing should be stopped'. They also allow you to see what are the highest and lowest values and the value at which most scores cluster.

For instance, you might be interested in the take-up of science and arts/social science subjects at A (advanced) level in a particular sixth-form college. After asking each boy what subjects he is studying at A level you could divide the boys into those taking mainly science subjects and those taking mainly arts/social science subjects.

It would be clearer if we counted up the number of boys in each category. This would give the **frequency** of occurrence in each category (see Exhibit 3.1). There are 26 boys studying science and 17 studying arts/social science at this college. We might be interested in comparing these numbers with the girls' choice of subjects. There are 23 girls studying science and 44 girls studying arts/social science at the same college. So 26 boys and 23 girls study science. Does this mean that boys and girls are about equally interested in science subjects? No, because there are more girls than boys. Twenty-six of a total of 43 boys are studying science compared with 23 of a total of 67 girls.

We need to give these figures a common base for comparison. The calculation of proportions provides this common base.

PROPORTIONS

Proportions are the number of cases belonging to a particular category divided by the total number of cases. The sum of the proportions of all the categories will always equal one. Exhibit 3.2 expresses the frequencies of girls' and boys' subject choices in terms of proportions: 0.605 of the boys study science, but only 0.343 of the girls.

PERCENTAGES

Percentages are proportions multiplied by 100. Thus the total of all the percentages in any particular group (boys or girls) equals 100 per cent. Thus at

Subject studied	Frequencies of boys (f)
Science	♂♂♂♂♂♂♂♂♂♂♂♂♂♂♂♂♂♂♂♂♂♂♂♂♂♂ = 26
Arts/social sciences	♂♂♂♂♂♂♂♂♂♂♂♂♂♂♂♂♂ = 17
Total	43

Exhibit 3.1   *A levels studied in a hypothetical sixth-form college*

A-level subject	Boys		Girls	
	Frequency (*f*)	Proportions (*p*)	Frequency (*f*)	Proportions (*p*)
Science	26	$\frac{26}{43} = 0.605$	23	$\frac{23}{67} = 0.343$
Arts/ social science	17	$\frac{17}{43} = 0.395$	44	$\frac{44}{67} = 0.657$
Totals	43	1.0	67	1.0

Exhibit 3.2   *Frequencies and proportions for boys and girls*

this sixth-form college, 60.5 per cent of boys study science subjects, compared to 34.3 per cent of girls.

If you want to **round** a percentage to the nearest whole percentage point, then look at the digits after the decimal point. If these are .499 or below, then round the figure down – for example, $23/67 = 34.328$ per cent, or 34 per cent to the nearest whole number. If you have .500 or above, then round the figure up – for example, $17/43 = 39.535$ per cent, which is 40 per cent to the nearest whole number.[1]

RATIOS

Ratios are another way of expressing the different numbers studying science and arts/social science subjects. The ratio of boys studying science to boys doing arts/social science A levels is

$$\frac{\text{frequency of boys studying science}}{\text{frequency of boys studying arts/social science}} = \frac{26}{17}$$

If we divide by the denominator (17), this becomes

$$\frac{1.53}{1}$$

[1] There are other methods of rounding, for example just truncating the number at the decimal point or numbers ending in .5 rounding alternately up and down. However, these rules are hard to remember and so for simplicity in this book we will always round up numbers ending in .5.

This can be written as 1.53 : 1. There are about 1.5 boys studying science subjects for every 1 boy studying arts. Since we normally like to express numbers like this as whole numbers, both the denominator and the numerator can be multiplied by 2 to show that there are three boys studying science subjects for every two boys studying arts/social science:

$$\frac{1.53}{1} \times \frac{2}{2} = \frac{3.06}{2}$$

Looking at the girls, the ratio of girls studying science to girls studying arts/ social science is

$$\frac{\text{frequency of girls studying science}}{\text{frequency of girls studying arts/social science}} = \frac{23}{44} = \frac{0.52}{1}$$

Once again dividing by the denominator (44), there are about 0.5 girls studying science for every girl studying arts/social science, that is, there is one girl studying science for every two studying arts/social science. Alternatively, we

---

Summary of notation for proportions, percentages and ratios

The following list summarizes the statistical concepts introduced so far this chapter.

Frequency:
  The number of observations with attribute 1, f_1
  The number of observations with attribute 2, f_2
  Total number of observations, N
Proportion:

$$p = \frac{f_1}{N} \quad \text{or} \quad \frac{f_2}{N}$$

Percentage:

$$= \frac{f_1}{N} \times 100\% \quad \text{or} \quad \frac{f_2}{N} \times 100\%$$

Ratio:

$$= \frac{f_1}{f_2} \quad \text{or} \quad \frac{f_2}{f_1}$$

could arrive at the same conclusion by turning the ratio round and expressing it as follows:

$$\frac{\text{frequency of girls studying arts/social science}}{\text{frequency of girls studying science}} = \frac{44}{23} = \frac{1.91}{1}$$

There are 1.9 girls (2 if we round up) studying arts for every one studying science.

Proportions, percentages and ratios are alternative ways of comparing the relative amounts of something (in this example, the relative numbers of boys and girls taking science). Proportions and percentages are easy to convert from one to another and, while there is no hard-and-fast rule, social scientists tend to prefer to use percentages. In this case, the percentages show clearly that the arts and social sciences subjects are most popular among girls, and that science is slightly more popular than arts/social science among boys.

CODING VARIABLES FOR COMPUTER ANALYSIS

Before you can use SPSS to help you calculate a frequency distribution, you need to give each category of a variable a numeric code. In addition, you need to give each variable a variable name of no more than 8 characters, as described in Chapter 2.

Exhibit 3.3 shows the data for sex, marital status, age and social class for just

Case	Sex	Marital status	Social class	Age
1	Male	Single	SOCIAL CLASS IIIN	68
2	Male	Cohabiting	SOCIAL CLASS IIIN	38
3	Female	Single	SOCIAL CLASS II	18
4	Female	Cohabiting	SOCIAL CLASS IIIN	29
5	Female	Married	SOCIAL CLASS IIIN	62
6	Female	Widowed	SOCIAL CLASS IV	81
7	Male	Widowed	SOCIAL CLASS II	74
8	Female	Divorced	SOCIAL CLASS II	41
9	Female	Married	SOCIAL CLASS IIIN	59
10	Male	Married	SOCIAL CLASS IIIM	59
11	Female	Divorced	SOCIAL CLASS IIIM	74
12	Female	Married	SOCIAL CLASS IIIN	39
13	Male	Married	SOCIAL CLASS I	78
14	Female	Divorced	SOCIAL CLASS IV	45
15	Female	Married	SOCIAL CLASS IIIN	64
16	Male	Married	SOCIAL CLASS II	45

Exhibit 3.3   *Data for sex, marital status, social class and age for 16 respondents*

16 people, before numeric codes have been assigned to each category of each variable. This data set is in a file called GHS95_16CASES.SAV. For example, person 1 (case 1) is male, single, in social class III non-manual (IIIN) and aged 68.

The first variable, sex, is an example of a nominal variable which we can give the variable name SEX, and one possibility of coding this variable would be to assign codes as in Exhibit 3.4. Note that these codes have been assigned arbitrarily, so a code of 1 for males could equally have been 2, and vice versa for females.

The second variable, marital status, which we will call MARSTAT, could be coded as in Exhibit 3.5. Once again, since marital status is a nominal variable, we could have coded this variable in a completely different order.

Social class, the third variable, has been given the SPSS variable name SOCLASE, and is an example of an ordinal variable where it is possible to rank or order the categories of the variable. As an ordinal variable, you know that someone in class I possesses more of whatever it is – salary, prestige, status – that goes to measure class, but you do not know *how much more* of these qualities they possess than someone in class IV. There are only two ways you can code an ordinal variable, in either ascending order or descending order, and it generally does not matter which way you choose. So SOCLASE could be coded either as in scheme A or as in scheme B in Exhibit 3.6.

Finally, AGE, the respondents' age, is a variable measured at the interval level.

SEX	Coding scheme
Males	1
Females	2

Exhibit 3.4   *Coding for the variable* SEX

MARSTAT - Marital status	Coding scheme
Married	1
Cohabiting	2
Single	3
Widowed	4
Divorced	5

Exhibit 3.5   *Coding for the marital status (*MARSTAT*)*

SOCLASE - SOCIAL CLASS	Scheme A	Scheme B
Social class I	1	6
Social class II	2	5
Social class IIIN (Non-manual)	3	4
Social class IIIM (Manual)	4	3
Social class IV	5	2
Social class V	6	1

Exhibit 3.6   *Coding for social class (SOCLASE)*

Here, instead of assigning codes to each person's response we will use their actual response. So we will use their actual age in the data.

Exhibit 3.7 shows these four variables in the SPSS **Data Editor** after they have been coded.

FREQUENCY DISTRIBUTIONS IN SPSS

In order to get SPSS to carry out the frequency procedure you need to select **Analyze|Descriptive statistics ▶|Frequencies**... and select the variables from the variable list before clicking on **OK** (see Chapter 2, Exhibit 2.17). The resulting frequency table for SEX is seen in Exhibit 3.8.

The first column shows the numeric codes that have been assigned to each category, labelled by the respective value label. The columns headed **Frequency** and **Percent** show the number of cases in the category and the percentages of the whole data set in the category respectively. The columns headed **Valid Percent** and **Cumulative Percent** will be explained in a later section in this chapter.

Exhibit 3.9 shows the frequency distribution of the variable MARSTAT, and Exhibit 3.10 the distribution for SOCLASE.

If SPSS were asked for a frequency distribution for a variable which has many categories such as AGE, one would get a very, very long table, with a row for each different age. In the GHS data set the youngest respondent is 16 and the oldest 97, therefore there would be 82 rows in the table. This table is too large to comprehend easily and not very useful. The conclusion is that an SPSS frequency distribution is only suitable for variables which have a moderate number of categories. If you do have a variable such as age which has many categories, it is best to divide the variable first into a small number of groupings (for example, group **age** into age bands) and then find the frequency distribution of the grouped categories.

	sex	marstat	soclase	age
1	1	3	3	68
2	1	2	3	38
3	2	3	2	18
4	2	2	3	29
5	2	1	3	62
6	2	4	5	81
7	1	4	2	74
8	2	5	2	41
9	2	1	3	59
10	1	1	4	59
11	2	5	4	74
12	2	1	3	39
13	1	1	1	78
14	2	5	5	45
15	2	1	3	64
16	1	1	2	45

Exhibit 3.7   The **Data Editor** *in SPSS showing the variables* SEX, MARSTAT, SOCLASE *and* AGE

SEX SEX

		Frequency	Percent	Valid Percent	Cumulative Percent
Valid	1 Male	6	37.5	37.5	37.5
	2 Female	10	62.5	62.5	100.0
	Total	16	100.0	100.0	

Exhibit 3.8   *SPSS frequency output for* SEX

MARSTAT MARITAL STATUS

		Frequency	Percent	Valid Percent	Cumulative Percent
Valid	1 Married	7	43.8	43.8	43.8
	2 Cohabiting	2	12.5	12.5	56.3
	3 Single	2	12.5	12.5	68.8
	4 Widowed	2	12.5	12.5	81.3
	5 Divorced	3	18.8	18.8	100.0
	Total	16	100.0	100.0	

Exhibit 3.9   *SPSS frequency output for marital status (*MARSTAT*)*

SOCLASE SOCIAL CLASS OF INDIVIDUAL

	Frequency	Percent	Valid Percent	Cumulative Percent
Valid 1 SOCIAL CLASS I	1	6.3	6.3	6.3
2 SOCIAL CLASS II	4	25.0	25.0	31.3
3 SOCIAL CLASS IIIN	7	43.8	43.8	75.0
4 SOCIAL CLASS IIIM	2	12.5	12.5	87.5
5 SOCIAL CLASS IV	2	12.5	12.5	100.0
Total	16	100.0	100.0	

Exhibit 3.10   *SPSS frequency output for social class (*SOCLASE*)*

GROUPED FREQUENCY DISTRIBUTIONS

In order to group a continuous, interval variable, respondents are divided into appropriate or convenient intervals. The first task is to decide the boundaries of the intervals to be used. If we group AGE into ten-year age bands using the categories and codes in Exhibit 3.11, SPSS will produce the frequency distribution shown in Exhibit 3.12 using the GHS95_16case data.

Creating intervals in this way seems quite straightforward. However, we have profited by the fact the survey only recorded respondents' ages in whole years, for example as 29 years, not as 29 years, 4 months and 5 days or 29.342.

It is worth considering what would happen to a person aged 29.5 years using the coding scheme in Exhibit 3.11. Code 2 is assigned to those aged between 20 and 29 and code 3 is assigned to those aged between 30 and 39. It appears that those aged between 29 and 30 do not belong in either code. In order to cater for all possible codes we need to close up all the gaps between the intervals. We need to abut the intervals by creating **real class intervals** with **real class limits**.

Age Band	Code
10–19	1
20–29	2
30–39	3
40–49	4
50–59	5
60–69	6
70–79	7
80–89	8
90–99	9

Exhibit 3.11   *Coding for recoding age into ten-year age groups*

AGEGROUP

		Frequency	Percent	Valid Percent	Cumulative Percent
Valid	1	1	6.3	6.3	6.3
	2	1	6.3	6.3	12.5
	3	2	12.5	12.5	25.0
	4	3	18.8	18.8	43.8
	5	2	12.5	12.5	56.3
	6	3	18.8	18.8	75.0
	7	3	18.8	18.8	93.8
	8	1	6.3	6.3	100.0
	Total	16	100.0	100.0	

Exhibit 3.12   *SPSS frequency output for age group (AGEGROUP)*

REAL CLASS INTERVALS

To create real class limits around real class intervals, divide the distance between the stated class intervals by 2, subtract this from the lower limit and add it to the upper limit (see Exhibit 3.13).

Exhibit 3.14 displays all the stated and real class limits for the variable AGE as previously coded. Of course, AGE could be recoded in many different ways with correspondingly different real class intervals.

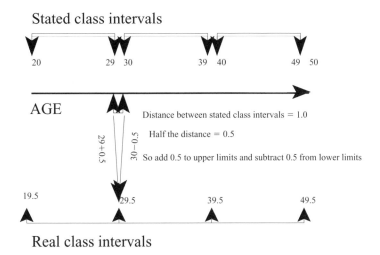

Exhibit 3.13   *The relationship between stated class intervals and real class intervals*

Stated class intervals	Real class intervals
10–19	9.5–19.5
20–29	19.5–29.5
30–39	29.5–39.5
40–49	39.5–49.5
50–59	49.5–59.5
60–69	59.5–69.5
70–79	69.5–79.5
80–89	79.5–89.5
90–99	89.5–99.5

Exhibit 3.14   *Stated class intervals and real class intervals for* agegroup

MIDPOINTS

Another important statistic when creating real class intervals is the midpoint of the real class interval. The midpoint of a real class interval is defined as the point exactly half-way between the lower and upper real class limit.

Midpoint of interval = real lower class limit

+ one half of size of class interval

For example,

$$\text{Size of the class interval} = 29.5\text{--}19.5 = 10$$

$$\text{Midpoint of the real class interval } 19.5\text{--}29.5 = 19.5 + \frac{10}{2} = 24.5$$

Exhibit 3.15 shows the midpoints of all the real class intervals for the variable AGE GROUP.

Procedure for grouped frequency distribution

1. Decide how many intervals to use. Between seven and ten intervals is a reasonable number. Too few and you lose too much information.
2. Find the size and number of the class intervals. Round the highest score up and the lowest score down to a convenient number. This will give you the range of scores. Then divide the range of the scores by the number of intervals, to arrive at a convenient interval size. For example, to create age bands from AGE, round the highest age, 97 up to 100 and the lowest, 16, down to 10, this gives a distribution of scores from 100 to 10, an range of 90. Divide this range by a convenient number of intervals so that you also get a convenient class interval size (usually a round number like 10 rather than an awkward number like 9). This naturally would yield nine intervals of size 10.
3. Count the number of cases in each stated interval and report these as frequencies (f). Report the total number of cases (N).
4. Calculate percentages for each interval.

Stated class intervals	Real class intervals	Midpoints
10–19	9.5–19.5	9.5 + 0.5(10) = 14.5
20–29	19.5–29.5	19.5 + 0.5(10) = 24.5
30–39	29.5–39.5	34.5
40–49	39.5–49.5	44.5
50–59	49.5–59.5	54.5
60–69	59.5–69.5	64.5
70–79	69.5–79.5	74.5
80–89	79.5–89.5	84.5
90–99	89.5–99.5	94.5

Exhibit 3.15   *Midpoints of real class intervals for age group*

FREQUENCY TABLES FROM THE 1995 GHS

Finally, let us look at the frequency distributions using the large GHS 1995 data set. Exhibits 3.16 and 3.17 show the frequency tables for SEX and MARSTAT. If we report the percentages to the nearest whole number by rounding, we see that 48 per cent are male and 52 per cent are female. Looking at marital status, 65 per cent are married or cohabiting, 20 per cent are single and the rest (15 per cent) are widowed, divorced or separated.

Exhibit 3.18 demonstrates a frequency table for the grouped variable AGEGROUP. This variable was derived from the original data by recoding the variable AGE according to the scheme in Exhibit 3.11.

The frequency table of the final variable, SOCLASE, is described below and illustrates the problem of how one deals with non-response codes.

SEX SEX

		Frequency	Percent	Valid Percent	Cumulative Percent
Valid	1 Male	2218	47.9	47.9	47.9
	2 Female	2415	52.1	52.1	100.0
	Total	4633	100.0	100.0	

Exhibit 3.16   *SPSS frequency output for sex from the GHS 1995 data set*

MARSTAT MARITAL STATUS

		Frequency	Percent	Valid Percent	Cumulative Percent
Valid	1 Married	2653	57.3	57.3	57.3
	2 Cohabiting	346	7.5	7.5	64.7
	3 Single	934	20.2	20.2	84.9
	4 Widowed	378	8.2	8.2	93.0
	5 Divorced	226	4.9	4.9	97.9
	6 Separated	94	2.0	2.0	100.0
	7 Same sex cohab	2	.0	.0	100.0
	Total	4663	100.0	100.0	

Exhibit 3.17   *SPSS frequency output for marital status from the GHS 1995 data set*

AGEGROUP

		Frequency	Percent	Valid Percent	Cumulative Percent
Valid	1.00 10–19	255	5.5	5.5	5.5
	2.00 20–29	758	16.4	16.4	21.9
	3.00 30–39	938	20.2	20.2	42.1
	4.00 40–49	806	17.4	17.4	59.5
	5.00 50–59	689	14.9	14.9	74.4
	6.00 60–69	570	12.3	12.3	86.7
	7.00 70–79	427	9.2	9.2	95.9
	8.00 80–89	170	3.7	3.7	99.6
	9.00 90–99	20	.4	.4	100.0
	Total	4633	100.0	100.0	

Exhibit 3.18   *SPSS frequency output for age group from the GHS 1995 data set*

MISSING VALUES IN SPSS

When you are coding the responses to a survey prior to computer analysis, *every* response must be coded,[2] even if the respondent refused to answer or if the question was inapplicable. For instance, there may be two questions in a survey, the first asking if the respondent is employed and the second asking about the respondent's occupation. Clearly, if the respondent is not employed, then the next question is inapplicable. However, you must assign a code to this non-response but then you are able to indicate that this code is special by assigning it as a **missing value**.

Consider the variable age measured on an interval scale. Some people may refuse to answer this question and be given a non-response code of −9. If you then wanted to work out the average age of all the respondents, you would want to make sure that the −9 code is not included in the analysis. Declaring a value as a missing value ensures that that value is excluded from any calculations.

In Exhibit 3.19, the frequency table for SOCLASE, notice that some people have never worked or did not answer (DNA) and have been given the code −9. We do not know their social class and therefore would want to exclude them from any further consideration in our analysis. This has been done by declaring the code they have been assigned (−9) as a **missing value** in SPSS. The effect of this is that the 216 respondents who have been given code −9 have been excluded from the percentage calculation seen in the column headed **Valid Percent**. Percentages calculated in this way are usually the ones that you are interested in and the ones that you report in your analysis.

---

[2] You can leave the data as a blank in SPSS. The data value will be treated as a missing value – a **system missing value**.

SOCLASE SOCIAL CLASS OF INDIVIDUAL

		Frequency	Percent	Valid Percent	Cumulative Percent
Valid	1 SOCIAL CLASS I	189	4.1	4.3	4.3
	2 SOCIAL CLASS II	1110	24.0	25.1	29.4
	3 SOC CLASS IIIN	1050	22.7	23.8	53.2
	4 SOC CLASS IIIM	956	20.6	21.6	74.8
	5 SOCIAL CLASS IV	796	17.2	18.0	92.8
	6 SOCIAL CLASS V	298	6.4	6.7	99.6
	7 ARMED FORCES	18	.4	.4	100.0
	Total	4417	95.3	100.0	
Missing	-9 DNA:NEVER WORKED	216	4.7		
Total		4633	100.0		

Exhibit 3.19   *SPSS frequency output for social class from the GHS 1995 data set*

DEFINING MISSING VALUES IN SPSS

To define a code as a missing-value code for any particular variable, you need that variable's **Define Variable** dialog box (see Exhibit 3.20), obtained by double-clicking the grey column heading for that variable in the **Data Editor** window. Then select **Missing Values** and type the value you wish to define as missing into the **Define Missing Values** screen as in Exhibit 3.20. Note that you are only allowed up to three different missing values.

EXPLORING THE DATA SET AND CREATING A CODEBOOK

Sometimes you do not know the names of the variables you are interested in using in your analysis. This is especially the case when you are conducting a secondary analysis of data that were collected by someone else. For instance, we might be interested in how many people have a telephone and know that a question on telephone use was asked in the General Household Survey, yet we do not know what variable name has been assigned to that question. There are two ways we could go about discovering this information. In the first place, we could use an on-screen facility in SPSS to help find out the variable name for this question and also find out the codes that have been assigned to the answers. In the long term, though, it is more useful to create a **codebook** with the same information, but for all the variables, which you can print out to refer to later.

To use the on-screen facility to discover the name of the variable that has asked the respondents about telephone use, select **Utilities|Variables**. . . from

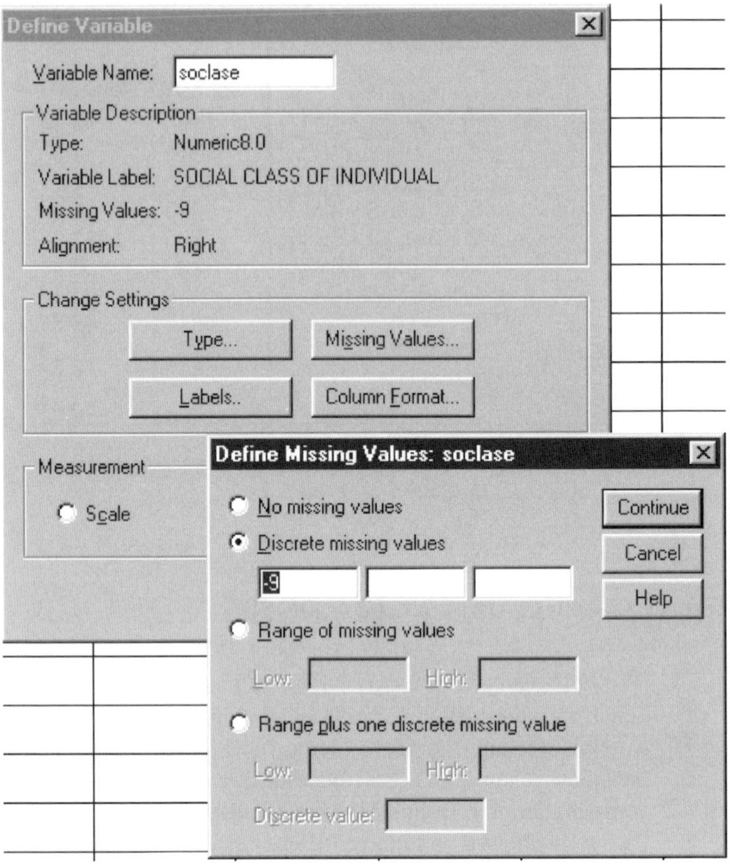

Exhibit 3.20   *Defining missing values in SPSS for social class*

the main menu to see the dialog box in Exhibit 3.21. A search of the list of variables in the left-hand side of the dialog box reveals a variable called PHONE. Selecting this variable displays its variable information in the right-hand side of the dialog box. Here we can see that those people who have a phone have been coded with a 1 and those who do not have a phone have been given code 2.

To create a codebook, select **Utilities|File info**. This provides you with text output with the details of all the variables in the file which can be saved or printed.

HOUSEHOLDS AND INDIVIDUALS IN THE GENERAL HOUSEHOLD SURVEY

As described in Chapter 1, the GHS consists of data about households and individuals within those households. Information about each household, such

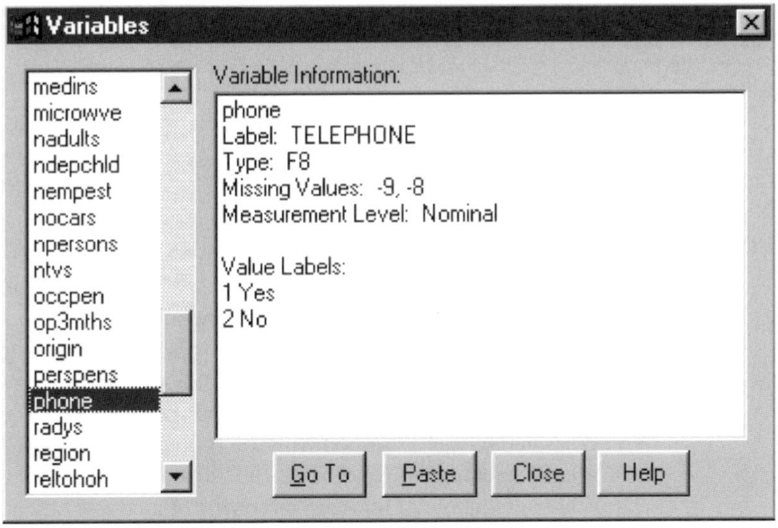

Exhibit 3.21   *Variable information in SPSS*

as telephone ownership, has been *spread* to each individual in that household. Therefore if three people live in one household and own a telephone, then it will be counted three times at the individual level. To get round this problem and to gain a correct percentage for telephone ownership at the household level, we need to select just one person from each household. This is the person who has been designated as *head of household*. So to continue with our investigation we first of all need to select heads of household. The variable RELTOHOH is coded 0 for those respondents who are heads of household.

Therefore we select **Data|Select cases**. . . and click on **If condition is satisfied** and then **If.** . . . The condition we type in the next dialog box is reltohoh = **0**. After selecting the correct cases, all we now need to do is to carry out a frequency procedure for the variable PHONE.

SUMMARY

This chapter has introduced frequencies, proportions and percentages for single variables. How to code nominal, ordinal and interval variables has been introduced as a preliminary procedure before using statistical software such as SPSS.

EXERCISES

Using the General Household Survey data (GHS95.SAV), answer the following questions. Remember to select only head of household data if the response is required at the household level.

1. What percentage of the households have a video recorder?
2. What percentage of households own more than three cars?
3. What percentage of respondents are Indian?
4. What percentage of households live in a semi-detached house?
5. What percentage of respondents live in Scotland?
6. What percentage of respondents are full-time students?
7. What percentage of respondents are retired?
8. What percentage of respondents left school under 15 years of age?
9. What percentage of households consist of a couple and no children?
10. What percentage of households have two or more colour TVs?

GRAPHICS FOR DISPLAY

4

CONTENTS

Research is not just about finding things out, but also about communicating new knowledge to people in a way which is clear and persuasive. In the previous chapter, we saw how a variety of statistics could be used to formulate conclusions about frequency distributions. In this chapter, we turn to graphical displays, which are useful for showing the form of a distribution to people who do not have a statistical background. The chapter focuses on two popular types of display for categorical data, pie charts and bar charts, both of which are often used in newspapers and academic articles to report on frequency distributions. For interval data, histograms and polygons are introduced.

GRAPHICAL METHODS FOR CATEGORICAL DATA

Most demographic variables such as sex, marital status and social class are categorical. Graphical methods for categorical data can be based on simple frequencies, proportions or percentages. These graphical methods are also appropriate for discrete, continuous variables.

PIE CHARTS

In the previous chapter we saw how we can calculate the proportion or percentage of cases in each category of a variable by expressing the number in the category as a proportion or percentage of the total. In a similar way, pie charts display the proportions or percentages in each category of a variable (as pieces of the pie) in relation to the whole or all the categories (represented by the entire pie), that is, as proportions of 1 or percentages of 100 per cent. Exhibit 4.1 is an example of a pie chart, showing the proportions of male and female sociology students attending an undergraduate programme.

To create a pie chart by hand you calculate the proportions of a circle which each category of a variable would occupy. Since the whole circle consists of 360°, you need to work out the proportions of 360° that each segment occupies. The result will be segments of a circle assigned in proportion to the frequencies in the categories. In Exhibit 4.1, there were 6 males out of a total of 32 students, corresponding to

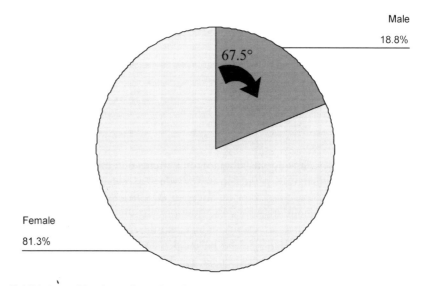

Exhibit 4.1   *Pie chart of gender of sociology undergraduates*

$$\frac{6}{32} \times 360° = 67.5°$$

or, in percentages,

$$\frac{6}{32} \times 100 = 18.8\%$$

The chart indicates clearly and strikingly the gender imbalance between sociology undergraduates in the statistics class. In practice, pie charts are more often used to display more than two categories and we can simplify the task by getting a computer to do the necessary calculations and draw the chart. SPSS will do this quite easily.

CREATING A PIE CHART IN SPSS

There are three sorts of pie chart in SPSS:

- summaries of groups of cases where each slice of the pie is a *category* of one variable;
- summaries of separate variables where each slice is a calculated *statistic* (i.e. sum or mean) of *several variables*;
- values of individual cases where each slice is a *case*.

We will explore only two of these pie charts: the summaries of groups of cases, the most popular method, and values of individual cases. Later on in the chapter these pie charts will be compared with similar bar charts.

SUMMARIES FOR GROUPS OF CASES

In the previous chapter we explored the frequency distribution of the variable MARSTAT, marital status (see Exhibit 3.17). However, to simplify the following graphical displays, we have recoded MARSTAT so that code 2 (cohabiting) and code 7 (same sex cohabiting) are combined into one cohabiting code and codes 5 (separated) and 6 (divorced) are combined into one separated/divorced category.

To create a pie chart in SPSS to show the distribution of marital status we need to select from the main menu **Graphs|Pie. . ..** We then have a choice of pie chart (see Exhibit 4.2). Since we wish to summarize the groups of people who fell into one marital status category or another, we select **Summaries for groups of cases** in the dialog box.

The dialog box in Exhibit 4.3 allows us to select the variable from the variable list box on the left-hand side and then transfer it over to the empty box by clicking on the ▶ button next to the **Define Slices by:** box and then clicking on **OK**. Exhibit 4.4 shows that just over half the respondents said that they were married. You may be surprised by the large size of the slice representing those

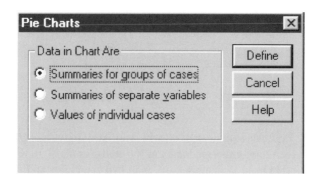

Exhibit 4.2   **Pie Charts** *dialog box*

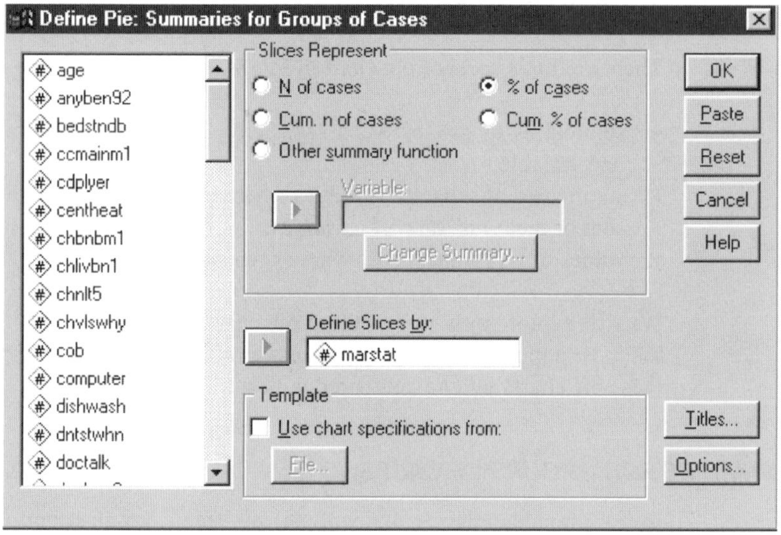

Exhibit 4.3   **Define Pie: Summaries for Groups of Cases** *dialog box*

who are widowed. This arises because on average women live longer than men, and so become widows when their husbands die.

VALUES OF INDIVIDUAL CASES

The other type of pie chart we consider here displays the values of individual cases. Suppose that we are interested in presenting the relative sizes of the populations of the countries of the European Union (EU). We would need to consider the **Values of individual cases** from the dialog box in Exhibit 4.2. The 'cases' here are the countries, and their populations are provided by the variable

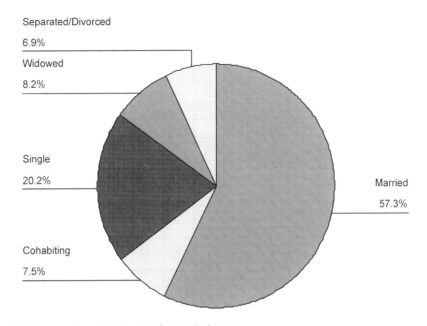

Separated/Divorced
6.9%

Widowed
8.2%

Single
20.2%

Cohabiting
7.5%

Married
57.3%

Exhibit 4.4   *Pie chart output for marital status*
Source: ONS, 1995

TOTPOP, total population. The data file called EU.SAV, selected from the SID data set, just contains data for the 15 EU member countries (Exhibit 4.5; see Appendix A for access to data).

We select TOTPOP as the variable represented by the slices and COUNTRY as the variable to label the slices (see Exhibit 4.6). The resulting pie chart is shown in Exhibit 4.7. In terms of population, the largest EU countries in 1991 were Germany, France, Italy and the UK, and these four made up well over half of the Union.

BAR CHARTS

Whereas pie charts are useful to show the relationship of parts to the whole, it is difficult to judge how much bigger one slice is compared to another. Often we want to compare the proportions that the categories occupy. For this a **bar chart**, a plot of frequencies or percentages against categories, is more useful. Bar charts emphasize the actual quantity or frequency in each category. An example is shown in Exhibit 4.8.

The bars may represent absolute magnitude (frequencies) or relative magnitude (proportion or percentage). The blocks are always of equal base width. The height is proportional to the frequency or percentage. The distance between the bars is of arbitrary width, chosen to ensure the bars are clearly distinguishable.

	country	totpop	popund14	pop15t64	pop.o64
1	Austria	7712001	1353000	5198001	1161000
2	Belgium	9956001	1783000	6675001	1498000
3	Denmark	5140000	867000	3483000	789999
4	Finland	4986000	970000	3351000	665000
5	France	56440000	11330003	37345010	7764987
6	Germany	79479010	12899006	54703996	11876008
7	Greece	10062000	1911000	6730000	1421000
8	Ireland	3503000	935000	2170000	398000
9	Italy	57663010	9480001	39629013	8553996
10	Luxembourg	378000	65000	261000	52000
11	Netherlands	14943000	2633000	10337999	1972001
12	Portugal	10354000	2142999	6869000	1342001
13	Spain	38959010	7708999	26093000	5157012
14	Sweden	8559001	1486001	5533000	1540000
15	United Kingdom	57395010	10860003	37535998	8999010

Exhibit 4.5 *Population data for countries in the European Union*
Source: World Bank, 1992
Filename: EU.SAV

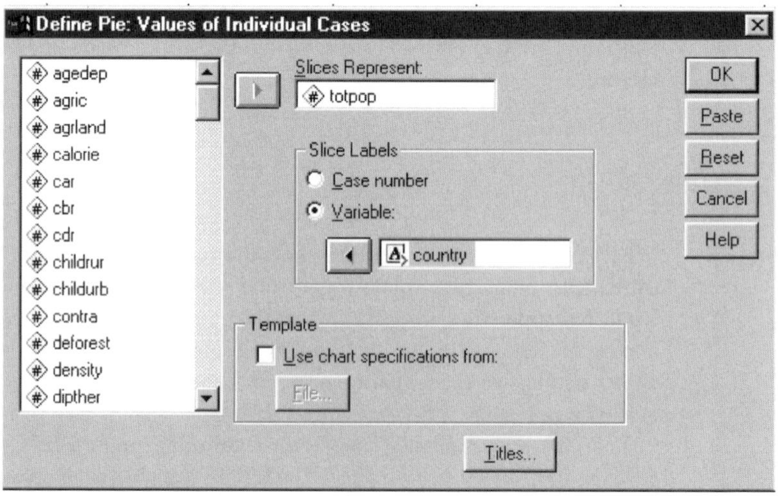

Exhibit 4.6 **Define Pie: Values of Individual Cases** *dialog box*

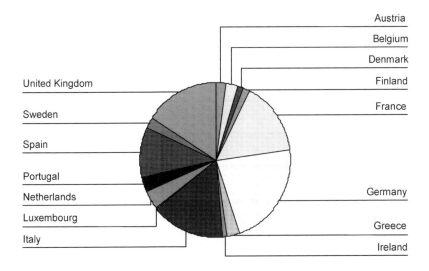

Exhibit 4.7   *Pie chart showing the population distribution in the European Union
Source: World Bank, 1992*

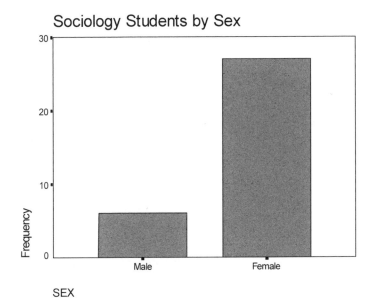

Exhibit 4.8   *Bar chart of sociology students by sex*

Exhibit 4.8 displays a bar chart of the proportion of male and female sociology students attending an undergraduate programme (the same data as used for the pie chart in Exhibit 4.1). Clearly, there are many more females studying sociology than males.

CREATING A BAR CHART IN SPSS

To create a bar chart select **Graphs|Bar chart**. . . . The dialog box shown in Exhibit 4.9 appears.

As with pie charts, there is a choice of bar chart. In this book we will only show you some of the bar charting possibilities of SPSS for Windows. Further examples can be seen in the *SPSS Base 8.0 Users Guide* (SPSS, 1998).

We start by selecting the default for which the data in the chart are **Summaries for groups of cases.** Then, by selecting the **Define** button while **Simple** is highlighted, we obtain the dialog box in Exhibit 4.10. Here we select MARSTAT to be the variable on the category axis. If we then click on **% of cases** and then on **OK** this would give us the bar chart in Exhibit 4.11.

Compare Exhibit 4.11 with Exhibit 4.4.

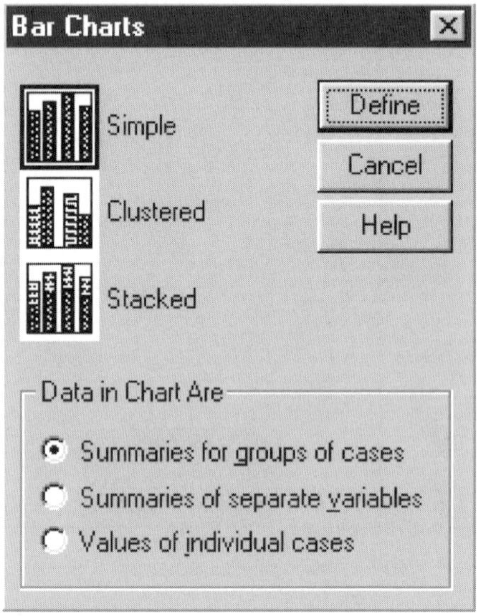

Exhibit 4.9   *Bar Charts dialog box*

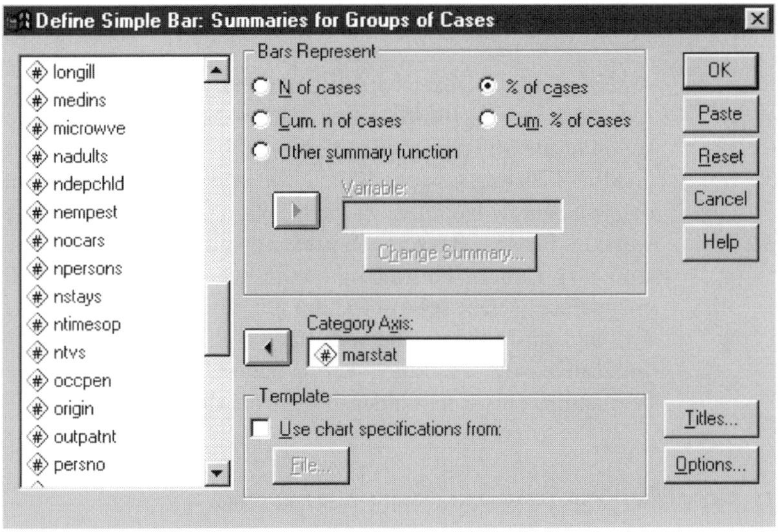

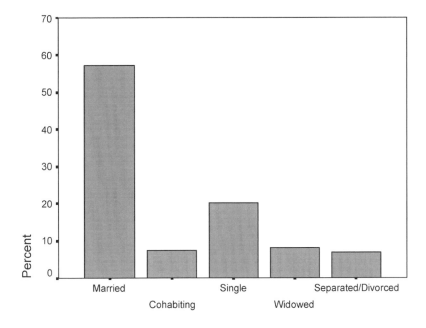

Exhibit 4.10   **Define Simple Bar: Summaries for Groups of Cases** dialog box

MARITAL STATUS

Exhibit 4.11   *Bar chart of marital status*
Source: ONS, 1995

BAR CHARTS OF VALUES OF INDIVIDUAL CASES

A second type of bar chart displays the values of a variable for a number of specific cases. To illustrate this kind of simple bar chart, we shall use the EU subset of the SID data seen in Exhibit 4.5.

After selecting **Graphs|Bar. . .**, we select the **Values of individual cases** to define a **Simple** bar chart. In the following dialog box, we select TOTPOP as the variable for the **Bars** to **Represent** and COUNTRY as the variable for the **Category Labels**. This dialog box in fact is very similar to Exhibit 4.6 used to create the pie chart seen in Exhibit 4.7. The resulting bar chart is seen in Exhibit 4.12 and can be compared with the pie chart of Exhibit 4.7. With the bar chart you can easily see which bar is tallest, i.e. which country has the largest population. This is far harder to see from the pie chart.

OTHER WAYS OF PRESENTING A BAR CHART

The examples so far have been of vertical bar charts where the categorical scale is on the horizontal axis and the frequencies or percentages are on the vertical

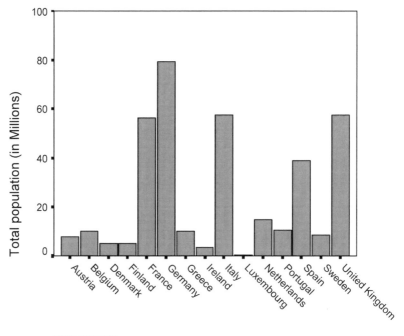

Exhibit 4.12   *Vertical bar chart of population in the European Union*
Source: World Bank, 1992

axis. Bar charts can also be presented so that the categorical scale is on the vertical axis and the frequencies or percentages are on the horizontal axis. This type of chart is called a **horizontal bar chart** and is useful when the category labels are too long to fit along the horizontal axis. The chart shown in Exhibit 4.13 was easily achieved by double-clicking on the vertical bar chart seen in Exhibit 4.12, thus opening the **Chart Editor**. Here, many changes can be made to the chart, including inverting the axis by clicking on the swap axis icon, ⬛.

COMPARING TWO CATEGORICAL VARIABLES USING PIE OR BAR CHARTS

We have demonstrated how single categorical variables can be presented graphically. The next step in analysis is often to explore the relationship between two variables. Chapter 8 describes how to present data in a table using **cross-tabulation**. The information can also be displayed in a graphical form using paired pie or bar charts.

PAIRED PIE CHARTS

Paired pie charts are useful for showing how the distribution of a variable differs according to the categories of a second variable. For example, the pie

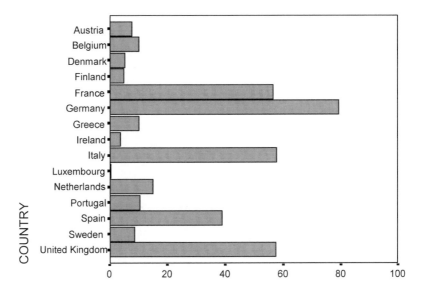

Exhibit 4.13   *Horizontal bar chart of population in the European Union*
Source: World Bank, 1992

charts in Exhibit 4.14 show marital status, but separately for males and females. Unfortunately, SPSS will not allow you to create a pie chart where the size of the circle for each pie chart is proportional to the number of cases, but in this example there were 48% males and 52% females and so the circles would have been of nearly equivalent sizes.

PAIRED PIE CHARTS IN SPSS

The pie chart in Exhibit 4.14 was *not* created using the **Graphs|Pie** procedure described at the beginning of this chapter. It was created using the **interactive graphics** facility included in the SPSS program in version 8.0. This new facility is used by selecting **Graphs|Interactive ▸|Pie ▸|Simple** to bring up the dialog box in Exhibit 4.15.

To create a paired pie chart in Exhibit 4.15 select MARSTAT as the **Slice By:** variable and SEX as the **Panel Variable**. In this feature, you select variables by 'grabbing' them with the mouse and dragging them across to the appropriate box.

Exhibit 4.14 plainly shows that there is a greater percentage of single men than single women and, as suspected, more females than males are widowed.

PAIRED BAR CHARTS

Another way of presenting the distribution of these data is to use a paired bar chart. The same General Household Survey data is presented as a paired or clustered bar chart in Exhibit 4.16.

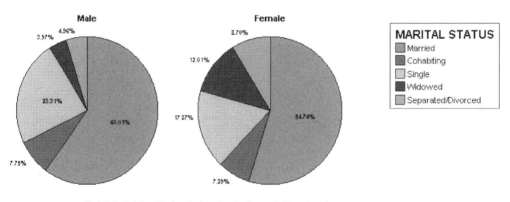

Exhibit 4.14   *Paired pie chart of marital status by sex*
Source: ONS, 1995

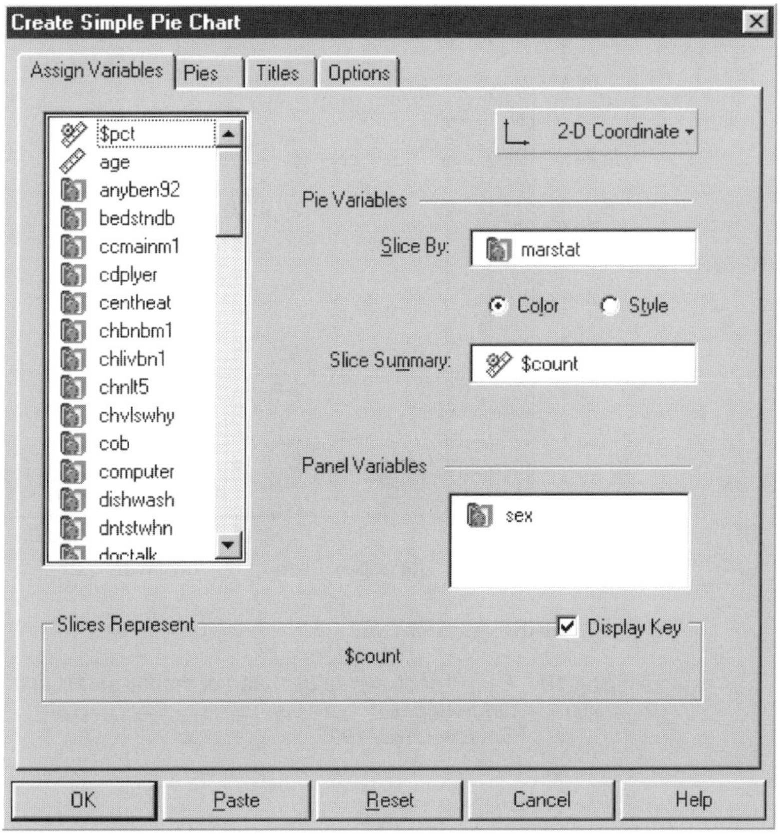

Exhibit 4.15   *Interactive graphics in SPSS: creating a simple paired pie chart*

PAIRED BAR CHARTS IN SPSS

Exhibit 4.16 was created by selecting **Clustered** as the bar chart type (rather than **Simple** as previously). Then (see Exhibit 4.17) the variable MARSTAT was selected as the **Category Axis** variable and SEX was selected as the variable to **Define Clusters by**. In addition, the button marked **Bars Represent...% of cases** was also selected.

As with the pie chart, the bar chart shows that a greater *proportion* of men than women are married and that more women than men are widowed. However, comparisons are easier to make using a bar chart with the bars adjacent to one another. Also note that had we selected **N of cases** rather than **% of cases**, we would have obtained a different chart (see Exhibit 4.18). Here you can see that, unsurprisingly, approximately the same number of men and women are married or cohabiting.

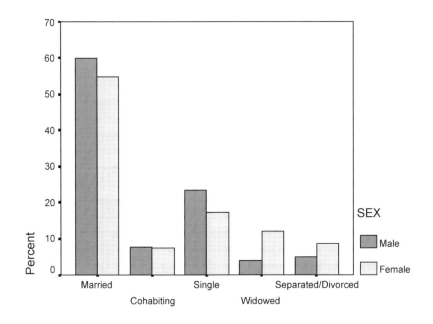

Exhibit 4.16   *Paired or clustered bar chart of marital status and sex in percentages*
Source: ONS, 1995

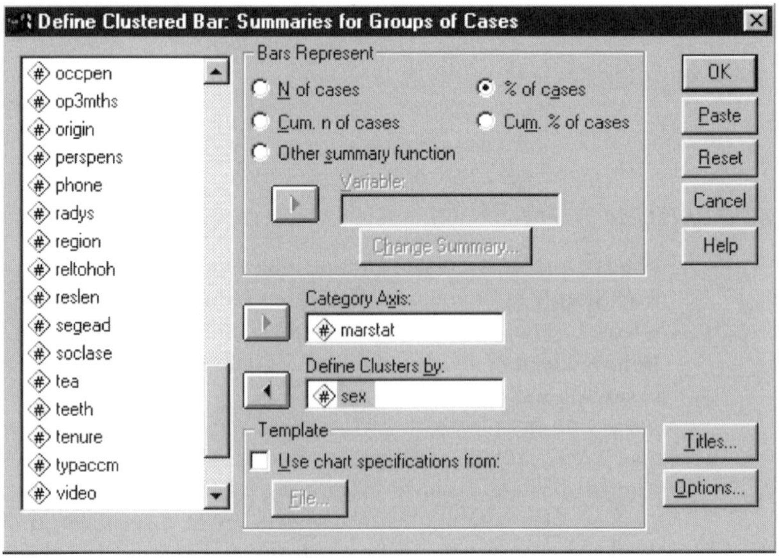

Exhibit 4.17   **Define Clustered Bar: Summaries for Groups of Cases** *dialog box*

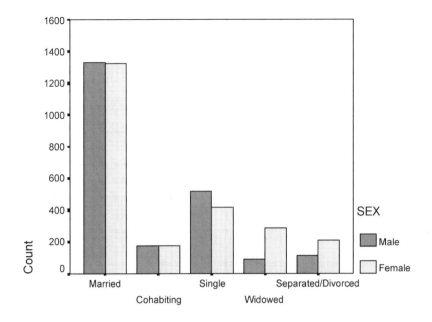

Exhibit 4.18 *Paired or clustered bar chart of marital status and sex using counts or frequencies*
Source: ONS, 1995

GRAPHICAL METHODS FOR CONTINUOUS DATA

Pie charts and bar charts are the appropriate graphical methods for nominal, ordinal and discrete, interval-level variables, but what would happen if we created a bar chart for a continuous interval-level variable? For instance, what happens if you request a bar chart of age? Age is a continuous variable but in most data sets, the General Household Survey included, it is *not* measured on a continuous scale. Age was measured *to the nearest whole year* and as such may appear to be a discrete variable. Another example is gross weekly earnings, which is measured to the nearest whole pound. If you ask SPSS for a bar chart of such a continuous variable it would create one, but there would be a bar for every category. Depending on how many categories there are, this could resemble the spikes on a seismograph. For example, Exhibit 4.19 demonstrates a bar chart of gross weekly income for those earning less than £1000 per week, taken from the 1995 GHS. It does not give a clear impression of the distribution of this variable. One way of simplifying this continuous distribution is to group the many categories into a discrete and manageable number and create a **histogram**.

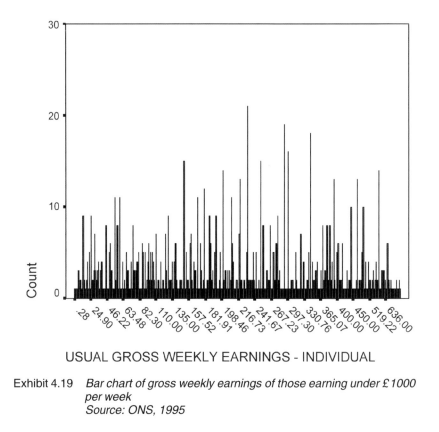

USUAL GROSS WEEKLY EARNINGS - INDIVIDUAL

Exhibit 4.19   *Bar chart of gross weekly earnings of those earning under £1000*
per week
Source: ONS, 1995

HISTOGRAMS

To create a histogram you first of all need to group the continuous variable
into class intervals as described in Chapter 3. Then the horizontal axis is
marked out using the midpoints of these real class intervals and the vertical
axis is labelled with the frequencies/count or percentages. In Exhibit 4.20 the
histogram of AGE, has the stated class interval of 20–29 picked out. This
interval has a real class interval of 19.5–29.5 and 758 cases are in this age
interval.

Histograms are like bar charts in that the height of the bars represents the
frequency or percentage of each category. However, whereas with bar charts
the width of the bar is completely arbitrary, the *width* of the bar in a
histogram represents the size of the intervals of the variable, and therefore
the *area* of the bar in a histogram represents the relative frequency of each
category (interval). We shall return to consider the importance of the area of
the bars representing the relative frequencies when we consider the normal
distribution in Chapter 7.

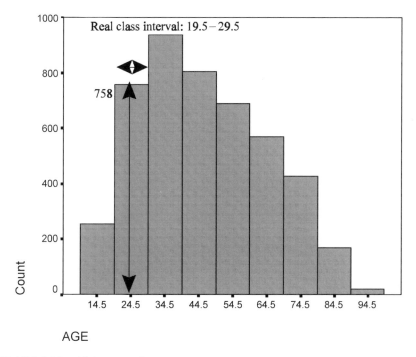

Exhibit 4.20   *Histogram of AGE*
               Source: ONS, 1995

HISTOGRAMS IN SPSS

Creating histograms in SPSS is quite easy since SPSS automatically groups the continuous variable into equal intervals. The following example has excluded the 32 respondents who earn more than £1000 per week using the selection criterion earnings <= **1000**.

To create the histogram of gross weekly earnings, select **Graphs| Histogram**... and select the variable EARNINGS taken from the GHS 1995 data set. Exhibit 4.21 shows the resulting histogram.

The grouping of the cases into intervals of £50 has simplified the chart compared with Exhibit 4.19, although it has now taken on a stepped appearance. Compare this histogram with that in Exhibit 4.22 which includes all the cases, even those earning over £1000 per week.

FREQUENCY POLYGONS

An alternative way of presenting continuous variables is to create a **frequency polygon**. This gives an impression of continuity by drawing straight lines between each plotted data point. Here the frequency of each class is plotted

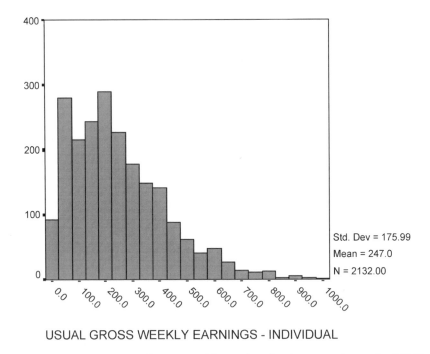

USUAL GROSS WEEKLY EARNINGS - INDIVIDUAL

Exhibit 4.21   *Histogram of gross weekly earnings for those earning under £1000*
               Source: ONS, 1995

against the *true upper limit* for each class interval. Exhibit 4.23 shows a frequency polygon for the GHS variable AGE. This graph can be compared to the histogram seen in Exhibit 4.20.

A **cumulative frequency polygon** is one where the frequencies are accumulated from the lowest class interval, step by step to the highest class interval. Exhibit 4.24 is a table showing the accumulated frequencies for each class interval, and Exhibit 4.25 shows the resulting cumulative frequency polygon.

If the accumulated frequencies are expressed as cumulative percentages, a **cumulative percentage polygon** is produced. This has the advantage that one can easily see the proportion of the distribution that occurs above or below a particular percentage. For instance, in Exhibit 4.26, the 50 per cent point has been indicated. From this line you can see that half of all the cases are aged above 45. The 50 per cent point is also referred to as the **median**, and we will meet it again in Chapter 5.

FREQUENCY POLYGONS IN SPSS

To draw a frequency polygon in SPSS of a continuous variable like age, you must first group age into age groups and then label the intervals with the upper

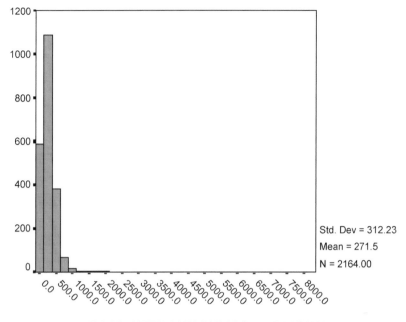

USUAL GROSS WEEKLY EARNINGS - INDIVIDUAL

Exhibit 4.22   *Histogram of gross weekly earnings for all respondents*
                Source: ONS, 1995

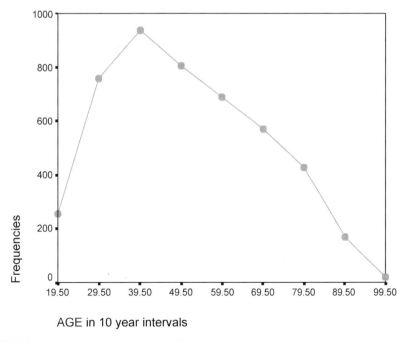

AGE in 10 year intervals

Exhibit 4.23   *Frequency polygon of AGE*
                Source: ONS, 1995

Stated limits	Midpoint	Frequency	Percent	Cumulative percent	Cumulative Frequency
10–19	14.50	255	5.5	5.5	255
20–29	24.50	758	16.4	21.9	255 + 758 = 1013
30–39	34.50	938	20.2	42.1	1013 + 938 = 1951
40–49	44.50	806	17.4	59.5	1951 + 806 = 2757
50–59	54.50	689	14.9	74.4	2757 + 689 = 3446
60–69	64.50	570	12.3	86.7	3446 + 570 = 4016
70–79	74.50	427	9.2	95.9	4016 + 427 = 4443
80–89	84.50	170	3.7	99.6	4443 + 170 = 4613
90–99	94.50	20	0.4	100.0	4613 + 20 = 4633
	Total	4633	100.0		

Exhibit 4.24   *Grouped variable* AGE *showing cumulative frequencies*

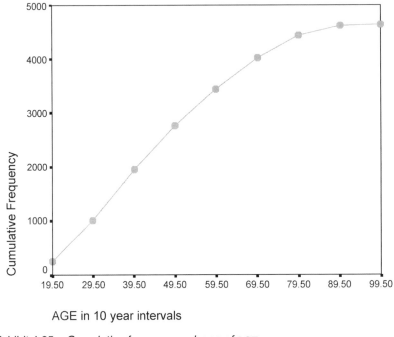

AGE in 10 year intervals

Exhibit 4.25   *Cumulative frequency polygon of* AGE
Source: ONS, 1995

class limit. Refer to Chapter 2 for a fuller explanation of how to do this, but Exhibit 4.27 displays the **Recode** dialog box to group the variable, AGE into AGEGROUP. Exhibit 4.28 displays the **Define Labels** dialog box to add the appropriate **Value Labels**.

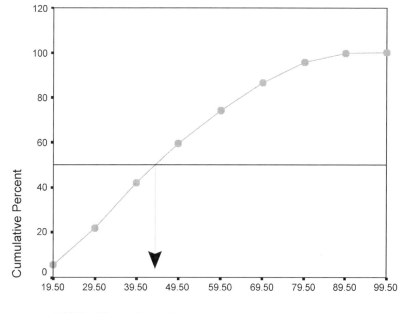

Exhibit 4.26   *Cumulative percentage polygon*
               Source: ONS, 1995

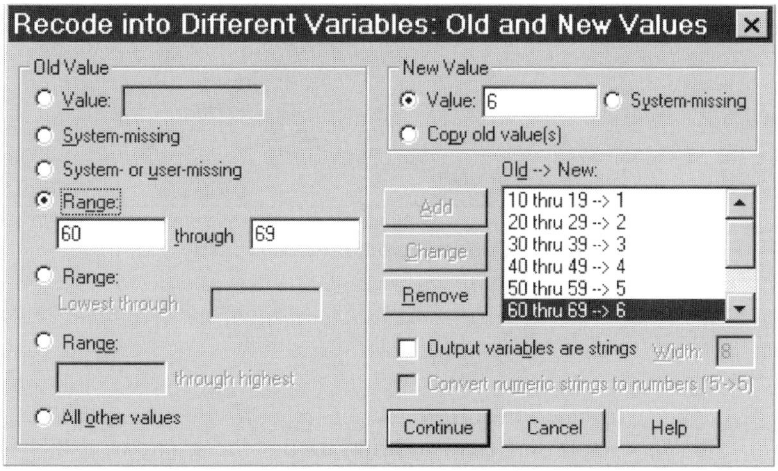

Exhibit 4.27   **Recode** *dialog box creating ten-yearly age groups*

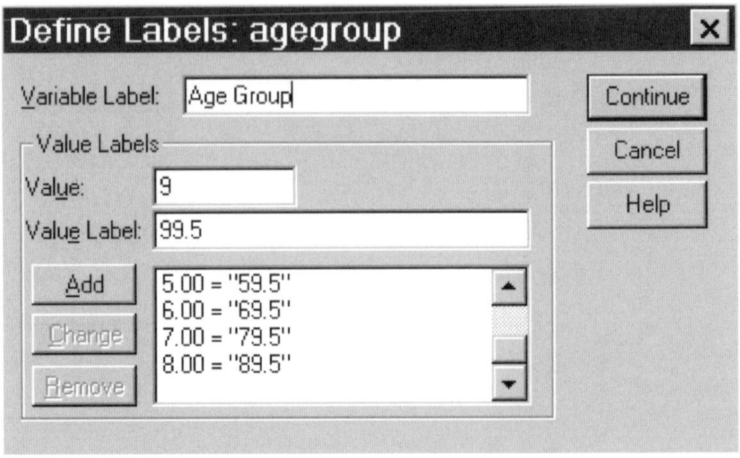

Exhibit 4.28   **Define Labels** *dialog box labelling age groups*

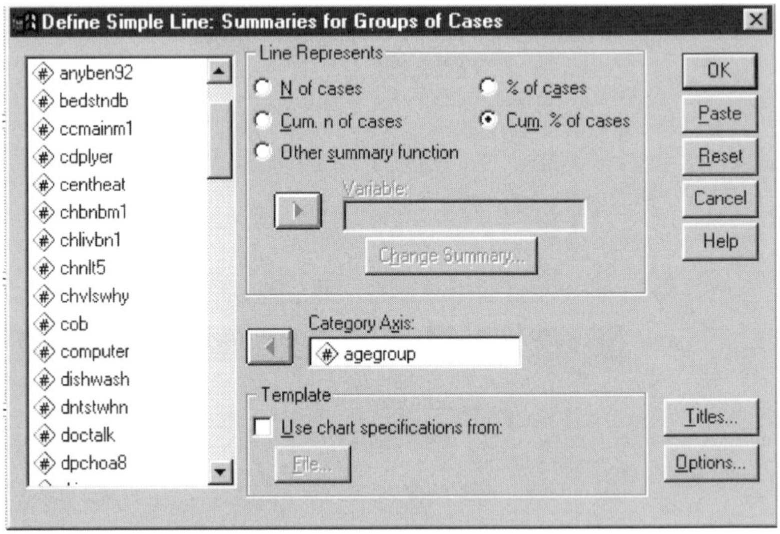

Exhibit 4.29   **Define Simple Line** *dialog box*

To draw a frequency polygon in SPSS, select **Graphs|Line**. . . and then **Define** a **Simple** line chart to bring up the dialog box in Exhibit 4.29. Here, select AGEGROUP for the category axis and, for the chart shown in Exhibit 4.26, select **Cum. % of cases**.

SUMMARY

In this chapter, we have seen how to create pie and bar charts for categorical and discrete variables, and histograms and polygons for continuous variables. This has been illustrated by step-by-step instructions using SPSS. There are many other types of charts and graphical display, but these are the most commonly used.

EXERCISES

Exercise

University students in Britain have (at the time of writing) been paying tuition fees for a year. The government reasoned that a university education leads to graduates benefiting from higher average earnings when they start work. You want to investigate this assertion to see if it is true.

Using the General Household Survey, look at a frequency distribution of the variable EDLEV, educational level. Recode EDLEV into three groups: those with higher qualifications (including teaching and nursing); those with any qualifications up to A levels; and those with no qualifications. Call this new variable QUALS.

Select only those in full-time employment using **Data|Select Cases...**, and use WKSTATE = 1 as the selection criterion.

Then recode, average weekly earnings (EARNINGS) into two categories: those earning above £275 per week and those earning below that amount. Call this new variable SALARY.

Create a clustered bar chart where the category axis is SALARY and define the clusters by QUALS. Make sure you select **Bars to represent % of cases**. Does gaining a degree or higher qualifications improve your chances of a higher salary?

Look at the same problem, but separately for men and women. This is done by selecting first men working full-time (WKSTATE = **1 and** SEX = **1**) and repeating the bar chart, and then women working full-time (WKSTATE = **1 and** SEX = **2**) and repeating the bar chart. Are there any differences for men and women?

MEASURES OF CENTRAL TENDENCY AND DISPERSION

5

CONTENTS

MEASURES OF CENTRAL TENDENCY

A frequency distribution allows us to see the overall pattern in the distribution of respondents on a variable. It is often also useful to summarize the distribution with a single number, a statistic called a **measure of central tendency**.

There are three main measures of central tendency, the **mode**, the **median** and the **mean**, each appropriate for a different level of measurement. Remember that the different levels of measurement describe the relationships between the categories of a variable (see Chapter 1).

THE MODE

The mode is the simplest measure of central tendency. It is simply the value of the observation that occurs most frequently in the distribution. Sometimes a distribution has more than one value with similarly large numbers of observations. This is called a **bimodal** distribution if there are two modal values or **multimodal** if there are more.

The mode can be calculated for nominal, ordinal or interval level variables, but it is the *only* measure of central tendency applicable to nominal variables.

In Exhibit 5.1, the modal value of the nominal variable, marital status, is *married*. Simply, there are more married people than of any other marital status. Note that the mode is always the value of the variable and *not* the number of cases. So the mode is the value 1 or its label, married.

For grouped data, the mode is the midpoint of the interval which has the largest frequency. Exhibit 5.2 displays the grouped variable, AGEGROUP. We see that the modal class interval is 30–39 so the mode is 34.5, the midpoint of that interval.

MARSTAT MARITAL STATUS

		Frequency	Percent	Valid Percent	Cumulative Percent
Valid	1 Married	2653	57.3	57.3	57.3
	2 Cohabiting	346	7.5	7.5	64.7
	3 Single	934	20.2	20.2	84.9
	4 Widowed	378	8.2	8.2	93.0
	5 Divorced	226	4.9	4.9	97.9
	6 Seperated	94	2.0	2.0	100.0
	7 Same sex cohab	2	.0	.0	100.0
	Total	4633	100.0	100.0	

Exhibit 5.1   *Frequency listing for marital status illustrating 'married' as the mode*
Source: ONS, 1995

AGEGROUP

	code: label:	midpoint	Frequency	Percent	Valid Percent	Cumulative Percent
Valid	1.00 10–19	14.5	255	5.5	5.5	5.5
	2.00 20–29	24.5	758	16.4	16.4	21.9
	3.00 30–39	34.5	938	20.2	20.2	42.1
	4.00 40–49	44.5	806	17.4	17.4	59.5
	5.00 50–59	54.5	689	14.9	14.9	74.4
	6.00 60–69	64.5	570	12.3	12.3	86.7
	7.00 70–79	74.5	427	9.2	9.2	95.9
	8.00 80–89	84.5	170	3.7	3.7	99.6
	9.00 90–99	94.5	20	.4	.4	100.0
	Total		4633	100.0	100.0	

Exhibit 5.2   *Frequency listing for age group demonstrating the mode is age group 30–39 with midpoint 34.5*

USING SPSS TO CALCULATE THE MODE

Measures of central tendency can be obtained in SPSS with an extension of the **Frequencies** command described previously. As explained in Chapter 2, you select **Analyze|Descriptive Statistics ▶|Frequencies. . .** and then the variable for analysis. However, this time, before you click on **OK**, click the button marked **Statistics** to bring up the dialog box in Exhibit 5.3.

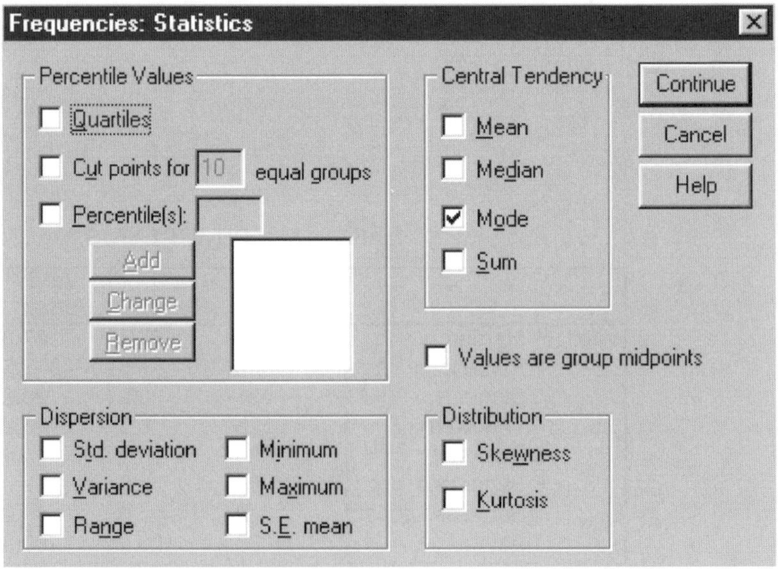

Exhibit 5.3   *The **Frequencies: Statistics** dialog box showing how to select the mode*

To calculate the mode simply select **Mode** from the **Central Tendency** box. Note, however, that if there are multiple modes, SPSS takes the lowest value.

PROPERTIES OF THE MODE

The mode, as the simplest measure of central tendency, has no mathematical properties; you cannot add, subtract, multiply or divide the mode. And one limitation with the mode is that it is possible to have more than one mode for a variable when two categories have exactly the same number of cases.

Another problem with the mode is illustrated by the following example. Imagine a hypothetical data set (A) of six cases with the following scores on a variable:

$$2\ 3\ 3\ 3\ 4\ 6$$

And here is a second data set (B), also with six cases and the following scores on another variable:

$$3\ 3\ 9\ 10\ 12\ 15$$

Both variables have a mode of 3, yet while a mode of 3 is clearly in the middle of A and describes its central tendency, this is not the case with B. The most frequent value, in this case, 3, is not necessarily the most typical value in data set B.

THE MEDIAN

The second measure of central tendency, used primarily for ordinal variables, but also appropriate for interval/ratio variables, is called the median. It is the middle value when the observations are arranged in order of magnitude. This means that there are as many scores or cases above the median as below it. The median identifies the *position* of an observation.

Consider the test scores from eleven students in Exhibit 5.4. To work out which is the middle value, we first have to rearrange them into ascending order and then mark the one which has as many values below as above (see Exhibit 5.5). Value 7 is positioned in the middle of this set of data. This median value allows you to summarize a set of numbers, the data set, with just one number or statistic.

8	2	12	4	5	2	7	15	10	7	5

Exhibit 5.4 *Test scores for eleven students*

1st	2nd	3rd	4th	5th	6th	7th	8th	9th	10th	11th
2	2	4	5	5	7	7	8	10	12	15

▲

Exhibit 5.5   *The test scores rearranged in ascending order showing the 'middle'*
or median value

The example above had an odd number of cases, so the middle data value has as many cases above as below. But what happens if we have an even number of observations? In Exhibit 5.6 there are two 'middle' observations. In this instance the median value lies half way between the 4th and 5th observations. The median value of this distribution is the average of the values of the two middle observations:

$$\text{median} = \frac{5+7}{2} = 6 \qquad (5.1)$$

A formula that can be applied to calculate the position of the median for any number of observations is:

$$\text{median} = \frac{(n+1)\text{th}}{2} \text{ observation} \qquad (5.2)$$

So

$$\text{median of 11 observations} = \frac{(11+1)\text{th}}{2} \text{ observation} = \text{6th observation} \quad (5.3)$$

and

$$\text{median of 8 observations} = \frac{(8+1)\text{th}}{2} \text{ observation} = \text{4.5th observation} \quad (5.4)$$

which we interpret as half-way between the 4th and the 5th observations.

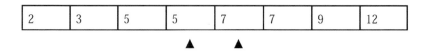

2	3	5	5	7	7	9	12

▲   ▲

Exhibit 5.6   *Eight scores in order showing two middle values*

PERCENTILES

As we have seen, the median value is the middle value of a set of observations arranged in order of magnitude. If the median value is 7, as with the eleven observations in Exhibit 5.5, 50 per cent of the observations have values *less* than 7. For this reason, it is also called the 50th percentile. Sometimes newspapers report on the number of people living below the 5th percentile in income, that is, the number in the bottom 5 per cent by income. The definition of **a percentile** is the smallest score below which a given percentage of cases fall. So if a salary of £26,000 is reported as the 95th percentile, it means that 95 per cent of the respondents have salaries *lower* than £26,000.

QUARTILES

Some percentiles are of particular importance. We have seen that the median is the 50th percentile. Each half of a distribution can be further divided to give **quartiles**. The **lower quartile** is half-way between the lowest value and the median and the **upper quartile** is half-way between the highest value and the median. We often write the lower quartile as Q_1, the median as Q_2 and the upper quartile as Q_3.

Equation (5.2), the formula for the position of the median, can also be written as

$$\text{median} = 0.5(n + 1)\text{th observation} \qquad (5.5)$$

In the same way, the formula for the 25th percentile or lower quartile can be written

$$\text{lower quartile} = 0.25(n + 1)\text{th observation} \qquad (5.6)$$

and the formula for the 75th percentile, or upper quartile can be written as

$$\text{upper quartile} = 0.75(n + 1)\text{th observation} \qquad (5.7)$$

Exhibit 5.7 demonstrates the calculation of the upper and lower quartiles for the set of 11 marks seen previously.

USING SPSS TO CALCULATE THE MEDIAN

While SPSS will calculate the median (by selecting **Analyze|Descriptive Statistics▸|Frequencies**... and changing the **Statistics**), it is easy to find the median category just by looking at the frequency table produced by SPSS. Consider the ordinal variable, SOCLASE, social class, from the 1995 General Household Survey. There are 4417 valid responses which could be any one of

1st	2nd	3rd	4th	5th	6th	7th	8th	9th	10th	11th
2	2	4	5	5	7	7	8	10	12	15

▲	▲	▲
Q_1	Q_2	Q_3
Lower quartile	Median	Upper quartile
0.25 (11+1)th obs.	0.5 (11+1)th obs.	0.75 (11+1)th obs.
= 3rd obs.	= 6th obs.	= 9th obs.
= 4	= 7	= 10

Exhibit 5.7   *Calculation of the median and the upper and lower quartiles*

seven values. See Exhibit 5.8 for a frequency listing of the seven valid responses, ranging from code 1 for those in class I to code 7 for those in the armed forces. In order to find the median value, look at the column headed cumulative percentages. We know that 50 per cent of the cases lies above the median and 50 per cent below, so we need to look in which category the middle observation falls. From Exhibit 5.8, we can see that 29.4 per cent are in the two highest classes. If we include the next category, Class IIIN (non-manual) we reach a cumulative percentage of 53.2. We crossed the 50 per cent point, or middle observation, somewhere in the Class IIIN group. Therefore, this category is the median category.

SOCLASE SOCIAL CLASS OF INDIVIDUAL

		Frequency	Percent	Valid Percent	Cumulative Percent
Valid	1 SOCIAL CLASS I	189	4.1	4.3	4.3
	2 SOCIAL CLASS II	1110	24.0	25.1	29.4
	3 SOC CLASS IIIN	1050	22.7	23.8	53.2 ←
	4 SOC CLASS IIIM	956	20.6	21.6	74.8
	5 SOCIAL CLASS IV	796	17.2	18.0	92.8
	6 SOCIAL CLASS V	298	6.4	6.7	99.6
	7 ARMED FORCES	18	.4	.4	100.0
	Total	4417	95.3	100.0	
Missing	-9 DNA:NEVER WORKED	216	4.7		
Total		4633	100.0		

Exhibit 5.8   *Calculating the median from the frequency output of the ordinal variable,* SOCLASE
Source: ONS, 1995

PROPERTIES OF THE MEDIAN

As with the mode, the median has no mathematical properties. You cannot add, subtract, multiply or divide the median. It only informs us of the point of the distribution at which there are 50 per cent of the cases above and 50 per cent below. We can say that at least half the respondents summarized in Exhibit 5.8 are of social class IIIN or below.

An advantage of the median is that it is unaffected by extreme values. For example, if the largest score in a distribution is made even larger, the median will not change. Consider the two sets of data in Exhibit 5.9. In both, the median remains at value 7, the 5th observation, regardless of the fact that the first set of numbers ranges from 2 to 15 and the second set from 2 to 99. For this reason, the median is known as a **resistant measure** of central tendency.

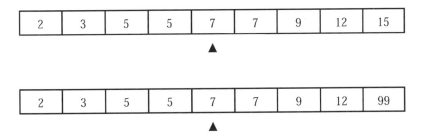

Exhibit 5.9   *Two sets of nine values demonstrating the resistant properties of the median*

THE MEAN

The third measure of central tendency, appropriate for interval/ratio variables but not for nominal or ordinal, is the arithmetic average or the mean. Unlike the median, which is based on the rank or position of a value, it is based on the actual values of scores. It allows us to compare groups on the basis of the amounts of a characteristic possessed by the group, relative to their size.

The arithmetic mean is calculated by summing all the values of the observations and then dividing by the number of observations. Consider five people with ages:

$$19, \quad 25, \quad 20, \quad 21, \quad 17$$

To calculate the mean age, you add up the ages and then divide by 5, the number of people. This would give a mean age of 20.4.

This procedure for calculating the mean can be expressed as a formula:

$$X = \frac{\sum\limits_{i=1}^{n} x_i}{n} \tag{5.8}$$

Let us break this formula down to its separate components. First of all, $\overline{X}$ (X bar) is the **mean**. The capital Greek letter, Σ, stands for 'the sum of'. Therefore, the expression

$$\sum_{i=1}^{n} x_i = x_1 + x_2 + x_3 + \ldots + x_n$$

means the sum of the value of all the xs from the first case, where $n = 1$ and therefore x is x_1, to the last case, n, where x is x_n.

Exhibit 5.10 shows the ages of the same five people, but with age called x, so person 1's age is called x_1 and person 2's age is called x_2 and so on. Substituting into the equation and, since $n = 5$, we get:

$$\sum_{i=1}^{5} x_i = x_1 + x_2 + x_3 + x_4 + x_5 = 19 + 25 + 20 + 21 + 17 = 102 \tag{5.9}$$

$$\therefore \overline{X} = \frac{102}{5} = 20.4 \tag{5.10}$$

confirming that the mean, $\overline{X}$, is 20.4 years.

THE MEAN OF A GROUPED VARIABLE

Although it is quite a familiar situation in a survey to be asked 'In which age or salary group do you belong?', then the researcher has a dilemma if they want to calculate the mean age or salary. They did not collect individual age data but collected grouped data.

Case number	AGE	Let's call AGE x
1	19	x_1
2	25	x_2
3	20	x_3
4	21	x_4
5	17	x_5

Exhibit 5.10   *Calculating the mean of* AGE

If SPSS is asked to give a frequency listing of the grouped variable, AGEGROUP, the result is the output seen in Exhibit 5.11. Asking SPSS to calculate the mean does not help – it gives you a mean of the codes, 1–9, a mean of 4.1448. Clearly, this is not the mean age but the mean of the *codes* given to the age groups.

To calculate the mean you need to assess the midpoint for each interval and then multiply that midpoint by the number of cases in that interval. The midpoint can be seen as the best estimate of all those in that category – in other words, the average age or salary of all those in that particular interval. If you then add up all the cumulative ages for each interval you arrive at a very large number which, if divided by the number of people, will give you a mean age, based on midpoint estimates. This procedure is demonstrated in Exhibit 5.12.

A short-hand way of describing this procedure to calculate the mean for grouped data is

$$\overline{X} = \frac{\sum_{i=1}^{n} f_i m_i}{n} \qquad (5.11)$$

AGEGROUP

		Frequency	Percent	Valid Percent	Cumulative Percent
Valid	1.00	255	5.5	5.5	5.5
	2.00	758	16.4	16.4	21.9
	3.00	938	20.2	20.2	42.1
	4.00	806	17.4	17.4	59.5
	5.00	689	14.9	14.9	74.4
	6.00	570	12.3	12.3	86.7
	7.00	427	9.2	9.2	95.9
	8.00	170	3.7	3.7	99.6
	9.00	20	.4	.4	100.0
	Total	4633	100.0	100.0	

Statistics

AGEGROUP

N	Valid	4633
	Missing	0
Mean		4.1448

Exhibit 5.11   *Inappropriate calculation of the mean of a grouped variable using SPSS*

Stated class intervals	Real class intervals	Midpoint (m_i)	Frequency (f_i)	$f_i m_i$
10–19	9.5–19.5	14.5	255	3697.5
20–29	19.5–29.5	24.5	758	18571
30–39	29.5–39.5	34.5	938	32361
40–49	39.5–49.5	44.5	806	35867
50–59	49.5–59.5	54.5	689	37550.5
60–69	59.5–69.5	64.5	570	36765
70–79	69.5–79.5	74.5	427	31811.5
80–89	79.5–89.5	84.5	170	14365
90–99	89.5–99.5	94.5	20	1890
		Total	4633	212878.5
			212878.5/4633 = 45.95	

Exhibit 5.12   *Calculation of the mean of the grouped variable* AGEGROUP

where f_i is the number of cases in an interval, and m_i is the midpoint of the interval and n is the total number of cases.

The sum of the product of the frequencies (f_i) and the midpoint (m_i) of each interval equals 212,878.5. It is a simple task to divide this number by the *total* number of valid cases, 4633, to give a grouped mean of 45.95:

$$\text{grouped mean} = \overline{X} = \frac{212{,}878.5}{4633} = 45.95 \qquad (5.12)$$

PROPERTIES OF THE MEAN

The mean is adversely affected by extreme values. Using the data from the example of the calculation of the median, consider what happens to the value of the mean (Exhibit 5.13).

As we saw, the median is not affected by changing the last score from 15 to 99. The median is called a resistant statistic because it is not affected by extreme values. However, the mean is not a resistant measure, and is greatly affected by the one extreme value of 99, changing from 7.2 to 16.6. In different circumstances, this can either be an advantage (the value of the mean summarizes the values of all the scores) or a disadvantage (its value is sensitive to the precise value of the scores).

Exhibit 5.14 summarizes the values of the three measures of central tendency – the mode, median and mean – for the variables AGE and AGEGROUP. The statistics for AGE were provided by the computer but the statistics for AGEGROUP, except the median which is just included for completeness, are those that we have calculated by hand. Notice that the values for the grouped variable are remarkably similar to those of the ungrouped variable. This demonstrates the validity of using grouped data where ungrouped data are not available. Notice also that the modes, using either variable, are much lower than

| 2 | 3 | 5 | 5 | 7 | 7 | 9 | 12 | 15 |

▲

Median   =7
Mean   =7.2

| 2 | 3 | 5 | 5 | 7 | 7 | 9 | 12 | 99 |

▲

Median   =7
Mean   =16.6

Exhibit 5.13   *Two sets of values demonstrating how the mean is affected by extreme values*

Statistic	Ungrouped value Calculated by SPSS	Grouped value Calculated by hand
Mode	31	34.5
Median	45	(44.5)**
Mean	45.97	45.95
Valid cases: 4633 Source: 1995 General Household Survey		

Exhibit 5.14   *Comparing the mode, the median and the mean for the grouped and ungrouped variable age*
** It is possible to calculate the median for grouped variables but the formula is quite complicated. Here the result is provided for comparative purposes only.

either the means or the medians. This is because there are more people in the lower age groups; the distribution is said to be **skewed**. In the next section we will be investigating the shape of the distribution, but this table demonstrates the dangers of relying on any one measure of central tendency which may not be a good summary of the overall distribution. If the distribution is skewed in one direction then a good resistant measure to use is the median.

Another distribution which is often skewed is income (see Exhibit 5.15). Most cases are in the lower-income brackets, yet a few individuals may have huge incomes and these will raise the mean, making it unrepresentative of the sample as a whole. In Exhibit 5.15 the mean weekly earnings are £272, yet the median is much lower at £219. This is a clear indication of a skewed distribution.

Statistics

EARNINGS USUAL GROSS WEEKLY EARNINGS: INDIVIDUAL

N	Valid	2164
	Missing	2469
Mean		271.5209
Median		218.5450
Mode		230.76

Exhibit 5.15   *The mode, median and mean for usual gross weekly earnings*
                Source: ONS, 1995

SUMMARY OF MEASURES OF CENTRAL TENDENCY

Three measures of central tendency, the mode, median and the mean, were introduced as ways of summarizing the distribution of a variable. Exhibit 5.16 shows the appropriate measures of central tendency for different levels of measurement. It will be noted that although a measure may be primarily intended for one level of measurement, it may in certain circumstances, for example a skewed distribution, be the most suitable measure for another.

		Level of measurement of the variable		
	Interval/Ratio	Nominal	Ordinal	Interval/Ratio
Level of measurement of the statistic used	Nominal *mode*	✔	✔ but may not be the best measure	✔ but may not be the best measure
	Ordinal *median*	‼ Logical errors	✔	✔, in fact as a resistant measure may be the best if distribution is skewed
	Interval/Ratio *mean*	‼ Logical errors	‼ Logical errors	✔

Exhibit 5.16   *Summary of levels of measurement and appropriate measures of*
                central tendency

THE SHAPE OF A DISTRIBUTION

In the previous chapter we saw how it was possible to create a histogram of a continuous variable by grouping the categories and making the areas in the bars of the chart proportional to the frequencies of each group. Exhibit 5.17 is a histogram of the variable AGE, grouped into 10-year intervals. It displays an uneven stepped outline.

Exhibit 5.18 and 5.19 also display histograms of this variable, but with decreasing intervals: first 5 years, then 1 year. Because age was only measured using one-year intervals we cannot reduce the intervals size below 1.

As we reduce the interval size the steps get smaller and the outline of the distribution becomes smoother. If we continued to reduce the interval size and increased the sample size we could further 'smooth' the steps of the histogram until it formed a perfectly smooth outline. However, because age was measured on a discrete, yearly, interval, Exhibit 5.19 is as 'smooth' as we can get with these data. A line has been drawn on Exhibit 5.20 to show a possible outline or silhouette.

As Exhibit 5.20 demonstrates, the distribution of a continuous variable can have a shape, in addition to a measure of central tendency which summarizes the distribution. The shape can be described in terms of several quantities: the number of modes, skewness, kurtosis and spread.

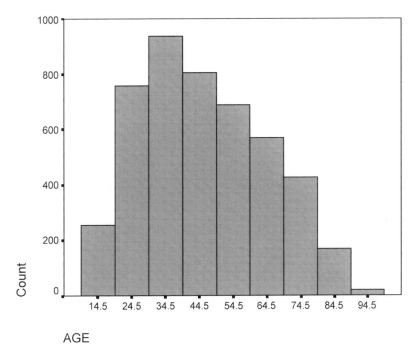

Exhibit 5.17   *Histogram of age in ten-yearly intervals*

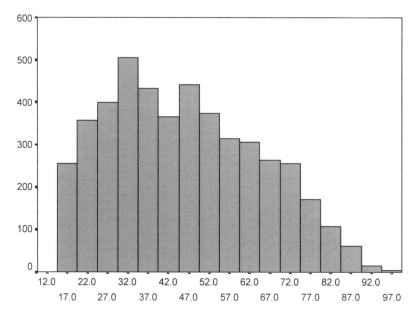

AGE in 5-year intervals

Exhibit 5.18   *Histogram of age in five-yearly intervals*

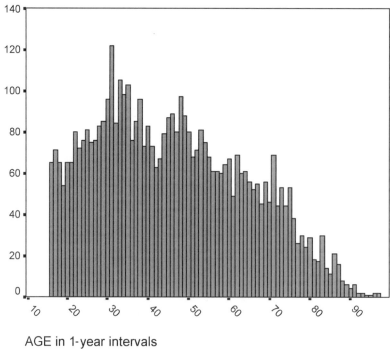

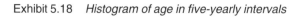

AGE in 1-year intervals

Exhibit 5.19   *Histogram of age in one-yearly intervals*

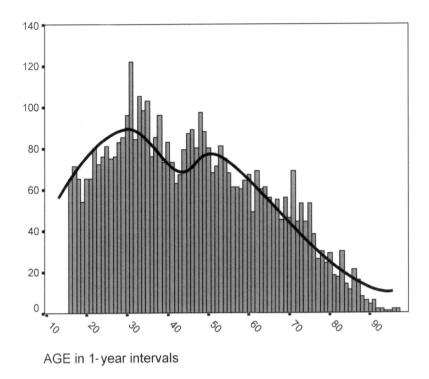

AGE in 1-year intervals

Exhibit 5.20   *Histogram of age with a curve superimposed to demonstrate the 'shape' of the distribution*

NUMBER OF MODES

The distribution can be unimodal (have one peak), bimodal (have two peaks) or it can be multimodal (with several peaks).

SKEWNESS

The tail of the peak (or peaks) can be stretched out to the left (the lower values), in which case we say that the distribution has **negative skew**, or it may be stretched out to the right, the higher values, when it has **positive skew**. Or it may lean neither to the left or right and be **symmetrical** (see Exhibit 5.21).

KURTOSIS

If the peak is pointed, which indicates that many observations are closely clustered around the mode, then the distribution is called a **leptokurtic** distribu-

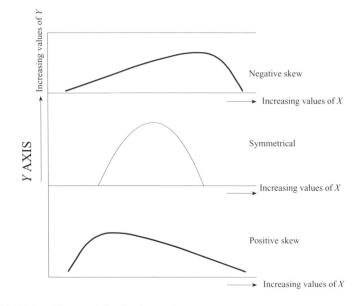

Exhibit 5.21   *Shape of distributions: skewness*

tion and to have **positive kurtosis**. If, on the other hand, the distribution is widely spread out, it is called **platykurtic** and is said to have a **negative kurtosis**. However, if it has an even spread then it is **mesokurtic** (see Exhibit 5.22).

MEASURES OF DISPERSION OR SPREAD

We have seen so far that we can describe variables in terms of their measure of central tendency (mode, median or mean) and, for continuous variables, the shape of the distribution. There is a further, and very important, feature of distributions for continuous variables and that is their spread or dispersion.

If all cases within a sample have the same value for a variable, for example all respondents in a survey earned £20,000, that variable, salary, would have no spread. There would be no variation as far as salary is concerned. The highest value would equal the lowest value and in this sample it would seem that everyone earned the same, £20,000. There would be no point in looking at differences between men's and women's earnings. In fact, there would be no point in trying to explain salary differential between any subgroups because there is none. In this hypothetical situation, salary is not a *variable*, it is a *constant*. However, in reality there is usually wide variation between individuals' salaries. This variation is what makes social research interesting. For these

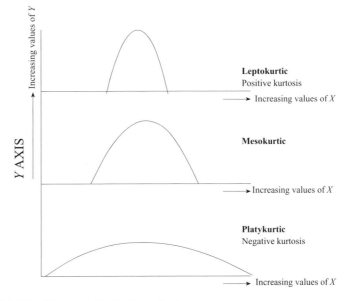

Exhibit 5.22   *Shape of distributions: kurtosis*

reasons we need to find ways of describing the spread of values caused by the variation. We can then measure the spread, compare different subpopulations (e.g. males and females) and possibly explain the variation.

We will start with the simplest way of describing variation, the **range**, and then go on to more sophisticated measures, the **variance** and **standard deviation**.

THE RANGE

The range is the highest value of a distribution minus the lowest value. This is one of the weaknesses of using the range as a measure of variation: it relies on only two values. Consider:

$$2, \ 5, \ 6, \ 7, \ 9, \ 99 \qquad \text{range} = 99 - 2 = 97$$

$$2, \ 5, \ 6, \ 7, \ 9, \ 11 \qquad \text{range} = 11 - 2 = 9$$

Clearly, the value of 99 in the first set of numbers is at odds with the rest of the numbers and the range of 97 gives a false impression of the actual values.

In addition, the range can depend on the size of the population or sample. Generally, you get a larger range for larger populations where you have a greater chance of extreme values.

INTERQUARTILE RANGE

One way round the problem of relying on just two values for the range is to calculate the **interquartile range** (IQR). The IQR is simply the value for the lower quartile subtracted from the value for the upper quartile:

$$\text{IQR} = \text{upper quartile } (Q_3) - \text{lower quartile } (Q_1) \qquad (5.13)$$

Whereas the range relies on the values of the highest and the lowest values, the IQR ignores the values of the highest 25 per cent and the lowest 25 per cent of cases. Exhibit 5.23 summarizes these two measures of spread in a symmetrical distribution.

USING SPSS TO COMPUTE THE RANGE AND INTERQUARTILE RANGE

To illustrate how SPSS provides a value for the range for a set of values, consider the data in Exhibit 5.24 for two sets of marks for ten students, one for a sociology exam and one for a psychology exam. This is the MARKS.SAV data set which you may have created in Chapter 2.

We select **Analyze|Descriptive Statistics ▶|Frequencies**.... After selecting the variable of interest, we select **Statistics**... in the **Frequencies** dialog box. In the **Statistics** dialog box (Exhibit 5.25) we would select **Range** in the box marked **Dispersion**. In addition, we could select **Mean, Mode** and **Median** in the **Central Tendency** box and **Quartiles** in the **Percentile Value** box.

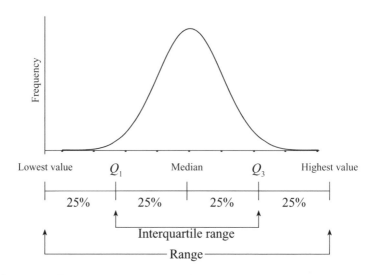

Exhibit 5.23   *The relationship between the range and the interquartile range*

	sociolog	psycholo
1	55.00	49.00
2	45.00	55.00
3	66.00	45.00
4	34.00	56.00
5	67.00	73.00
6	53.00	37.00
7	78.00	12.00
8	45.00	85.00
9	57.00	58.00
10	60.00	63.00

Exhibit 5.24   *Sociology and psychology marks for ten students*
            Source: MARKS.SAV

Before clicking **OK** in the main **Frequencies** dialog box, we need to deselect **Display frequency tables**. This ensures that we do not get a long listing of individual frequency counts, just the statistic(s) we asked for. The result from SPSS is shown in Exhibit 5.26.

The **Frequencies** procedure does not calculate the IQR for you but it is very easy to find it for yourself using the values of the 25th and 75th percentiles.[1]

$$Q_3 \qquad Q_1$$

Sociology: $66.25 - 45 = 21.25$

Psychology: $65.5 - 43 = 22.5$

So the sociology marks have a range of 44 and an IQR of 21.25, while the psychology marks have a range of 73 and an IQR of 22.5. The psychology marks have a lower minimum and a higher maximum than the sociology marks.

[1] The **Explore** procedure in SPSS for Windows will give you an IQR statistic.

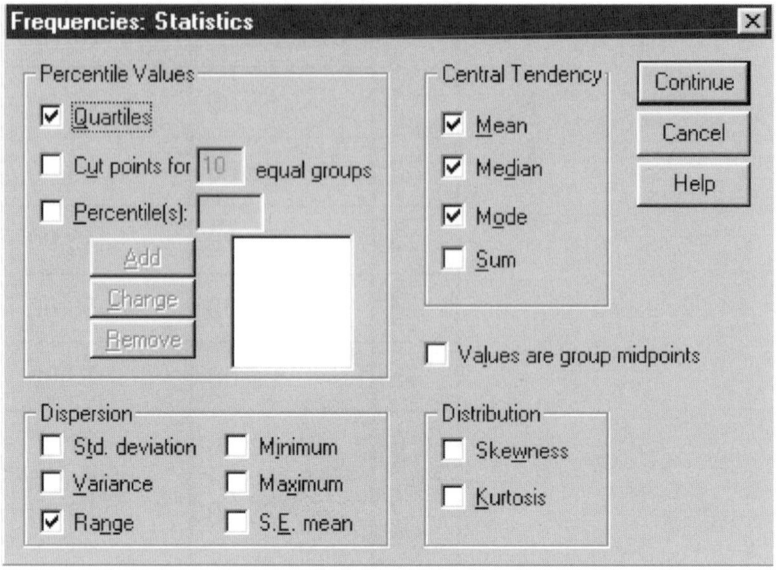

Exhibit 5.25   The **Frequencies: Statistics** dialog box. Calculation of the quartiles and range in SPSS

Statistics

		PSYCHOLO	SOCIOLOG
N	Valid	10	10
	Missing	0	0
Mean		53.3000	56.0000
Median		55.5000	56.0000
Mode		12.00[a]	45.00
Range		73.00	44.00
Percentiles	25	43.0000	45.0000
	50	55.5000	56.0000
	75	65.5000	66.2500

[a] Multiple modes exist. The smallest value is shown

Exhibit 5.26   **Frequencies: Statistics** output in SPSS showing the range and quartiles

These extreme values, however, are ignored in the calculation of the interquartile range, resulting in similar values for the sociology and psychology IQRs.

The IQR and the range are based on the *position* of the observations, not on their actual values. If we want to assess the spread of a variable in a way which takes into account all the observations, we need to use the actual values of the data and consider how they are distributed around the average value. We need to know *how far* each mark is above or below the mean. A measure of variation that does consider the values of each observation is the **variance**.

THE VARIANCE

The variance (denoted by s^2) is based on the deviations or distances of each observation from the central or average observation. In Exhibit 5.27 each sociology mark and the mean value have been placed on a line. In addition, we have calculated how far each mark is from the mean and made a note of it.

If we then add up all these deviations each side of the mean we find that they sum to identical amounts; $+48$ above the mean and -48 below the mean. So if we added these deviations together we would end up with zero. Clearly this measure is not going to get us far. However, there is one way we can end up with a positive deviation, and that is to calculate the *square of each deviation* and sum these squared deviations. Exhibit 5.28 charts these calculations for the sociology marks.

However, we have not quite arrived at a measure of spread because our figure for the sum of the squared deviations will obviously get bigger as we have greater numbers of observations and therefore deviations to sum. So we need to divide by the number of observations to control for the number of cases.

However, although this gives us a good measure when we have gathered information from the whole population of interest, it tends to *underestimate* the value of the variance when we have only collected information from a sample. In other words, we need to divide by slightly less than the number of respondents in order to get a slightly larger value for the variance. This *fudge factor* turns out to be the number of cases less than one. So, since we have only collected

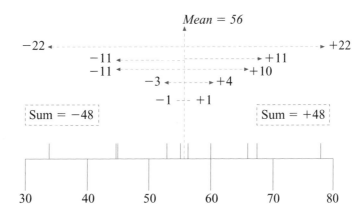

Exhibit 5.27   *Distances from the mean for each sociology mark*

Sociology Mark X	Mean ($\overline{X}$)	Mark−Mean ($X-\overline{X}$)	$(X-\overline{X})^2$
55	56	−1	1
45	56	−11	121
66	56	10	100
34	56	−22	484
67	56	11	121
53	56	−3	9
78	56	22	484
45	56	−11	121
57	56	1	1
60	56	4	16
SUM (Σ) =		0	1458

Exhibit 5.28   *Calculation of the sum of the deviations from the mean for each mark*

marks from 10 students we need to divide the sum of the squared deviations by $N - 1$ or $10 - 1$, or 9.

$$s^2 = \frac{1458}{10 - 1} = \frac{1458}{9} = 162 \qquad (5.14)$$

The short-hand way of writing these instructions for the calculation of the variance for a sample is

$$s^2 = \frac{\sum(X - \overline{X})^2}{N - 1} \qquad (5.15)$$

where s^2 is the sample variance. And the formula for a population is

$$\sigma^2 = \frac{\sum(X - \mu)^2}{N} \qquad (5.16)$$

where σ^2 is the population variance and μ is the population mean.

Both Equations (5.15) and (5.16) both involve the subtraction of the mean from each value. An alternative formula which provides a short-cut for the calculation of the variance by hand is

$$s^2 = \frac{\sum X^2 - (\sum X)^2/N}{N - 1} \qquad (5.17)$$

Exhibit 5.29 demonstrates the steps necessary to calculate the variance of the psychology marks using equation (5.17). Using this formula you only need two columns in the table of calculations; one for the mark and one for the mark squared. Then it is relatively quick and simple to sum each column to provide the sum of all the marks and the sum of all the squared marks.

USING SPSS TO CALCULATE THE VARIANCE

As with the calculation of the range, we select **Analyze|Descriptive Statistics ▶|Frequencies**. . . . This time, however, we select **Variance** in the **Statistics**. . .

Psychology Mark X	x^2
49	2401
55	3025
45	2025
56	3136
73	5329
37	1369
12	144
85	7225
58	3364
63	3969
Sum = Σ = 533 $\therefore (\Sigma x)^2$ = 284,089	Sum = Σ = 31,987 $\therefore \Sigma x^2$ = 31,987

$$s^2 = \frac{\Sigma x^2 - (\Sigma x)^2/N}{N-1}$$

Equation 1.1

$$s^2 = \frac{31987 - 284089/10}{10-1} = \frac{31987 - 28408.9}{9} = 397.57$$

Exhibit 5.29   *Calculation of the variance using the alternative formula*

dialog box (see Exhibit 5.3). The result is shown in Exhibit 5.30. The variance of the psychology marks (397.57) is greater than that for the sociology marks (162). This confirms what we have already seen when we calculated the range. The psychology marks are more spread out and show greater variation.

THE STANDARD DEVIATION

The variance is calculated by summing *squared* deviations. This means that the units of variance are on a squared scale. For example, if the data were measured in pounds, the variance would be in pounds squared. To create a measure of variation on the same scale as the original marks data we need to take the square root of the variance which is called the **standard deviation**.

The standard deviation (denoted by *s* or SD) is the square root of the summed deviations divided by the number of cases. For a sample, the denominator is the number of cases minus one. The formula for the standard deviation is

$$s = \sqrt{\frac{\sum(X - \overline{X})^2}{n - 1}}$$ (5.18)

The larger the standard deviation, the more spread out are the data. Conversely, the smaller the standard deviation, the less spread out and the more similar are the data. A standard deviation of 0 occurs when all scores are the same so there is no deviation around the mean.

To see what it means to have two distributions with different standard deviations, imagine two ambulance crews, crew A in North London and crew B in South London, both with an average response time of 10 minutes. However, the standard deviation for the response times for crew A is 9 minutes and the standard deviation for crew B is 5 minutes. Where would you rather live?

If you live in North London and called the ambulance out enough times you would wait 10 minutes on average for it to arrive. However, since North London has the larger standard deviation you may have to wait considerably longer on any one occasion or you may be lucky and it would arrive in just a few minutes. In South London, where the response time has a smaller standard deviation, the times will be closer to the average of 10 minutes, and they will deviate from the

Statistics

		PSYCHOLO	SOCIOLOG
N	Valid	10	10
	Missing	0	0
Variance		397.57	162.00

Exhibit 5.30   *The variance output in SPSS using the **Frequencies** procedure*

mean to a lesser degree than those in North London. So your chances of having to wait a long time for an ambulance crew are greater if you live in North London than if you live in the South.

What is the likelihood of making a wrong guess about the chances of getting a slow ambulance? If certain conditions are satisfied the chance of guessing wrongly can be quantified. These conditions are to do with the shape of the distribution. If the distribution of the variable you are interested in, be it exam marks or ambulance response times, forms a specific shape of curve, you can use the properties of this special sort of curve to quantify the chances of getting any particular range of scores or times. This special shape is called a **normal curve** and is the subject of the next chapter.

SUMMARY OF MEASURES OF SPREAD

In this chapter we have considered the range, the interquartile range, the variance and the standard deviation as alternative measures of spread. Exhibit 5.31 summarizes the notation we have used for these measures of spread.

EXERCISE ON THE MEAN, MODE AND MEDIAN

Exhibits 5.32–5.34 show the outputs from SPSS when asked to display frequencies for a number of variables from the 1995 General Household Survey. For each variable do the following:

(a) Find the mode.
(b) *If applicable*, find the median.
(c) *If applicable*, find the mean.
(d) Write brief comments about your conclusions from considering the values of the mode, median and the mean.

Type of Statistic	Sample	Population
Variance	s^2	σ^2 (sigma)
Standard deviation	s	σ
Mean	$\overline{X}$	μ (mu)
Number of observations	N	N

Exhibit 5.31   *Notation for the variance and standard deviation*

NADULTS NUMBER OF ADULTS IN HOUSEHOLD

		Frequency	Percent	Valid Percent	Cumulative Percent
Valid	1	812	32.8	32.8	32.8
	2	1286	52.0	52.0	84.9
	3	267	10.8	10.8	95.7
	4	91	3.7	3.7	99.4
	5	13	.5	.5	99.9
	6	2	.1	.1	100.0
	7	1	.0	.0	100.0
	Total	2472	100.0	100.0	

Exhibit 5.32   *Frequency output for number of adults in household*

HHTYPF1 HOUSEHOLD TYPE F

		Frequency	Percent	Valid Percent	Cumulative Percent
Valid	1 1 PERSON ONLY	703	28.4	28.5	28.5
	2 2+ UNREL ADULTS	60	2.4	2.4	30.9
	3 M.CPLE, DEP CH	595	24.1	24.1	55.0
	4 M.CPLE, INDEP CH	159	6.4	6.4	61.5
	5 M.CPLE, NO CH	712	28.8	28.8	90.3
	6 LONE P, DEP CH	152	6.1	6.2	96.5
	7 LONE P, INDEP CH	72	2.9	2.9	99.4
	8 2+ FAMILIES	14	.6	.6	100.0
	9 SAME SEX COHAB	1	.0	.0	100.0
	Total	2468	99.8	100.0	
Missing	-9	4	.2		
Total		2472	100.0		

Exhibit 5.33   *Frequency output for household type*
Note. M.CPLE -married couple
CH   -children
Lone P -lone parent
UNREL -unrelated

EXERCISE ON MEASURES OF SPREAD

NB. In all the following exercises, assume you have a population and use N rather than $N - 1$ in the calculation of the standard deviation.

1. Guess which of the following two lists has the larger standard deviation. Check your guess by computing the standard deviation for both lists.

EDLEV HIGHEST EDUCATIONAL QUALIFICATION

		Frequency	Percent	Valid Percent	Cumulative Percent
Valid	1 HIGHER DEGREE	53	1.1	1.5	1.5
	2 FIRST DEGREE	335	7.2	9.3	10.7
	3 TEACHING QUAL	65	1.4	1.8	12.5
	4 OTH HIGHER QUAL	239	5.2	6.6	19.2
	5 NURSING QUAL	73	1.6	2.0	21.2
	6 GCE A LEVEL 2+	161	3.5	4.5	25.6
	7 GCE A LEVEL 1	284	6.1	7.9	33.5
	8 GCSE&OLV5+, SG1–2	461	10.0	12.8	46.3
	9 GCSE&OLV1–4, NOCQ	73	1.6	2.0	48.3
	10 GCSE&OLV1–4, NOCQ	316	6.8	8.8	57.0
	11 COMM Q, NO O LEVS	148	3.2	4.1	61.1
	12 CSE GRD 2–5	117	2.5	3.2	64.4
	13 APPRENTICESHIP	92	2.0	2.5	66.9
	15 FOREIGN QUALS	61	1.3	1.7	68.6
	16 OTHER QUALS	31	.7	.9	69.5
	17 NO QUALS	1102	23.8	30.5	100.0
	Total	3611	77.9	100.0	
Missing	-9 NEV WENT TO SCH	1022	22.1		
Total		4633	100.0		

Exhibit 5.34   *Frequency output for educational level*
GCE A level   -General Certificate of Education Advanced Level
GCSE   -General Certificate of Secondary Education
OLV   -General Certificate of Education Ordinary Level
CSE   -Certificate of Secondary Education
CM Q   -Commercial qualifications
NOCQ   -No commercial qualifications

List A	7	8	8	8	10	13
List B	8	8	9	9	9	11

2.   (a) For each list of numbers work out the mean and the standard deviation.

List A	4	3	6	4	4	3
List B	11	10	13	11	11	10

(b) How is list A related to list B? How does this relationship carry over to the average? The standard deviation?

3.   Repeat Exercise 2 for the following two lists:

List A	4	3	6	4	4	3
List B	8	6	12	8	8	6

4.   Repeat Exercise 2 for the following two lists:

List A	0	-3	5	-4	-4	3
List B	0	3	-5	4	4	-3

GRAPHICS FOR ANALYSIS

6

EXPLORATORY DATA ANALYSIS

Exploratory methods are designed to give you an idea about the range, shape and structure of the data collected. They include simple graphical methods that are quick to carry out and interpret. Interpretation therefore tends to be visual and impressionistic. These methods tend to be used as a first step in any analysis, to give you ideas about further areas to explore and as the prelude to a more rigorous analysis where ideas you have formed about the data can be tested.

STEM AND LEAF DIAGRAMS

Stem and leaf diagrams are one of the simplest exploratory techniques, and are used to display either discrete or continuous data which have at least two significant places, for instance tens and units. The first significant place becomes the stem, and the second the leaf.

To illustrate this technique, consider the following twelve numbers. . .

11, 23, 24, 35, 36, 36, 39, 42, 47, 48, 55, 58

If the tens are considered the 'stem' and the units the 'leaf', we could distribute the numbers in the pattern seen in Exhibit 6.1. Here there is a general trend for more numbers on the 3 stem than any other.

EXPLORING THE SOCIAL INDICATORS OF DEVELOPMENT DATA SET USING A STEM AND LEAF DIAGRAM

One of the most sensitive indicators of the relative well-being of people living in different countries is their average life expectancy. Despite its name, life expectancy is actually calculated on the basis of people's average age of death. Life expectancy in this sense is a good measure of the average state of a nation's health. If, for example, a high proportion of children die while they are still young, this will be reflected in a low average life expectancy.

Exhibit 6.2 displays the life expectancies for 38 countries on the American continent taken from the SID data set. The data have been rounded to two significant figures. Numbers ending with .1 to .4 have been rounded down and those ending with .5 to .9 have been rounded up. The highest life expectancy is that of Canada with a value of 77 and the lowest is that of Haiti at 54. In Exhibit 6.3 the data have been displayed with three 'stems', 5, 6, and 7.

Exhibit 6.3 has many 'leaves' on the 6 and 7 stems and it is difficult to see any pattern in the data. If each stem were split into two then we would get a clearer picture of the distribution of life expectancy. Exhibit 6.4 shows what is known as a **two-line stem and leaf** diagram where each stem has been split into

Stem (tens)	Leaf (units)	
1	1	
2	3 4	i.e. 23 then 24
3	5 6 6 9	i.e. 35 then 36, 36, 39
4	2 7 8	i.e. 42 then 47 and 48
5	5 8	i.e. 55 then 58

Exhibit 6.1   *Simple stem and leaf diagram*

Americas		
LIFE Expectancy		
	Guatemala	63
Antigua and Barbuda 74	Guyana	64
Argentina 71	Haiti	54
Bahamas, The 69	Honduras	65
Barbados 75	Jamaica	73
Belize 68	Martininque	76
Bermuda 69	Mexico	70
Bolivia 60	Nicaragua	65
Brazil 66	Panama	73
Canada 77	Paraguay	67
Chile 72	Peru	63
Colombia 69	Puerto Rico	76
Costa Rica 75	St. Lucia	72
Cuba 76	St. Vincent	70
Dominica 75	Suriname	68
Dominican Republic 67	Trinidad and Tobago	71
Ecuador 66	United States	76
El Salvador 64	Uruguay	73
Grenada 70	Venezuela	70
Guadeloupe 74	N=38	

Exhibit 6.2   *Life expectancy data for countries in the Americas*
           Source: World Bank, 1992

Stem	Leaf
5	4
6	0 3 3 4 4 5 5 6 6 7 7 8 8 9 9 9
7	0 0 0 0 1 1 2 2 3 3 3 4 4 5 5 5 6 6 6 6 7

Exhibit 6.3   *Simple stem and leaf diagram for life expectancy in the Americas*
           Source: World Bank, 1992

two, using an asterisk (*) to indicate a stem with leaves from 0 to 4 and a full stop (.) to indicate a stem with leaves from 5 to 9.

Exhibit 6.4 demonstrates a clearer pattern in the data, with most countries' life expectancies falling on the 7* stem, between 70 and 74. We could refine this pattern even further by dividing the stems not just into two leaves but into five. Exhibit 6.5 shows a **five-line stem and leaf** diagram. The notation for the leaves is as follows:

Stem	Leaves
5*	4
5.	
6*	0 3 3 4 4
6.	5 5 6 6 7 7 8 8 9 9 9
7*	0 0 0 0 1 1 2 2 3 3 3 4 4
7.	5 5 5 6 6 6 6 7

Exhibit 6.4   *A two-line stem and leaf diagram for life expectancy in the Americas*
            Source: World Bank, 1992

*   0s and 1s
t   2s and 3s ... *t*wos and *t*hrees
f   4s and 5s ... *f*ours and *f*ives
s   6s and 7s ... *s*ixes and *s*evens
.   8s and 9s

Exhibit 6.5 tends to spread the data out too much, so the two-line stem and leaf diagram of Exhibit 6.4 would be the best way of representing these data.

PAIRED STEM AND LEAF DIAGRAMS

We can use the same procedure to compare the life expectancies of the countries of America (Exhibit 6.2) and Africa (see the data in Exhibit 6.6) using a **paired two-line stem and leaf** diagram.

Life expectancy in the African countries ranges from a minimum of 39 to a maximum of 71, so the stem in Exhibit 6.4 needs to be extended to start at 3. (35 to 39). The same stem is used to display the life expectancies in both the American and African countries (see Exhibit 6.7). The data for the African countries are displayed on the left-hand side of the diagram and for the American on the right-hand side.

In Exhibit 6.7 we can see the differences in the distribution of life expectancies between Africa and American countries. Africa has the most countries with life expectancies on the 4. stem (i.e. between 45 and 49) in comparison with America where most countries are on the 7^* stem.

Arranging the data like this allows us to see the maximum and minimum values at a glance, as well as showing the overall spread of the data. In Exhibit

Stem	Leaves
5t	
5f	4
5s	
5.	
6*	0
6t	3 3
6f	4 4 5 5
6s	6 6 7 7
6.	8 8 9 9 9
7*	0 0 0 0 1 1
7t	2 2 3 3 3
7f	4 4 5 5 5
7s	6 6 6 6 7
7.	

Key: * = 0,1 t = 2, 3 f = 4,5 s = 6, 7 . = 8,9

Exhibit 6.5   *A five-line stem and leaf showing life expectancy in the Americas*
               Source: World Bank, 1992

6.7 the data for African countries are more spread out than those for America. We might also consider the African country with a life expectancy of 39 (Guinea-Bissau) or the American country with a life expectancy of 54 (Haiti) in relation to the rest of the data. Are these countries unusual in some way? Maybe they do not belong with the rest of their group. Or perhaps these data may be the result of a typographical error. Studying such cases often reveals unexpected insights into the data or leads to the early detection of an error that might have gone undiscovered until much later in the analysis. Cases that do not seem to 'fit in' with the rest of the data are called **outliers**. The reason why Haiti and Guinea-Bissau are outliers is not because the data are wrong, but probably because both countries were ruled by corrupt dictators for much of the recent past.

As well as noting outliers, it is also useful to identify the most usual or typical

AFRICA			Liberia	54
			Libya	62
			Madagascar	51
COUNTRY	LIFE Expectancy		Malawi	46
Algeria	65		Mali	48
Angola	46		Mauritania	47
Benin	50		Mauritius	70
Botswana	67		Morocco	62
Burkina Faso	48		Mozambique	47
Burundi	47		Namibia	57
Cameroon	57		Niger	45
Cap Verde	66		Nigeria	52
Central African Rep	49		Rwanda	48
Chad	47		Sao Tome	67
Comoros	55		Senegal	47
Congo	53		Seychelles	71
Cote d'Ivoire	55		Sierra Leone	42
Egypt, Arab Republic	60		Somalia	48
Equatorial Guinea	47		South Africa	62
Ethiopia	48		Sudan	50
Gabon	53		Swaziland	57
Gambia, The	44		Tanzania	48
Ghana	55		Togo	54
Guinea	43		Tunisia	67
Guinea-Bissau	39		Uganda	47
Kenya	59		Zaire	52
Lesotho	56		Zambia	50
			Zimbabwe	61
			Number of cases listed: 51	

Exhibit 6.6 *Life expectancy data for countries in Africa*
Source: World Bank, 1992

case in respect of the variable concerned. In the previous chapter we saw how the median identified the case located in the middle position when the cases are arranged in ascending order. It would be useful if we could incorporate this information into our exploratory graphical analysis. The median, at the 50% position, as well as the lower and upper quartiles (at the 25% and 75% position respectively) are all used in the exploratory data analysis technique called a **boxplot**.

BOXPLOTS

A **boxplot** is a diagram which represents the spread of the data based on the position or order of each data point or case. From a boxplot you can easily

Africa	stem	America
9	3	
4 3 2	4*	
9 8 8 8 8 8 8 7 7 7 7 7 7 7 6 6 5	4.	
4 4 3 3 2 2 1 0 0 0	5*	
9 7 7 7 6 5 5 5	5.	4
2 2 2 1 0	6*	0 3 3 4 4
7 7 7 6 5	6.	5 5 6 6 7 7 8 8 9 9 9
1 0	7*	0 0 0 0 1 1 2 2 3 3 3 4 4
	7.	5 5 5 6 6 6 6 7
	8*	

Exhibit 6.7   *Paired stem and leaf diagram comparing life expectancy in Africa*
and America
Source: World Bank, 1992

identify those cases that are positioned in the middle of the ranked data set and
also those cases at either extreme, the outliers.

Consider the data in Exhibit 6.8. In Exhibit 6.9 the quartiles have been drawn
in as short horizontal lines against the scale on the left-hand side. If we were to
draw vertical lines to join the Q_1 and Q_3 horizontal lines, we would form a box
which contains 50 per cent of the cases. This, of course, would define the
interquartile range (IQR) described in Chapter 5. Some of the other data points,
outside the box, may be outliers. A useful definition of an outlier is that it is
more than $1\frac{1}{2}$ times the box length or IQR above or below the box. So in Exhibit
6.9

$$IQR = Q_3 - Q_1 = 10 - 4 = 6$$

and therefore

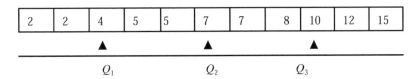

Exhibit 6.8   *The lower quartile, the median and the upper quartile*

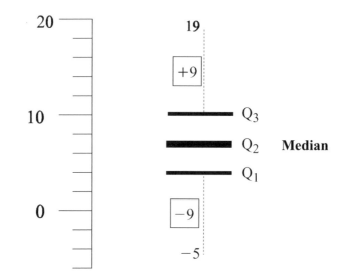

Exhibit 6.9   *The position of the quartiles in boxplots*

$$1.5 \times \text{IQR} = 1.5 \times 6 = 9$$

So the boundaries of the main body of the data, beyond which lie the outliers, are

$$\text{upper boundary} = Q_3 + 1.5 \text{ IQR} = 10 + 9 = 19$$

and

$$\text{lower boundary} = Q_1 - 1.5 \text{ IQR} = 4 - 9 = -5$$

Clearly, in this set of data there are no outliers since all the data points are within the range -5 to 19.

In addition, if a data point is more than three box lengths above or below the box, then it will be called an **extreme outlier**.

The main body of the data therefore consists of those data points that fall between $1\frac{1}{2}$ times the IQR above the upper quartile and $1\frac{1}{2}$ times the IQR below the lower quartile (see Exhibit 6.10).

Exhibit 6.10 shows the notation involved in drawing outliers and extreme outliers and introduces the **inner** and **outer fences**: the boundaries that define the outliers and extreme outlier positions.

In addition, a complete boxplot would also include those data points that are the highest and lowest values *that are not* outliers. These are indicated by a vertical line extending from the top and bottom of the box and ending in a small T. These values are called the adjacent values and their appearance led to these diagrams to be called **box and whisker** diagrams. See Exhibit 6.11 for the full

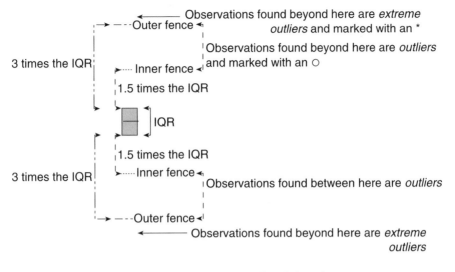

Exhibit 6.10   *Outliers and extreme outliers in boxplots*

Exhibit 6.11   *Notation for boxplots*

notation for a box and whisker plot. Exhibit 6.12 shows the completed boxplot for the small dataset seen in Exhibit 6.8.

The data in Exhibit 6.13 on life expectancies in the American continent are used to demonstrate how to create a box and whisker plot. Summary statistics for this data are presented in Exhibit 6.14. The resulting boxplot is displayed in Exhibit 6.15.

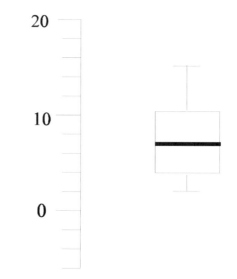

Exhibit 6.12   *The completed boxplot*

COUNTRY LIFE Expectancy	COUNTRY LIFE Expectancy
Antigua and Barbuda 73.75	Guatemala 63.16
Argentina 71.23	Guyana 64.17
Bahamas, The 68.96	Haiti 54.36
Barbados 75.12	Honduras 64.88
Belize 67.91	Jamaica 73.18
Bermuda 68.90	Martinique 76.10
Bolivia 59.98	Mexico 69.70
Brazil 66.16	Nicaragua 64.74
Canada 77.43	Panama 72.65
Chile 71.96	Paraguay 67.30
Colombia 68.80	Peru 62.72
Costa Rica 75.15	Puerto Rico 75.70
Cuba 75.87	St. Lucia 71.52
Dominica 74.91	St. Vincent 70.37
Dominican Republic 67.00	Suriname 67.86
Ecuador 66.11	Trinidad and Tobago 70.98
El Salvador 63.56	United States 76.04
Grenada 69.72	Uruguay 72.98
Guadeloupe 74.41	Venezuela 70.12

Exhibit 6.13   *Life expectancy on the American continent*
Source: World Bank, 1992

The box plot in Exhibit 6.15 shows that life expectancy in the American continent has a median value of 69.93. Haiti is clearly demonstrated as an outlier, but only just, confirming our previous analysis using stem and leaf diagrams.

Statistic	Value
Median	69.93
Upper quartile	73.91
Lower quartile	66.15
IQR	7.76

Exhibit 6.14   *Statistics for life expectancy on the American continent*
Source: World Bank, 1992

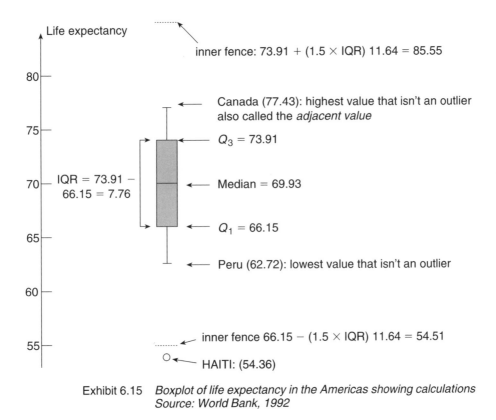

inner fence: 73.91 + (1.5 × IQR) 11.64 = 85.55

Canada (77.43): highest value that isn't an outlier
also called the *adjacent value*

$Q_3 = 73.91$

IQR = 73.91 −
66.15 = 7.76

Median = 69.93

$Q_1 = 66.15$

Peru (62.72): lowest value that isn't an outlier

inner fence 66.15 − (1.5 × IQR) 11.64 = 54.51

HAITI: (54.36)

Exhibit 6.15   *Boxplot of life expectancy in the Americas showing calculations*
Source: World Bank, 1992

CREATING STEM AND LEAF DIAGRAMS AND BOXPLOTS IN SPSS

The exploratory data analysis procedure within SPSS is called **Explore**. The following example uses the World Bank data file, SID.SAV, which must be opened before any analysis can proceed. To use **Explore** to create a stem and leaf plot and a boxplot you need to select **Analyze|Descriptive Statistics ▶|Explore**. . . . The dialog box in Exhibit 6.16 appears.

Life expectancy in the 171 countries in the SID data file is recorded in years in the variable LIFEX. Click once on the variable name, LIFEX, and then click on the upper button to insert it into the **Dependent List:** box. The **Factor List** box is only used when creating multiple boxplots (which we shall do in the next section). Then click on **OK** to get SPSS to carry out the procedure.

By default, SPSS will create a stem and leaf diagram and a boxplot with the **Explore** procedure as well as calculating some summary statistics, called **Descriptives** in SPSS. The summary statistics are seen in Exhibit 6.17, the stem and leaf diagram is seen in Exhibit 6.18 and the boxplot in Exhibit 6.19.

We can see from the plot that countries fall into two bands: the majority for which life expectancy is in the range 60 to 78 years, and a smaller group with life expectancies ranging from a low of 38 to 59. We might suspect that the two bands correspond roughly with countries from the developed and the less developed areas of the world.

In this case, a boxplot is not a particularly useful representation of the data. This is because, as we have seen from the stem and leaf plot, the distribution of life expectancy is bimodal – it has two peaks, one for the less developed and one for the developed countries – and the boxplot does not show this. A more useful picture would be obtained if we were able to construct separate box plots for poor and the rich countries. As a first step towards this, we shall get SPSS to draw box plots for each continent side by side, so that they can easily be compared.

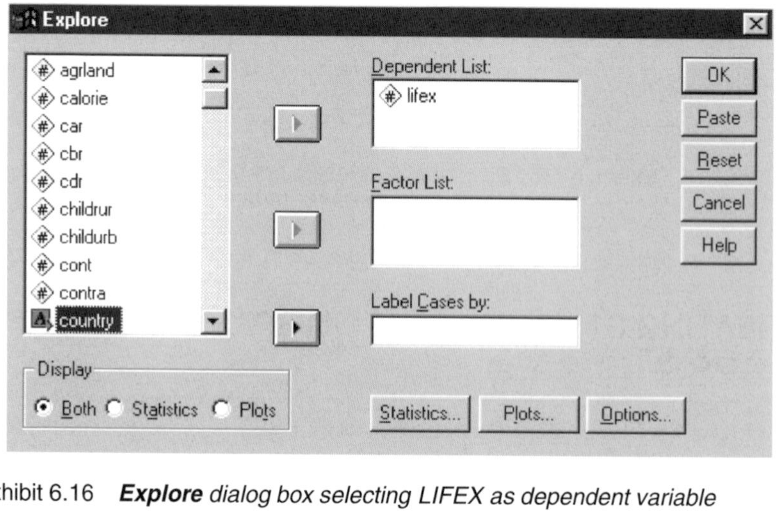

Exhibit 6.16   ***Explore*** *dialog box selecting LIFEX as dependent variable*

Descriptives

			Statistic	Std. Error
LIFEX Life expectancy at birth, overall (years)	Mean		64.1093	.8020
	95% Confidence Interval for Mean	Lower Bound	62.5261	
		Upper Bound	65.6926	
	5% Trimmed Mean		64.4849	
	Median		66.5929	
	Variance		109.344	
	Std. Deviation		10.4568	
	Minimum		38.82	
	Maximum		78.81	
	Range		39.98	
	Interquartile Range		17.4986	
	Skewness		−.552	.186
	Kurtosis		−.926	.370

Exhibit 6.17　*Descriptives for life expectancy produced by the* **Explore** *procedure in SPSS*
Source: World Bank, 1992

```
Life expectancy at birth, overall (years) Stem-and-leaf Plot

   Frequency      Stem & Leaf

       1.00        3 . 8
       4.00        4 . 1234
      22.00        4 . 5566666677777788888999
      15.00        5 . 000011112334444
      11.00        5 . 55556677899
      22.00        6 . 0011111222223344444444
      31.00        6 . 5555666666666677777788899999999
      35.00        7 . 00000000001111111222222223334444444
      29.00        7 . 55555555566666666667777777788

   Stem width:      10.00
   Each leaf:        1 case(s)
```

Exhibit 6.18　*Stem and leaf plot of life expectancy*
Source: World Bank, 1992

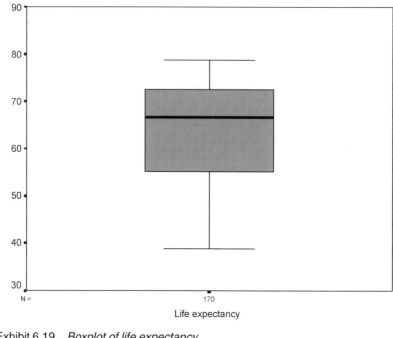

Exhibit 6.19   *Boxplot of life expectancy*
Source: World Bank, 1992

MULTIPLE BOXPLOTS

A multiple boxplot enables one to compare subsets of observations. In this example we shall compare life expectancies for different continents. As before, we select **Analyze|Descriptive Statistics ►|Explore**... and the dialog box in Exhibit 6.20 will appear. Select LIFEX as the dependent variable as before, but this time move CONT (continent) into the **Factor List:** box. A separate boxplot will be created for every value of the variable CONT, that is, for Africa (value 1), Americas (2), Austral/Asia (3) and Europe (4).

The dialog box shows that COUNTRY has been chosen to **Label Cases by**. As we shall see, countries with extreme values of life expectancy will be labelled using the country names stored in this variable.

Click on **OK** and SPSS will carry out the **Explore** procedure which, in addition to creating summary statistics and a stem and leaf diagram as before, will also create the boxplots shown in Exhibit 6.21. It is clear that Africa has by far the lowest average life expectancy of the four continents, and Europe the highest.

The outliers in the American and Austral/Asian continents have been labelled by country name. Haiti has the lowest life expectancy in the American continents and Afghanistan the lowest in the Austral/Asian continents. The data

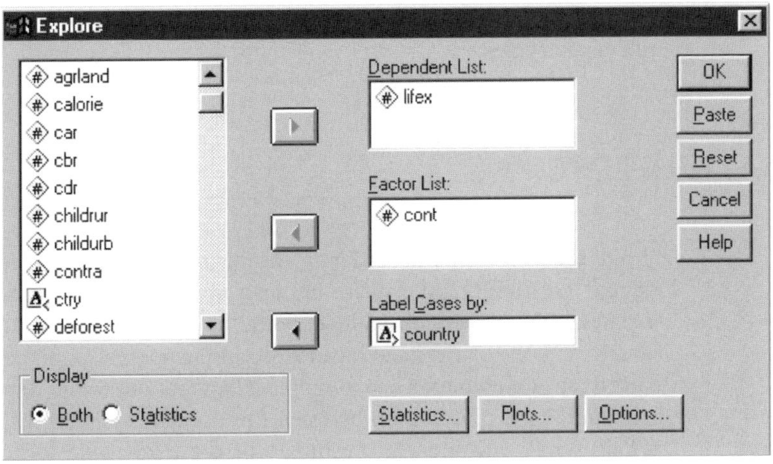

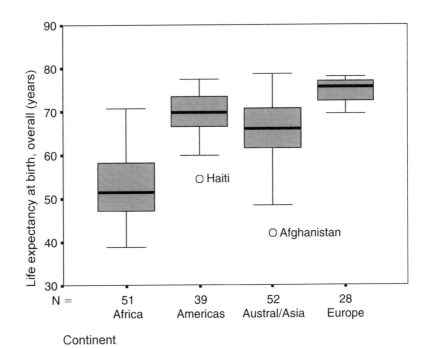

Exhibit 6.20   **Explore** *dialog box*

Exhibit 6.21   *Multiple boxplot of life expectancy by continent*
Source: World Bank, 1992

for the countries in Africa and Europe do not contain any countries with extreme life expectancies.

SCATTERPLOTS

While the continents do differ in the degree to which the economies of their nations are rich or poor, there are also great variations within continents. For example, the Americas include both the United States, one of the richest countries in the world, and Guyana, one of the poorest. A better way of exploring the effect of a country's economic development on its life expectancy would be to examine the relationship between life expectancy and gross national product (GNP). GNP is a monetary estimate of the total value of goods and services produced by a country. Because countries with large populations will produce more than small ones simply as a consequence of their greater number of people, we usually use the GNP per head of population, rather than the raw total. We therefore want to look at the relationship between life expectancy and GNP per head, or, as it is often called, GNP per capita.

Exhibit 6.22 shows the values of life expectancy (LIFEX) and gross national product per head (GNP) for a small number of countries taken from the SID data set. Exhibit 6.23 plots these data. One country, Portugal, with a life expectancy of 74.9 and a GNP of US$4900, has been marked to show how the points in the plot are located. Since we are supposing that GNP may have an effect on life

COUNTRY	LIFEX Life expectancy at birth, overall (years)	GNP Gross national product per capita ($US)
The Gambia	44.24	260.00
Mauritania	46.63	500.00
Uganda	46.89	220.00
Ethiopia	47.99	120.00
Nigeria	51.53	290.00
Pakistan	55.79	380.00
Tunisia	66.73	1440.00
Mauritius	69.79	2250.00
China	70.16	370.00
Chile	71.96	1940.00
Kuwait	74.06	16160.00
Portugal	74.93	4900.00
Sweden	77.59	23760.00
Hong Kong	77.70	11490.00
Japan	78.81	25890.00

Exhibit 6.22   *A small subset of 15 countries from the SID 1992 data set*

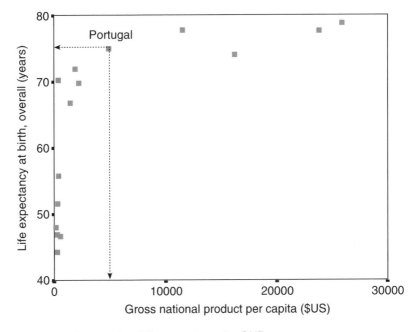

Exhibit 6.23   *Scatterplot of life expectancy by GNP*
                Source: World Bank, 1992

expectancy, GNP is the **independent** variable and life expectancy the **dependent** variable. It is usual to plot the dependent variable as the vertical or *Y*-axis.

To create a **scatterplot** (or scattergram) like this, but showing data from all 171 countries, open the SID.SAV file and select: **Graphs|Scatter**.... We want a simple scatterplot, so select **Simple** and then click on **Define** (see Exhibit 6.24).

Exhibit 6.25 shows the **Simple Scatterplot** dialog box, where LIFEX has been chosen as the dependent or *Y*-axis variable and GNP as the independent or *X*-axis variable. Exhibit 6.26 shows the results produced by SPSS. Although GNP cannot possibly be less than zero, the left-hand end of the horizontal axis

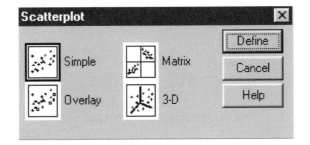

Exhibit 6.24   **Scatterplot** *dialog box*

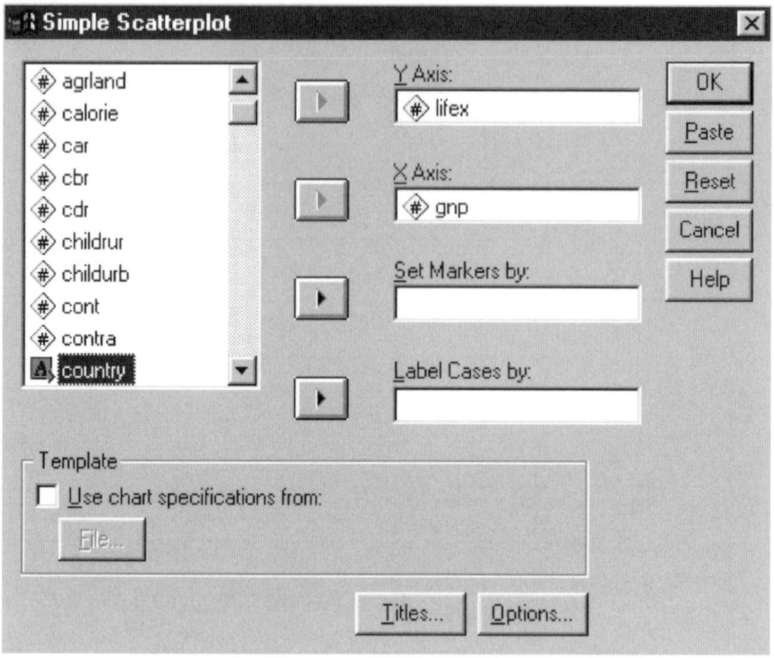

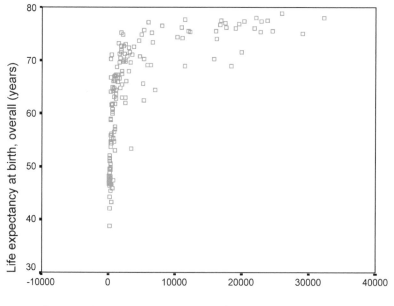

Exhibit 6.25   ***Simple Scatterplot*** *dialog box*

Exhibit 6.26   *Scatterplot of GNP and life expectancy*
Source: World Bank, 1992

of the scatterplot is labelled −10,000. This is to enable you to see the values clustered around zero more clearly.

The scatterplot in Exhibit 6.26 shows that the relationship follows a curve from the lower left to the upper right. As GNP per capita increases, so does life expectancy. This confirms what we had expected – the richer the country, the longer the population lives. This is presumably because rich countries spend more on health, education, nutrition and other resources which prolong life.

If you roughly connect up the points on the scatter plot by eye, it is clear that the relationship between GNP per head and life expectancy follows a curve which starts by going almost vertically upwards and then changes so that it is close to horizontal. This means that in the poorer countries small increases in GNP correspond to very large increases in life expectancy. However, quite large increases in GNP per head make little difference to life expectancy in the richer countries. In later chapters, we shall see that statistical methods will allow us to quantify these conclusions, to find out how much longer one could expect to live for a given increase in GNP per head. For the moment, however, it is enough to know that it appears that even small additions to GNP per head in poor countries could make substantial improvements to their populations' life expectancy.

SUMMARY

This chapter has introduced exploratory graphical techniques such as stem and leaf diagrams, boxplots and scatterplots as tools in data analysis.

EXERCISES

1. In this exercise we explore the infant mortality rate data from the SID data set.

    (a) Create a boxplot of infant mortality rate (INFMOR) using the **Explore** procedure. Infant mortality rate is the annual number of deaths of

Infant mortality				
Statistic	Africa	Americas	Austral/Asia	Europe
Median				
Maximum				
Minimum				

Exhibit 6.27

infants under one year of age per 1000 live births. What is the median value of infant mortality?

(b)   Compare infant mortality in the four continents by creating multiple boxplots with CONT as the factor variable. Which continent has the lowest infant mortality? Fill in the table in Exhibit 6.27.

2.   Explore the relationship between infant mortality and female illiteracy. Female illiteracy in this data set is defined as the proportion of the population 15 years of age and older who cannot read and write a short simple statement about everyday life. Since both infant mortality and female illiteracy are measured on a continuous scale, the relationship between them is best investigated using a scatterplot. Does it look as though there is a relationship? If so, describe it.

THE NORMAL CURVE 7

CONTENTS

HISTORY OF THE NORMAL CURVE

The French mathematician, Abraham de Moivre (1667–1754) first published the formula for the normal curve in 1733 arising from his studies of probability and chance, probably informed by his coffeehouse soirées with the gentlemen of London. However, the formula is more often associated with Karl Friedrich Gauss (1777–1855) and another name for the normal curve is the Gaussian curve. In the eighteenth century the increased growth of the use of scientific instrumentation, especially for astronomical measurements, led Gauss and others to measure their reliability. They found that repeated measurements of the same quantity using an instrument gave rise to different results which could be represented by the following statement:

observed measurement = true measurement + error

They then discovered that if the observed measurements were plotted as a frequency distribution the resulting distribution approximated a characteristic curve, a normal or Gaussian curve. For instance, if repeated measurements were taken of the distance between two mountain peaks some measurements would overestimate the 'true' value and some would underestimate it (see Exhibit 7.1).

It has been shown that data which are influenced by many independent random effects have an approximately normal distribution. Scientific measurements and exam marks are among the many examples. Some are biologically based like height and weight, but others, like seasonal temperature variations or stock market fluctuations, may come from the physical or social world. An example based on data about adult heights collected by the Department of Health in 1980 is seen in Exhibit 7.2 (Knight, 1984). Both graphs display normal curves, although the one for the females has a lower mean and smaller variance or standard deviation.

If we were to create a boxplot of a normal distribution, such as height or IQ, we would create a symmetrical plot with the median coinciding with the mean at the centre of the box and an even spread of cases above and below the box (see Exhibit 7.3).

THE FORMULA FOR A NORMAL PROBABILITY DISTRIBUTION

The formula for the normal curve is given by

$$Y = \frac{1}{\sigma\sqrt{2\pi}}e^{-(x-\mu)^2/2\sigma^2} \qquad (7.1)$$

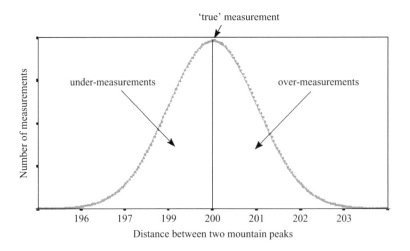

Exhibit 7.1   *Measurement of the distance between two mountain peaks*

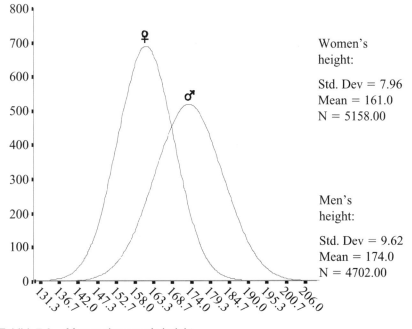

Exhibit 7.2   *Men and women's height*
               Source: Department of Health data collected in 1980

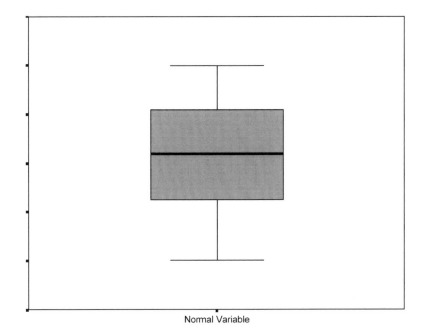

Normal Variable

Exhibit 7.3   *Boxplot of a normal distribution*

where Y is the height of the curve for a given value of X, σ the standard deviation and μ the mean, and e $= 2.71828$ and $\pi = 3.14159$. The point in presenting this formula is not for you to memorize it but to demonstrate that since e and π are both constants, the value of Y only depends on the mean and the standard deviation. Therefore the shape of the curve – how high it is or how spread out it is – is a function of its mean and standard deviation.

There are many different normal curves, differing according to their means and standard deviations. A large value for the standard deviation will result in a spread-out curve and a small value for the standard deviation means a narrow curve. Exhibit 7.4 demonstrates three normal curves.

PROPERTIES OF NORMAL CURVES

All normal curves have the following properties. They are:

- *bell-shaped*. The most frequent observations occur at the midpoint of the curve. These observations are the most probable outcome. As you move away from midpoint, the observations become less frequent.
- *symmetrical*. That is, the left half is a mirror image of the right half. The implication of this is that the mean, mode and median all have same value and coincide at the centre.
- *continuous*. Theoretically, the values the variable can assume are infinite and measured on a truly continuous scale.
- *asymptotic*. The two tails never touch the X axis because there is always some probability that more extreme values will occur.

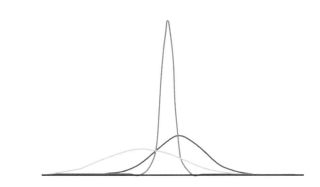

Exhibit 7.4   *Three normal curves*

THE NORMAL DISTRIBUTION AS A THEORETICAL DISTRIBUTION

Although Gauss and others collected repeated measurements which they plotted to form a normal curve, it would have taken many, many measurements, in fact an infinite number, before a smooth curve would have been produced. So the normal curve is a *theoretical curve*, an idealized version of the distribution, against which we can compare the distribution we actually obtain in our research.

If many measurements are taken, most would cluster around the middle or 'true' measurement. Any single measurement will most probably fall near the centre and will be least likely to occur in the tails.

In Exhibit 7.5 it can be seen that there are more observations with a value of 199 than of 198. So the chances of getting a measurement of around 199 are greater than getting a measurement of around 198. This is what is meant by a **distribution of probabilities**. You will notice that the phrase *around 199* was used. This is because there are an infinite number of values between any two X values, and the probability of obtaining any one particular value is infinitesimally small. For this reason we can only talk of the probability between two values when all the infinitesimally small probabilities add up to a measurable probability. However, it is clear that the length of the vertical line under the curve around 199 is longer than the vertical line under the curve around 198. So a value around 199 is more probable than a value around 198. However, if we want to know the chances of obtaining a measurement *between* 198 and 199, we would have to sum the lengths of *all* the lines between a measurement of 198 and 199 (i.e. not just those at 198.1, 198.2, 198.3 and so on but also those at 198.12987665 and 198.45637298 etc.). This amounts to saying that what we

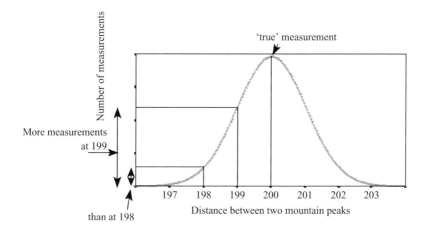

Exhibit 7.5   *Frequency of measurements at two different distances*

want is the *area* under the curve between the two measurements. If we can also find the total area under the curve, we can express our area of interest as a proportion of all possibilities, since the total area under the curve represents the probability of all possible measurements.

THE STANDARD NORMAL DISTRIBUTION

We have noted above that there are many different normal curves, each with different means and standard deviations. But if we were to pick just one representative curve, we could fully document this one curve, calculating the area under the curve at different points above and below the 'true' mean. Mathematicians have done just that. They chose to document the normal curve which has a mean equal to 0 and a standard deviation equal to 1 and then fixed the total area under the curve to equal 1. Using calculus, they calculated the proportions of the areas under the curve at intervals. Because the curve is symmetrical, the area below the mean of zero is equal to the area above the mean, and so they only needed to calculate the areas for half the curve. This information was then published as a statistical table and is to be found in most statistical textbooks (see Appendix B). This special normal curve, with a mean of 0 and a standard deviation of 1, is called the **standard normal curve** or **standard normal distribution**.

Exhibit 7.6 shows a normal curve with mean μ and standard deviation σ, and Exhibit 7.7 shows a standard normal curve with a mean of 0 and standard deviation of 1. The axis of the standard normal curve can be expressed in terms of standard deviation units or z **units**.

A table of the standard normal distribution (Appendix B) gives the area under the curve from the centre at $z = 0$ to any desired z value. For example, if we consult the table for z equal to one standard deviation ($z = 1$), it gives the value 0.3413. This means that there are 0.3413 units of the area under the curve between $z = 0$ and $z = 1$ (see Exhibit 7.8). Because the total area under the

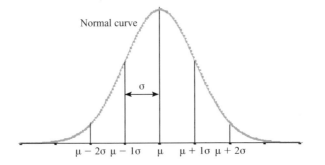

Exhibit 7.6   *A normal curve with mean μ and standard deviation σ*

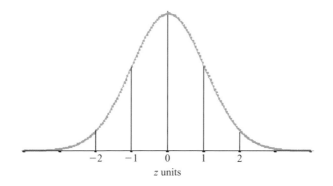

Exhibit 7.7   *The standard normal curve with mean 0 and standard deviation 1.*

curve is 1, by definition, we can also say that the proportion of the area of the whole distribution which is shaded in Exhibit 7.8 is 0.3413.

A way of writing this symbolically is

$$P(0 \leqslant z \leqslant 1) = 0.3413.$$

We can read this in two ways. It says that the *P*roportion of the curve lying between *z* values of 0 and 1 is 0.3413. It also says that the *P*robability of getting an observation with a *z* value between 0 and 1 is 0.3413. Moreover, this means that about 34 per cent of cases will fall between the mean and a *z* score of 1. This is because we know that all cases will be somewhere under the curve, and the shaded area represents 34 per cent of that total area.

To take this one step further, since the curve is symmetrical, 50 per cent of cases fall below the mean, and so $50 + 34.13 = 84.13$ per cent have a *z* score of 1 or less, and therefore $100 - 84.13 = 15.87$ per cent have a *z* score of more than 1 (see Exhibit 7.9).

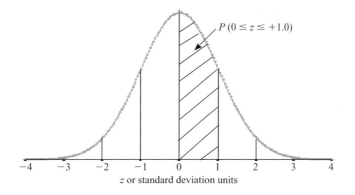

Exhibit 7.8   *Area under the normal curve between z = 0 and z = +1*

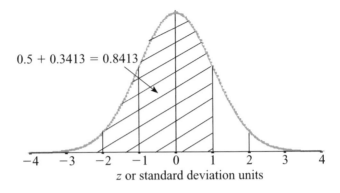

$$0.5 + 0.3413 = 0.8413$$

z or standard deviation units

Exhibit 7.9   *Area under the normal curve to the left of z = 1*

KEY AREAS UNDER THE NORMAL CURVE

We have seen that 0.3413 of the total area under the curve is between the mean and one standard deviation above the mean. Similarly, 0.3413 of the total area is between the mean and one standard deviation below the mean. This can be expressed as follows:

$$P(0 \leqslant z \leqslant 1) = 0.3413$$

and

$$P(-1 \leqslant z \leqslant 0) = 0.3413$$

As indicated in Exhibit 7.10, the shaded area between $z = -1.0$ and $z = +1.0$ occupies 68.26% of the total area under the curve. Thus, approximately 68 per cent of values will lie within one standard deviation of the mean.

Similarly, using the standard normal tables, we can calculate that the proportion of the area between $z = -2.0$ and $z = +2.0$ is 95.4 per cent, since

$$P(0 \leqslant z \leqslant 2) = 0.4772$$

and

$$P(-2 \leqslant z \leqslant 0) = 0.4772$$

Thus, approximately 95 per cent of values will lie within two standard deviations from the mean.

Again, for the area between $z = -2.5$ and $z = +2.5$,

$$P(0 \leqslant z \leqslant 2.5) = 0.4938$$

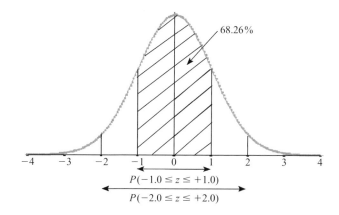

Exhibit 7.10   *The shaded area (between z = −1.0 and z = 1.0) is 68.26 per cent of the total area under the curve*

and

$$P(-2.5 \leqslant z \leqslant 0) = 0.4938$$

Thus, similarly, we can say that approximately 99 per cent of values lie within 2.5 standard deviations of the mean.

Finally, for the area between $z = -\infty$ (minus infinity) and $z = +\infty$ (plus infinity), note that

$$P(0 \leqslant z \leqslant \infty) = 0.5$$

and

$$P(-\infty \leqslant z \leqslant 0) = 0.5$$

which means that 100 per cent of values lie within an infinite number of standard deviations of the mean – recall our discussion of the properties of the normal curve, when we said there is always some probability that the more extreme values will occur, i.e. that the distribution is asymptotic.

Another way of looking at this would be to turn it around and instead of starting with the z values and finding out the area under the curve, we could start with a percentage under the curve and find out the range of z values. So, we could ask what is the z value above and below the mean that encloses 95 per cent of the values? Exhibit 7.11 lists the z values around the mean that contain 90 per cent, 95 per cent and 99 per cent of the values or cases.

% of values	z value on either side of the mean
90%	1.645
95%	1.960
99%	2.576

Exhibit 7.11   *z scores for three important percentages of cases*

STANDARDIZATION

We might now ask how are we going to use all this information about the standard normal curve. What about all the other normal curves, for instance the ones displaying men's height with a mean of 174 cm ($\sigma = 9.62$) and women's height with a mean of 161 cm ($\sigma = 7.96$) in Exhibit 7.2?

For the table of the standard normal curve to be useful in research, we need to 'standardize' data to bring its mean to 0 and its standard deviation to 1. Once we have done that, we can use the tabulated areas under the curve to express the probability of outcomes occurring for any normal curve. Standardization allows us to compare:

- variables with different means;
- variables with different standard deviations;
- scores expressed in differing original units.

To convert our empirical distributions to standard units we need to calculate z scores. These are given by

$$z = \frac{X - \overline{X}}{s} \tag{7.2}$$

To calculate the z score for any particular data point we subtract the value of the mean of all the data from the value of each data point and then divide by the standard deviation of the data. Thus, z scores are a way of transforming the data so that it is in z-units or standard deviation units.

As an example of the use of z scores, suppose that a student gets 56 per cent for an exam in sociological analysis and wants to know where he or she stands in relation to the rest of the group. The mean mark for all the students is 52 per cent and the standard deviation equal to 4. We shall assume that the marks are normally distributed. Calculating the z score for 56, we get:

$$z = \frac{56 - 52}{4} = \frac{4}{4} = 1 \tag{7.3}$$

So this student gained a mark which was one standard deviation above the average. Using the normal tables we see that 0.34 of the total area under the curve lies between the mean and a *z* score of 1. In addition, we know that 0.5 of the total area falls below the mean and so we can add both these proportions to conclude that 0.84 of the total area under the curve is below a *z* score of 1. Expressed as a percentage of cases, we can say that 84 per cent of students scored less than 56. Conversely, this student is in the top 16 per cent of the group. This is depicted in Exhibit 7.12.

Now consider the situation if the same student gets 56 per cent for data analysis and the mean for the data analysis marks is 65 per cent with a standard deviation of 6 per cent. Then

$$z = \frac{56 - 65}{6} = -\frac{9}{6} = -1.5 \qquad (7.4)$$

This time, the student's mark is 1.5 standard deviations *below* the average mark as indicated by the negative value. If we look this *z* value up in the 'The normal distribution' table in Appendix B we see that this corresponds to an area between the mean and the *z* score of 1.5 as 0.4332 and an area of 0.0668 beyond the *z* score. The negative sign just means that these areas are *below* the mean. If we convert this last area into percentages, we see that this student is now in the bottom 6.7 per cent of the group for data analysis (see Exhibit 7.13).

FINDING THE AREA UNDER THE STANDARD NORMAL CURVE BETWEEN TWO SCORES

Suppose you had a sample of 5-year-old children who were born of mothers who smoked and you wished to know what percentage fell within the usual height

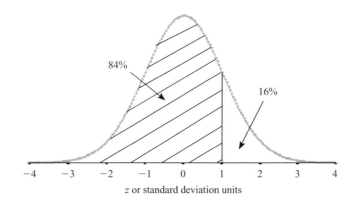

Exhibit 7.12   *The area under the normal curve for one positive z score. The shaded area (to the left of z = +1.0) is 84 per cent of the total area under the curve*

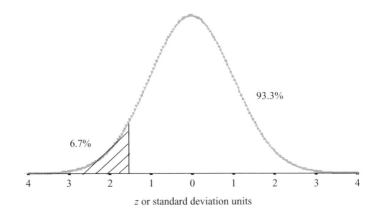

Exhibit 7.13   *The area under the normal curve for z, when z = 1.5, is 6.7 per cent of the total area under the curve*

range for that age group of between 105 and 115 cm. You calculate that the mean height for your sample is 107 cm and the standard deviation is 6 cm. Height is known to be normally distributed within the population.

First, calculate the z scores. For a raw score of 105, we obtain

$$z = \frac{105 - 107}{6} = -0.33 \tag{7.5}$$

and a raw score of 115 gives

$$z = \frac{115 - 107}{6} = 1.33 \tag{7.6}$$

Looking in tables for the areas under the normal curve between the z score and the mean, we get 0.1293 for $z = -0.33$ and 0.4082 for $z = 1.33$. The total area is therefore $0.1293 + 0.4082 = 0.5375$, or about 54 per cent of children in this group are likely to be within the usual height range (see Exhibit 7.14).

Consider now an example where there are two positive z scores, one of 0.5 and one of 1.55. The standard normal table indicates that 0.44 of the total area under the curve lies between the mean and a z score of 1.55 and that 0.19 of the total area is between the mean and a z score of 0.5. Since the areas overlap, the smaller area must be subtracted from the larger area to find out the area that falls between the scores (Exhibit 7.15). Hence, we find that 0.25 or 25 per cent of the area falls between a z score of 0.5 and 1.55.

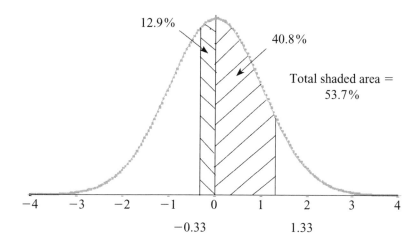

Exhibit 7.14 *Calculating the area between a positive and a negative z score*

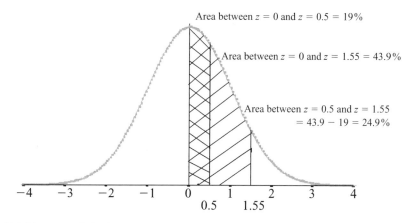

Exhibit 7.15 *Calculating the areas between two positive z scores*

TRANSFORMATIONS TOWARDS NORMALITY

We have seen how important a normal distribution is in being able to predict the probability of an event occurring. What can be done if the distribution is *not* normal? One solution is to **transform** the data to approximate a normal distribution.

Suppose we are interested in the distribution of infant mortality among the countries of the world as recorded in the World Bank data set (SID). SPSS will show the shape and spread of this variable (INFMOR), giving the statistics in Exhibit 7.16 and the boxplot in Exhibit 7.17.

Comparing the mean of 55 to the median of 42 indicates that the distribution of infant mortality is positively skewed. This conclusion is reinforced by

			Statistic	Std. Error
INFMOR Infant mortality rate (per thous. live births)	Mean		55.1131	3.3884
	95% Confidence Interval for Mean	Lower Bound	48.4241	
		Upper Bound	61.8022	
	5% Trimmed Mean		52.6585	
	Median		42.0600	
	Variance		1951.828	
	Std. Deviation		44.1795	
	Minimum		4.58	
	Maximum		169.36	
	Range		164.78	
	Interquartile Range		76.4200	
	Skewness		.670	.186
	Kurtosis		−.774	.370

Exhibit 7.16   *Descriptive statistics of infant mortality*
Source: SID, 1992

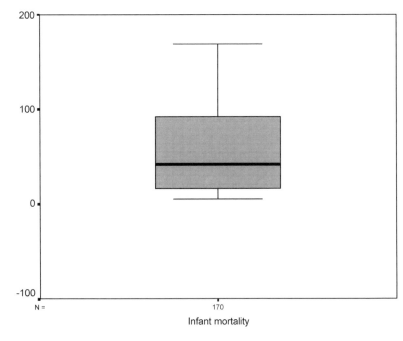

Exhibit 7.17   *Boxplot of infant mortality*
Source: SID, 1992

inspection of the boxplot with those countries with low infant mortality clustered more closely together below the median. Remember that the 'box' in the boxplot contains 50 per cent of all cases and the black line in the middle is drawn at the median or 50 per cent position when countries are ordered by their values for infant mortality.

The distribution is quite different from the boxplot of a normal curve seen in Exhibit 7.3, but it may be possible to transform the data so that there is a more even spread of countries above and below the median line so that it more closely resembles the normal shape. Transforming data means applying some arithmetic operation to *all* the data points with the result that the points become measured on some different scale. For example, to compare salaries in France with those in London you need to convert francs to pounds sterling before a meaningful comparison can be made. To transform degrees Celsius to degrees Fahrenheit, you multiply by a fraction (9/5) and add a constant (32).

However, both these examples of transformation just move the data points up or down. They do not change the relative distance between the pairs of data points and certainly do not change the order of the data points. Looking again at the boxplot in Exhibit 7.17, we need to spread out the data points below the median and squash together the values above the median. A transformation which will perform that kind of change is the logarithmic function. The logarithm or log of a number is another number which indicates the power to which (usually) 10 must be raised to produce that number. So the log of 100 is 2 because 10^2 (i.e. 10×10) is equal to 100.

Notice that in Exhibit 7.18 the lower data values are being spread out on the log scale and the higher values are squashed in.

Exhibit 7.19 gives a larger range of log values for comparison. These are logs to the base 10. It is also possible to use logarithms to other bases, but the general effect is always the same. It is also possible to use other transformations such as the square root or powers: the choice of which transformation to use depends on the shape of the original curvilinear relationship (see Marsh, 1988).

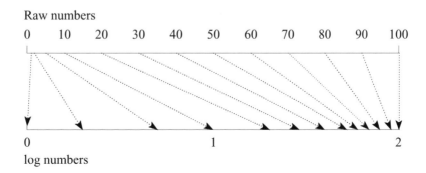

Exhibit 7.18   *Transforming raw numbers to log to the base 10 numbers*

Original data (x)	Transformed data (log x)
0.0001	−4
0.001	−3
0.01	−2
0.1	−1
1	0
10	1
100	2
1000	3
10,000	4

Exhibit 7.19   *The logarithmic scale*

TRANSFORMATIONS IN SPSS

Using infant mortality as an example, the following explains how transformations can be accomplished in SPSS. A log transformation will be applied to the variable INFMOR and the transformed values stored in the new variable LOGINF.

Click on **Transform|Compute...**, and the dialog box in Exhibit 7.20 should

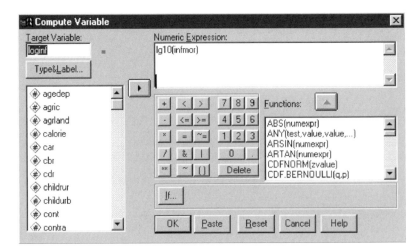

Exhibit 7.20   *The **Compute Variable** dialog box in SPSS creating a log transformation*

			Statistic	Std. Error
LOGINF	Mean		1.5610	3.317E-02
	95% Confidence	Lower Bound	1.4955	
	Interval for Mean	Upper Bound	1.6265	
	5% Trimmed Mean		1.5699	
	Median		1.6238	
	Variance		.187	
	Std. Deviation		.4325	
	Minimum		.66	
	Maximum		2.23	
	Range		1.57	
	Interquartile Range		.7641	
	Skewness		−.288	.186
	Kurtosis		−1.206	.370

Exhibit 7.21   *Descriptive statistics of the transformed variable, log infant mortality*
                Source: SID, 1992

appear. Type in the new variable name, **LOGINF**, in the **Target Variable:** box followed by **LG10(INFMOR)** in the **Numeric Expression** box.

Summary statistics for the new transformed variable, log infant mortality, are shown in Exhibit 7.21. Comparing these with the statistics for the untransformed INFMOR (Exhibit 7.16), it can be seen that the mean and the median are now more similar. Repeating the **Boxplot** in SPSS but this time using the transformed variable we obtain Exhibit 7.22. Notice that the boxes above and below the median are similar in size, indicating that the transformed variable has a distribution which more closely resembles the normal.

Exhibit 7.23 lists the data for both the original and the transformed variables for values of the raw and logged variable for the first 15 countries listed alphabetically. This demonstrates that the position of each country relative to others stays the same, even after the logarithmic transformation.

SUMMARY

The normal distribution has been introduced as a probability distribution, and examples have been given of the uses and importance of the normal curve through the standardization of a distribution of z scores. The importance of the normal distribution has been emphasized. Finally, the concept of using an arithmetic transformation to produce a more normal curve from an otherwise skewed distribution has been discussed. This technique will be used in more advanced statistical procedures, particularly in linear regression, to be introduced in later chapters.

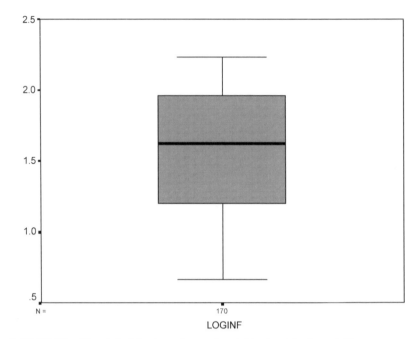

Exhibit 7.22   *Boxplot of the transformed variable, log infant mortality*
Source: World Bank, 1992

COUNTRY	INFMOR	LOGINF
Australia	7.22	.86
Austria	8.82	.95
Belgium	8.86	.95
Barbados	10.44	1.02
Bermuda	15.40	1.19
Antigua_and_Barbuda	19.20	1.28
Bahamas, The	24.96	1.40
Albania	25.44	1.41
Argentina	29.12	1.46
Bahrain	31.88	1.50
Botswana	37.74	1.58
Belize	44.60	1.65
Brazil	57.48	1.76
Algeria	66.50	1.82
Bolivia	91.92	1.96
Bangladesh	104.54	2.02
Benin	112.90	2.05
Bhutan	122.48	2.09
Angola	129.64	2.11
Afghanistan	169.36	2.23

Exhibit 7.23   *Data for infant mortality showing the raw and transformed data*

EXERCISES

1. Using the table for the areas under the normal distribution (Appendix B), find the probability that a normally distributed variable will have a z score. . .

   (a) above 1.2
   (b) below 0.55
   (c) between -0.5 and 1.7
   (d) below -0.75
   (e) above 2.3
   (f) between 0.3 and 1.8
   (g) greater than -0.45
   (h) greater than 0.66
   (i) less than 1.99
   (j) less than -2.4

   For each, draw a sketch and shade in the area.

2. If a variable is normally distributed for a set of cases, use the tables for the area under the curve to find z scores that define the following percentage of cases . . .

   (a) the top 18 per cent
   (b) the 5 per cent of cases with the lowest values
   (c) the middle 68 per cent
   (d) the middle 26 per cent
   (e) the top 45 per cent

PART III

BIVARIATE ANALYSIS

INTERVAL DATA: CORRELATION AND REGRESSION

8

CONTENTS

Looking at the distribution of one variable in terms of its measure of central tendency, spread and shape is an important step in any research sequence, but it is often of more interest to see in what ways the distribution of another variable can affect that of the first variable. This step in the research sequence is called bivariate analysis and is the subject of this chapter. By means of a simple example, this chapter will explore the relationship between two variables, how the distribution of one variable varies with the distribution of another variable. At the end of the chapter another example will be given using the SID data with the help of SPSS.

A SIMPLE EXAMPLE OF A BIVARIATE RELATIONSHIP

Suppose five girls have taken a statistics test and obtained the marks seen in Exhibit 8.1. From these figures we can calculate the girls' average mark to be 65 (by adding all the marks together as in Exhibit 8.2 and dividing by the number of people, as explained in Chapter 5). To get an idea of how spread out the marks are, we can then calculate a measure of dispersion such as the variance:

$$\text{variance} = \frac{\sum \text{squared deviations}}{\text{number of people} - 1} = \frac{650}{5 - 1} = 162.5 \qquad (8.1)$$

Because the variance, 162.5, is expressed in squared units, it is not comparable with the original marks, ranging from 50 to 80. However, when we take the *square root* of the variance we will then return to the same unit of measurement as the original data. As explained in Chapter 5, this measure is called the **standard deviation**:

$$\text{standard deviation} = \sqrt{\text{variance}} = \sqrt{162.5} = 12.7 \qquad (8.2)$$

Name	Statistics test mark
Jessica	50
Amelia	65
Helen	55
Sarah	80
Katy	75

Exhibit 8.1   *Test marks for five hypothetical cases*

MARK	Deviation from the mean (**Mark** – mean)	Squared deviations
50	50 – 65 = –15	225
65	65 – 65 = 0	0
55	55 – 65 = –10	100
80	80 – 65 = 15	225
75	75 – 65 = 10	100
Σ = 325	Σ = 0	Σ = 650

Exhibit 8.2 *Calculation of the sum of squared deviations*

BIVARIATE ANALYSIS AND ASSOCIATION

So far in this example we have just been looking at one variable using univariate statistics. We will now introduce a second variable, which we think is related to the test scores that we are interested in. Such a variable could be how much time each girl spends revising each day. There may be other variables we could think of that may relate to the test score, such as how well each girl has done in previous tests, but in bivariate analysis we are only interested in the relationship between just two variables. Analysing more than two variables is the realm of **multivariate analysis**.

Exhibit 8.3 shows the number of hours each girl spent studying every day and how the data might look in SPSS. Here the statistics test marks are given the variable name MARK, and the times spent studying are given the variable name WORKHRS.

Let us now explore this second variable in conjunction with the first. We want to know if there is any relationship between the two variables. Are they associated in any way? Two variables are said to be associated if the values of one variable vary, in a consistent way, with the values of the other variable. One way of looking at this is to examine the variation above and below the means for each variable. Exhibit 8.4 plots each girl's mark and the hours she spent studying. The horizontal line in each plot marks the means for each separate variable and the arrowed lines measure the 'errors' or deviations for each data point above and below the means.

Generally we see a similar pattern between the deviations from the mean (arrowed lines) in the two plots. The marks that are above the mean (Sarah and

	name	mark	workhrs
1	Jessica	50	1
2	Amelia	65	2
3	Helen	55	3
4	Sarah	80	4
5	Katy	75	5

Exhibit 8.3   *Hypothetical data for marks gained and study time per day*

Katy) correspond with study times that are also above the mean and a mark that is below the mean (Jessica) corresponds to a study time also below the mean. There is not a perfect correspondence, since Helen has a mark below the mean but a study time that is on the mean, but our task now is to calculate a measure that reflects the extent of this association, a **measure of association**. If we simply added up all the deviations we would have the same problem as we did with the variance in that we would end up with a total error of zero. With the calculation of the variance we solved this problem by squaring each deviation, but in this case we could simply *multiply* each pair of deviations together to create the **cross-product**. If the deviations are either both positive or both negative then we arrive at a positive cross-product, indicating deviations in the same direction. But if one is positive and one negative, the resulting cross-product will be negative, indicating that the deviations are in different directions. So if we want to measure the extent of the association we should add up all the cross-products. Then, to obtain an average, we could divide by the number of observations (in fact we divide by $n - 1$ as we did before in the calculation of the variance). We would then arrive at a measure known as the **covariance**. Exhibit 8.5 takes you through the calculation of the covariance, which we can summarize in the following formula:

$$Cov_{xy} = \frac{\sum(X - \bar{X})(Y - \bar{Y})}{(N - 1)}$$ (8.3)

However, the problem with the covariance is that it is dependant on the units of measurement. If MARK had been measured out of 1000 rather than 100 then we would have arrived at a value for the covariance which was ten times as great (see Exhibit 8.6).

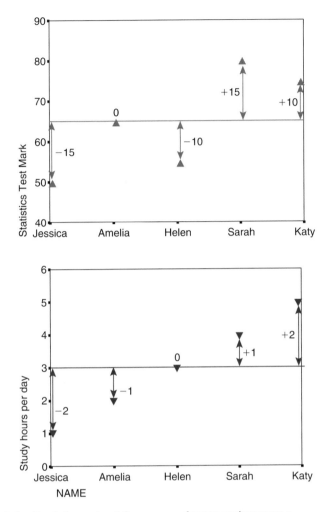

Exhibit 8.4   *Deviations about the means of* MARK *and* WORKHRS

COVARIANCE AND THE CORRELATION COEFFICIENT

In order to get round the problem of differing units and to give us a measure that we can use to compare between different pairs of variables, we would need to standardize our measure. In Chapter 7 we introduced standardization, but to remind you, equation (8.4) displays the formula. Subtract the mean from each score and then divide the result by the standard deviation:

$$z = \frac{X - \overline{X}}{s} \qquad (8.4)$$

Data		Deviations		
WORKHRS	MARK	$X - \bar{X}$	$Y - \bar{Y}$	Cross-product
X	Y	$X - 3$	$Y - 65$	
1	50	−2	−15	30
2	65	−1	+ 0	0
3	55	0	−10	0
4	80	+1	+15	15
5	75	+2	+10	20
$\bar{X} = 3$	$\bar{Y} = 65$			$\Sigma = 65$ $\therefore \text{Covariance} = \dfrac{65}{4} = 16.25$

Exhibit 8.5   *Calculation of the covariance*

Data		Deviations		
WORKHRS	MARK	$X - \bar{X}$	$Y - \bar{Y}$	Cross-product
X	Y	$X - 3$	$Y - 5$	
1	500	−2	−150	300
2	650	−1	+ 0	0
3	550	0	−100	0
4	800	+1	+150	150
5	750	+2	+100	200
$\bar{X} = 3$	$\bar{Y} = 650$			$\Sigma = 650$ $\therefore \text{Covariance} = \dfrac{650}{4} = 162.5$

Exhibit 8.6   *Calculation of the covariance changing one variable by a factor of 10*

Here s is the standard deviation of the set of data and $\bar{X}$ is its mean.

If you compare equations (8.3) and (8.4) you will notice that $(X - \bar{X})$, the deviation from the mean, appears in both but that to effect standardization in equation (8.4) the deviation is divided by the standard deviation, s. If you remember, the covariance was calculated by *multiplying* the deviations together to create the cross-product, so we could standardize the covariance by dividing by the *product* of the standard deviations, that is, multiply both standard deviations together and divide the covariance by this number. The result of this calculation is called the **Pearson product moment correlation coefficient**, for which the formula is written

$$r = \frac{Cov_{xy}}{s_x s_y} = \frac{\sum(X - \overline{X})(Y - \overline{Y})}{(N - 1)s_x s_y} \tag{8.5}$$

The correlation coefficient ranges from -1.0, a perfect negative correlation where an increase in one variable is accompanied by a proportionate decrease in the other variable, to $+1.0$, a perfect positive correlation where an increase in one variable is accompanied by a proportionate increase in the other variable. A value of zero indicates no linear relationship at all.

We have already calculated the standard deviation for X, so if we calculate the value for Y, we can substitute those figures into the equation, along with the value for the covariance, which we have previously calculated, to arrive at a value for the correlation coefficient:

$$r = \frac{16.25}{1.58 \times 12.75} = 0.806 \tag{8.6}$$

Now all we need to do is interpret this value for r. Since r ranges from -1.0 to $+1.0$, a value of 0.806 would be considered a high positive correlation. The interpretation of r is discussed in more detail in the next section in relation to scatterplots.

CORRELATION AND SCATTERPLOTS

One way of visualizing a relationship between two interval-level variables such as marks and study time is to create a scatterplot. Exhibit 8.7 shows the scatterplot of these two variables created using SPSS. We can definitely see that there is an upward trend in the data points, a positive correlation, as confirmed by our correlation coefficient of 0.806. Chapter 6 describes how to create scatterplots using the **Graphs** procedure in SPSS.

Exhibit 8.8 shows some other examples of scatterplots and their correlation coefficients. The more tightly clustered the points are, the closer the correlation coefficient is to 1.0 or -1.0. Plot A demonstrates a strong negative correlation, with a coefficient close to -1.0 and plot B demonstrates a strong positive correlation with the coefficient close to 1.0. Loose clustering, as seen in plots E and F, will have a correlation coefficient approaching zero, indicating no linear relationship, while intermediate clustering, as seen in plots C and D, will exhibit weak correlations around -0.5 or 0.5.

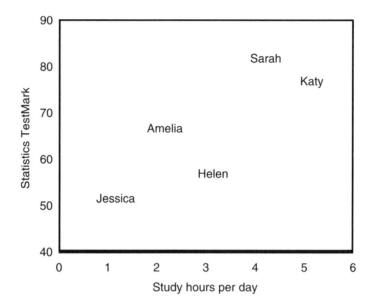

Exhibit 8.7   *Scatterplot of marks gained and study hours per day*

Summary of the correlation coefficient

- The correlation coefficient is a measure of the degree of association.
- It can be positive or negative, depending on direction of slope.
- It measures the extent to which the two variables covary.
- It ranges from -1.0 to $+1.0$.

BIVARIATE ANALYSIS AND EXPLANATION

Correlation does not imply causation or the ability to 'explain' a dependency of one variable on another. It is simply a measure of association that tells us whether two variables vary together. If we are interested in trying to 'explain' the behaviour of one variable, the dependent variable, using the predictive power of another variable, the independent or predictor variable, we need to use **simple regression analysis**. If we have two or more independent or predictor variables we would use **multiple regression analysis** (see Chapter 12).

If we return to our original example, marks gained is the dependent variable, and study hours is one independent or predictor variable. Our model is that time spent in revision before the test may predict, or explain, the performance in the statistics test. We hope to go beyond simple correlation where the variation in

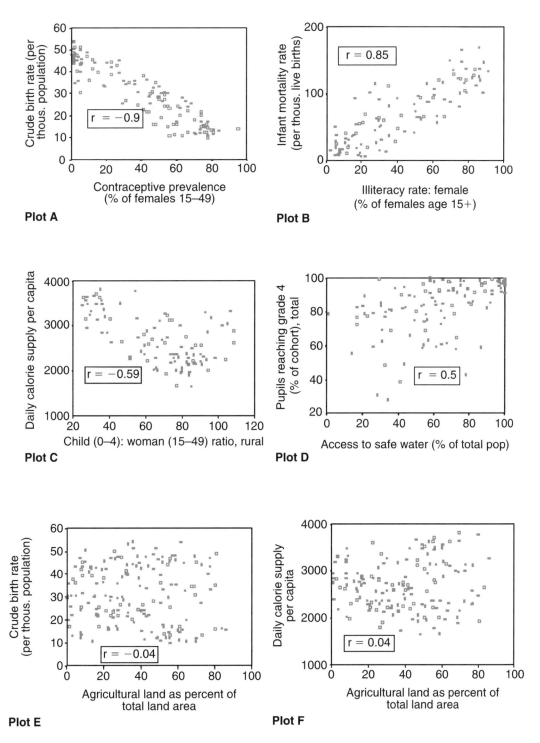

Exhibit 8.8   *Six scatterplots showing different correlation coefficients*
Source: World Bank, 1992

the marks is reflected by a similar variation in time spent studying. We are introducing a time-ordering into our analysis. Time spent studying precedes the exam and subsequent mark. If a girl spends few hours studying, does this lead to a low mark? Another way of putting this is, can we can 'explain' the variation in marks by the variation in time spent studying? We can also ask, does the mark obtained by each girl depend upon the time she spends studying? Because a girls' mark may depend on her study time, MARK is the dependent variable and WORKHRS the independent variable. The dependent variable is also often called the **Y variable** and the independent variable, the **X variable**.

   Looking again at the scatterplot in Exhibit 8.7, we can see an upward trend in the data points. It does seem that spending more time studying leads to a better mark. But the data points are not perfectly aligned; it is not a 'perfect' relationship. Exhibit 8.9 however, shows just such a 'perfect' relationship. All the points fall on an obvious straight line. According to this line, for every hour spent studying, the student can expect an increase of 20 percentage points. We could say that

$$\text{marks} = 20 \text{ times number of hours spent studying} \qquad (8.7)$$

and using the symbols Y for marks and X for time spent studying, we could express the relationship as

$$Y = 20X \qquad (8.8)$$

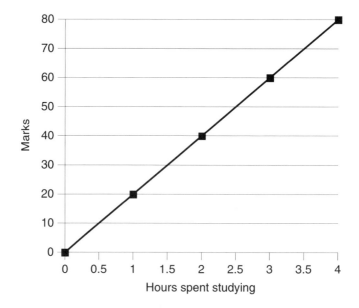

Exhibit 8.9   *Perfect relationship between marks and hours spent studying*

Now consider Exhibit 8.10. Here we see that even if a student spends no time studying, he or she can expect a mark of 10 per cent. This time we could express the relationship as

$$\text{marks} = 10 + 20 \text{ times hours spent studying} \tag{8.9}$$

or

$$Y = 10 + 20X \tag{8.10}$$

This equation is called the **regression equation** and can be used to describe the relationship between two continuous variables, in this case the relationship between marks and hours spent studying.

THE EQUATION FOR A STRAIGHT LINE

Using the symbol Y, for the dependent variable and X for the independent variable, we can express the equation for a straight line relationship as follows:

$$Y = a + bX \tag{8.11}$$

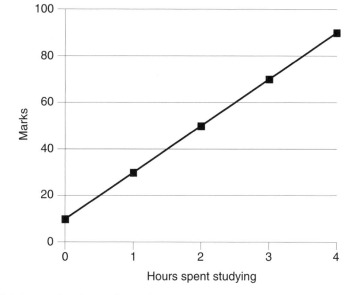

Exhibit 8.10   *Another perfect relationship between marks and hours spent studying*

where a, called the a coefficient or the **intercept**, is the value of Y where the line crosses the Y axis (where $X = 0$) and b, called the b coefficient or the **slope**, is the difference in Y for a unit difference in X. Note that a and b may be positive or negative.

Exhibit 8.11 shows four possible regression lines and their corresponding equations. If the regression line crosses the positive side of the Y axis, the a coefficient will be positive, as in (a) and (c). The reverse is true for the coefficient a in (b) and (d). The sign for the b coefficient depends on the direction of the slope of the line. If the line rises from lower left to upper right, it has a positive slope and the value for b will be positive. If it falls from upper left to lower right, it has a negative slope and the value for b will be negative.

Returning to the data in Exhibit 8.7, there is no obvious straight line through the points, although a clear trend is visible. We could, nevertheless, draw a line between the data points in such a way that it is as close as possible to all the points. The method used to position the line to minimize the distances between the data points and the line is called **ordinary least squares** (OLS). Imagine trying out one line and measuring how close it is to all the data points, then trying another line, and so on until you find the line that produces the smallest sum of the squares of the distances from the data points to the line. However,

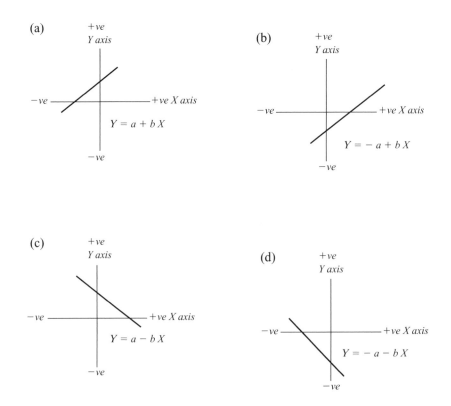

Exhibit 8.11   *The four possible straight line relationships*

finding the position of the line by trial and error would be tedious and a simpler way is to use the following formulae. To calculate the slope, b, use

$$b = \frac{\sum(X - \bar{X})(Y - \bar{Y})}{\sum(X - \bar{X})^2} \tag{8.12}$$

Once b has been calculated, the intercept a can be calculated from

$$a = \bar{Y} - b\bar{X} \tag{8.13}$$

Exhibit 8.12 shows how you can systematically calculate the sums of the products, $(X - \bar{X})(Y - \bar{Y})$ and $(X - \bar{X})^2$ before using them in the equations. These sums of the products can be substituted into the equations as follows:

$$b = \frac{\sum(X - \bar{X})(Y - \bar{Y})}{\sum(X - \bar{X})^2} = \frac{65}{10} = 6.5 \tag{8.14}$$

and

$$a = \bar{Y} - b\bar{X} = 65 - 6.5 \times 3 = 45.5 \tag{8.15}$$

So the regression equation is

$$Y = 45.5 + 6.5X \tag{8.16}$$

which we interpret as

$$\text{marks} = 45.5 + 6.5 \times \text{number of hours spent studying} \tag{8.17}$$

Data		Deviations		Products	
MARKS	WORKHRS	$Y - \bar{Y}$	$X - \bar{X}$	$(X - \bar{X})(Y - \bar{Y})$	$(X - \bar{X})^2$
Y	X	$Y - 65$	$X - 3$		
50	1	−15	−2	30	4
65	2	0	−1	0	1
55	3	−10	0	0	0
80	4	15	1	15	1
75	5	10	2	20	4
$\bar{Y} = 65$	$\bar{X} = 3$			$\sum(X - \bar{X})(Y - \bar{Y}) = 65$	$\sum(X - \bar{X})^2 = 10$

Exhibit 8.12   *Calculation of the slope, b, in the regression equation*

Exhibit 8.13 shows the position of the regression line using the values for the coefficients *a* and *b* calculated above.

THE 'FIT' OF THE REGRESSION LINE

Exhibit 8.14 shows the same scatterplot as in Exhibit 8.13, but dotted lines represent the deviations or **'residuals'** from each data point to the fitted line. The smaller the deviations, the better the fit of the line to the data – the closer to a perfect fit. Notice that the regression line goes through the means of both *X* and *Y*.

If there were no deviations or residuals, then we would have a perfect fit. So in order to estimate the 'fit' of the model, we need to measure these deviations or residuals. To do this we need to know the values of *Y* through which the regression line passes, for each value of *X*. This is simply done by working out the **predicted** value of *Y* for each value of *X* using the regression equation, as seen in Exhibit 8.15. This predicted or **fitted** value is called '*Y*-hat' and is written with a circumflex: $\hat{Y}$.

Having found the predicted values for *Y*, we still need to measure the lengths of the deviations, which is easily done by subtracting the fitted value from the actual value $(Y - \hat{Y})$. This procedure is very similar to that used to calculate the

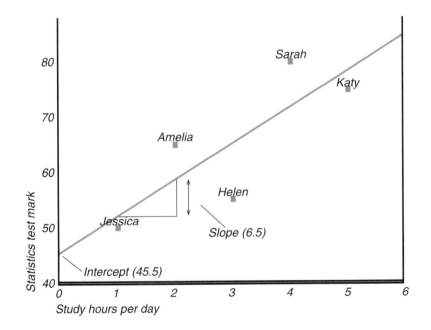

Exhibit 8.13   *The regression line*

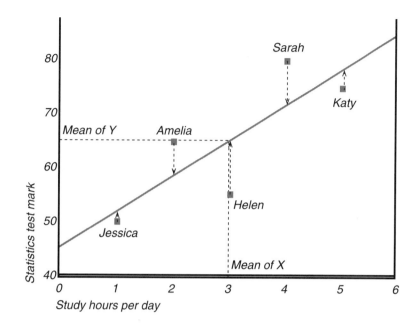

Exhibit 8.14   *The regression line and deviations from the regression line*

	Y	X	$\hat{Y}$ = 45.5 + 6.5 × X			
	Y	X	$\hat{Y}$ Fitted value using the equation		$(Y - \hat{Y})$	$(Y - \hat{Y})^2$
	50	1	52	(45.5 + 6.5 × 1)	−2	4
	65	2	58.5	(45.5 + 6.5 × 2)	6.5	42.25
	55	3	65	(45.5 + 6.5 × 3)	−10	100
	80	4	71.5	(45.5 + 6.5 × 4)	8.5	72.25
	75	5	78	(45.5 + 6.5 × 5)	−3	9
Sum	325	15	325.0		0	227.5
Mean	65	3	65		0	Variance = 227.5/N −1 = **56.9**

Exhibit 8.15   *Calculation of the variance of the regression*

total variance of Y, except that instead of subtracting the mean of Y, $\overline{Y}$, from each value of Y, we subtract the 'fitted value', $\hat{Y}$, from each value of Y.

However, as with the calculation of the variance, the sum of these residual deviations is always exactly zero. The sum of the deviations cannot therefore be used as a good measure of how well the line fits the data points. Instead, as with variance, we take the squares of the deviations and calculate the mean of these squared deviations. This measure, the variance of the residuals or **unexplained variance**, takes into account the average size of the squared deviations and provides a measure of 'fit' for the regression line. Obviously, the smaller the residual variance, the better the 'fit'.

Remember, we started off with a total variance of 162.5 (see equation (8.1)) before we thought of using another variable as a predictor variable. After the regression the residual variance has been reduced to 56.9 (Exhibit 8.15). Discovering the relationship between MARKS and WORKHRS has helped to explain some of the variation in the dependant variable MARKS.

Not surprisingly,

$$\text{Total variance} = \text{explained variance} + \text{unexplained variance} \qquad (8.18)$$

Therefore

$$162.5 = \text{variance explained by } X + 56.9 \qquad (8.19)$$

so

$$\text{variance explained by } X = 162.5 - 56.9 = 105.6 \qquad (8.20)$$

We can now measure how well the regression line 'fits' in terms of explained and unexplained variance.

$$\frac{\text{unexplained variance}}{\text{total variance}} = \text{proportion of unexplained or residual variance} \quad (8.21)$$

$$= \frac{56.9}{162.5} = 0.35 \text{ or } 35\% \qquad (8.22)$$

Similarly,

$$\frac{\text{explained variance}}{\text{total variance}} = \text{proportion of variance explained by the regression}$$

$$\qquad (8.23)$$

$$= \frac{105.6}{162.5} = 0.65 = 65\% \qquad (8.24)$$

The quantity calculated in equations (8.23) and (8.24) is called 'r **squared**' (r^2) or the **coefficient of determination** and is a measure of how well the regression line fits the data points. When there are multiple (more than two) variables, R^2 is used. Thus we can say that 65 per cent of the variance in mark is explained by the variation in number of hours spent studying. That still leaves 35 per cent of unexplained variance, variance that may be explained by some other, as yet, unmeasured variable totally unrelated to our one X variable, or it may simply be due to random variation. For this reason, the regression equation is more properly written as follows:

$$Y = a + bX + \varepsilon \tag{8.25}$$

where the ε component represents an error term that accounts for all the other factors that may have an effect on the Y variable.

REGRESSION FOR PREDICTION

Imagine that a sixth girl sat the statistics test, but we do not know her mark. The best guess for the sixth girl's mark would be the average of all the other five girls' marks, 65 per cent. However, we also have discovered a relationship between hours spent studying and marks gained. It seems that the longer one spends studying, the better the mark. Therefore, if we know how long someone has spent studying we could make a better prediction of their expected mark. If we are told that the sixth girl had spent $2\frac{1}{2}$ hours studying, we can use the regression equation

$$\text{marks} = 45.5 + 6.5 \times \text{number of hours spent studying} \tag{8.26}$$

to predict her mark to be

$$\text{marks} = 45.5 + 6.5 \times 2.5 = 62\% \tag{8.27}$$

The additional information about her study time allows us to predict marks with greater accuracy.

THE RELATIONSHIP BETWEEN CORRELATION AND REGRESSION

Let us once again consider a perfect relationship as seen in Exhibit 8.16. Note that if you add the respective standard deviations (31.6 for Y and 1.6 for X) to each of their means (40 for $\overline{Y}$ and 2 for $\overline{X}$), those coordinates are also intersected by the plotted line.

Exhibits 8.17 and 8.18 demonstrate the general pattern of a perfect positive correlation and a perfect negative correlation where, for an increase in one standard deviation of X, you get a corresponding increase (positive correlation) or decrease (negative correlation) of one standard deviation in Y. The position where the two means intersect is called the point of averages. This line is called the **standard deviation line** or **SD line**.

X	Y
0	0
1	20
2	40
3	60
4	80
$\overline{X} = 2$	$\overline{Y} = 40$
$SD = 1.6$	$SD = 31.6$

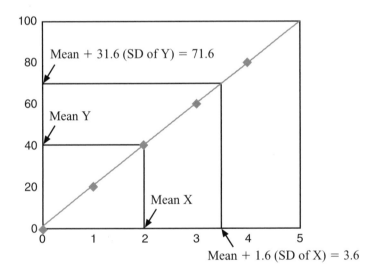

Exhibit 8.16   *The standard deviation line in perfect correlation*

THE RELATIONSHIP BETWEEN THE STANDARD DEVIATION LINE AND THE REGRESSION LINE

Exhibit 8.19 shows the calculation of z or standardized scores for MARK and WORKHRS, and Exhibit 8.20 the scatterplot of the z scores. In addition, Exhibit 8.20 shows the best-fitting regression line and the SD line.

If MARK and WORKHRS were perfectly correlated the regression and SD lines would coincide, and someone with a study time one standard deviation above

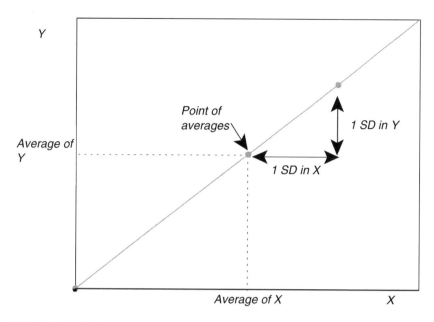

Exhibit 8.17   *Perfect positive correlation*

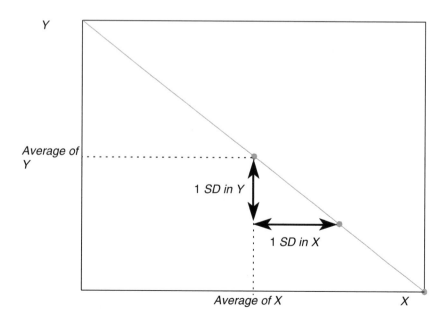

Exhibit 8.18   *Perfect negative correlation*

Data		Deviations		Squared deviations		z SCORES	
WORKHRS	MARK	$X - \bar{X}$	$Y - \bar{Y}$			$\dfrac{X - \bar{X}}{s_x}$	$\dfrac{Y - \bar{Y}}{s_y}$
X	Y	$X - 3$	$Y - 5$	X^2	Y^2	z (WORKHRS)	z(MARK)
1	50	-2	-15	4	225	-1.26	-1.18
2	65	-1	$+0$	1	0	-0.63	0
3	55	0	-10	0	100	0	-0.78
4	80	$+1$	$+15$	1	225	0.63	1.18
5	75	$+2$	$+10$	4	100	1.26	0.78
$\bar{x} = 3$	$\bar{y} = 65$			10	650		

Note: Standard deviation $X\ (s_x) = \sqrt{\dfrac{10}{5-1}} = 1.58$

Standard deviation $Y\ (s_y) = \sqrt{\dfrac{650}{5-1}} = 12.75$

Exhibit 8.19   *Creation of standard or z scores for* MARK *and* WORKHRS

average would also have a mark one standard deviation above average. Comparing the regression line and the SD line, we see that someone with a study time one standard deviation above average can expect a mark which is slightly less than one standard deviation above average. This is further demonstrated in Exhibit 8.21, where an area of Exhibit 8.20 has been enlarged. The relationship is that for an increase of one standard deviation in WORKHRS we can expect an increase of only r times one standard deviation in MARK. More generally, associated with each increase of one standard deviation in x there is an increase of only r times the standard deviation in y. Since the standard deviation of MARK is 1.58 and of WORKHRS is 12.75 (Exhibit 8.19), for every 1.58 hours additional study ($1s_x$) one would expect an increase in marks of

$$r \times s_y = 0.806 \times 12.75 = 10.28 \qquad (8.28)$$

Therefore an increase of 1.0 hour in study time leads to an increase of

$$\frac{r \times s_y}{s_x} = \frac{10.28}{1.58} = 6.5 \qquad (8.29)$$

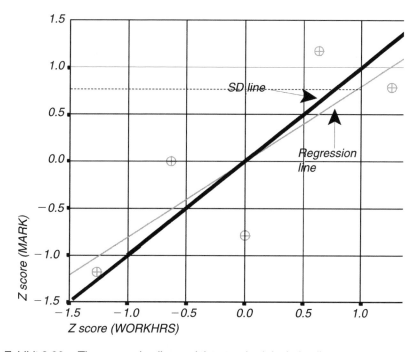

Exhibit 8.20   *The regression line and the standard deviation line*

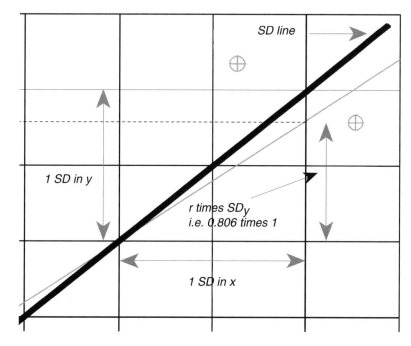

Exhibit 8.21   *Part of Exhibit 8.20 enlarged*

The last result is the value of the regression equation's b (slope) coefficient:

$$Y = 45.5 + 6.5X \tag{8.30}$$

THE RELATIONSHIP BETWEEN r AND r^2, THE PROPORTION OF VARIANCE EXPLAINED

We previously calculated r^2 for our example to be 0.65 or 65 per cent. This is a measure of the proportion of variance explained by the regression. The relationship between the correlation coefficient and r^2 is that the correlation coefficient is the square root of r^2, or

$$r = \sqrt{r^2}$$

so $r = \sqrt{0.65} = 0.806$.

ASSUMPTIONS OF REGRESSION

There are several assumptions underlying the use of regression analysis. One is that the residuals, the differences between the predicted values and the data points, are distributed normally. In addition, these residuals must bear a linear relationship with the predicted values and the variance must be the same for all predicted values.

USING SPSS FOR REGRESSION ANALYSIS

The following example uses the very small (just 5 cases) marks and work hours data set which is in a file called REGRESS.SAV (see Appendix A for access).

To perform a regression analysis in SPSS select **Analyze|Regression ▸|Linear** ... and the dialog box in Exhibit 8.22 will appear. MARK has been selected as the dependent variable, WORKHRS as the independent variable and NAME for case labels.

The output from SPSS is in several sections (see Exhibit 8.23), including the Model Summary, the analysis of variance (ANOVA), Coefficients and Residual Statistics. We shall only explain aspects of the Model Summary (Exhibit 8.24), Coefficients (Exhibit 8.25) and ANOVA (Exhibit 8.26) output here.

The Model Summary displays the correlation coefficient (which it calls R) and the coefficient of determination (R square). The Coefficient output displays the a coefficient (which it calls Constant) and the b coefficient next to the

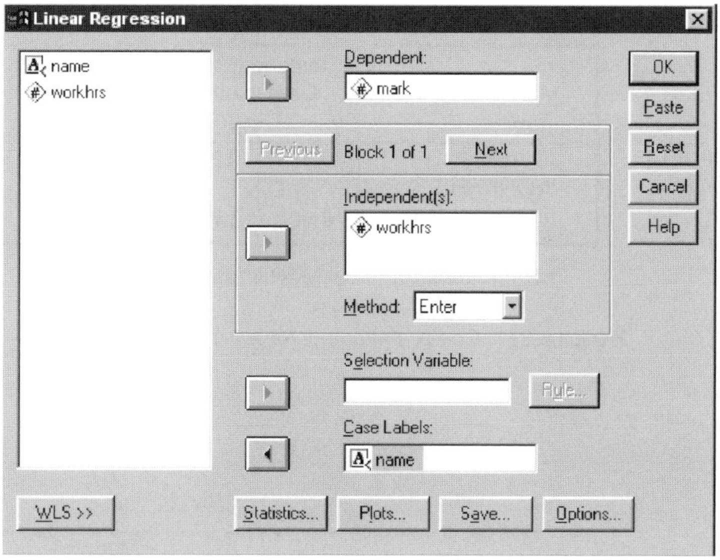

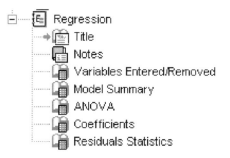

Exhibit 8.22   ***Linear Regression*** *dialog box*

Exhibit 8.23   *Regression output in the **Viewer** window*

Model Summary[b]

Model	R	R Square	Adjusted R Square	Std. Error of the Estimate
1	.806[a]	.650	.533	8.71

[a] Predictors: (Constant), WORKHRS Study hours per day
[b] Dependent Variable: MARK Statistics Test Mark

Exhibit 8.24   *Model summary for* MARK *and* WORKHRS

Coefficients[a]

Model	Unstandardized Coefficients		Standardized Coefficients	t	Sig.
	B	Std. Error	Beta		
1 (Constant)	45.500	9.133		4.982	.016
WORKHRS Study hours per day	6.500	2.754	.806	2.360	.099

[a] Dependent Variable: MARK Statistics Test Mark

Exhibit 8.25   *Coefficient output for* MARK *and* WORKHRS

ANOVA[b]

Model	Sum of Squares	df	Mean Square	F	Sig.
1 Regression	422.500	1	422.500	5.571	.099[a]
Residual	227.500	3	75.833		
Total	650.000	4			

[a] Predictors: (Constant), WORKHRS Study hours per day
[b] Dependent Variable: MARK Statistics Test Mark

Exhibit 8.26   *ANOVA output for* MARK *and* WORKHRS

variable WORKHRS. Both are displayed under the column heading *Unstandar-dized coefficients* and labelled *B*. Notice that the standardized coefficient (Beta) for WORKHRS is equal to the correlation coefficient, *r*.

The ANOVA output displays the sum of squared deviations, which were calculated in Exhibits 8.2 and 8.15.

ANOTHER EXAMPLE OF REGRESSION IN SPSS USING THE SID DATA SET

Let us look at another example using real data from the World Bank data set. Consider the scatterplot of variables from the SID data in Exhibit 8.27. Here we see that with increasing female illiteracy there is increasing infant mortality. Female illiteracy (ILLITF) is defined as the proportion of the female popula-tion 15 years or older who cannot, with understanding, both read and write a simple short statement on everyday life. Infant mortality (INFMOR) is defined as

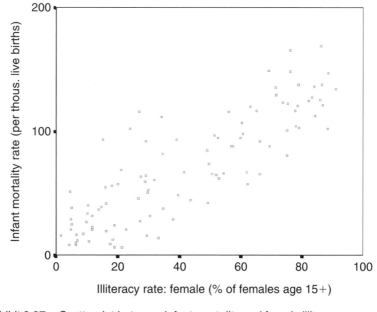

Exhibit 8.27   *Scatterplot between infant mortality and female illiteracy*
Source: World Bank, 1992

the number of deaths of infants under 1 year of age per 1000 live births in a
given year.

REGRESSION WITH RESIDUAL PLOTS

Selecting **Analyze|Regression ▸|Linear** ... in SPSS allows us to specify infant
mortality as the dependent variable and female illiteracy as the independent
variable. This time, however, we will create a **residual plot**. A residual plot will
allow us to ascertain if there are any cases that are unusual in any way and that
do not fit our model. We request a residual plot by selecting **Plots** ... in the
Linear Regression (Exhibit 8.22) dialog box and then specifying a plot of
standardized residuals (*****ZRESID**) against standardized predicted values
(*****ZPRED**) (see Exhibit 8.28).

   In addition, if we select **Statistics**... from the **Linear Regression** dialog box,
we can request **Casewise diagnostics** which will classify outliers as only those
cases more than two standard deviations from the regression line. This we do by
clicking on **Casewise diagnostics** and changing the **Outliers outside** box to 2
standard deviations (see Exhibit 8.29). We then click on **Continue** and then
OK in the **Linear Regression** dialog box (Exhibit 8.22).

   The SPSS output Model Summary (Exhibit 8.30) shows that R square is equal

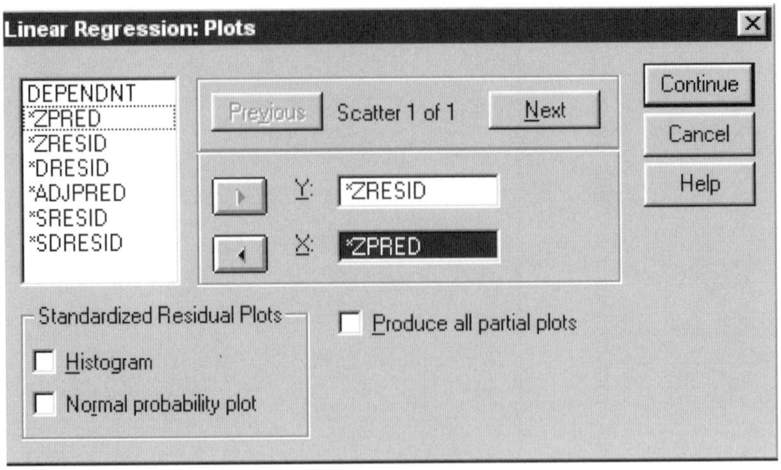

Exhibit 8.28   **Linear Regression: Plots** dialog box

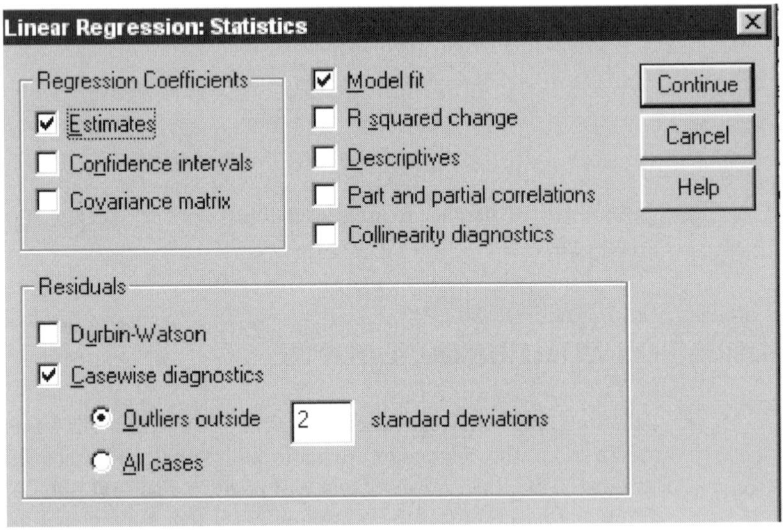

Exhibit 8.29   **Linear Regression: Statistics** dialog box

to 0.726 and therefore that 72.6 per cent of the variance in infant mortality is explained by female illiteracy.

From the Coefficients output (Exhibit 8.31) we can deduce that the regression equation is

$$\text{INFMOR} = 13.13 + 1.36 \ \text{ILLITF} + \varepsilon \tag{8.31}$$

Model Summary[b]

Model	R	R Square	Adjusted R Square	Std. Error of the Estimate
1	.852[a]	.726	.723	23.1717

a Predictors: (Constant), ILLITF Illiteracy rate: female
(% of females age 15+)
b Dependent Variable: INFMOR Infant mortality rate
(per thous. live births)

Exhibit 8.30   *Model Summary for* ILLITF *and* INFMOR

Coefficients[a]

Model	Unstandardized Coefficients		Standardized Coefficients	t	Sig.
	B	Std. Error	Beta		
1 (Constant)	13.134	4.176		3.145	.002
ILLITF Illiteracy rate: female (% of females age 15+)	1.363	.083	.852	16.519	.000

a Dependent Variable: INFMOR Infant mortality rate (per thous. live births)

Exhibit 8.31   *Coefficients for* ILLITF *and* INFMOR

The Casewise Diagnostics output presented in Exhibit 8.32 shows those cases that do not fit the model. We previously specified that those cases whose residuals are more than 2 standard deviations from the best-fitting regression line would be classified as outliers. Five countries have such large residuals: Lao PDR, Lesotho, Madagascar, Mali and Swaziland. All have positive standardized residuals and therefore have infant mortality rates much higher than that predicted by their female illiteracy. The Lao PDR, for example, has an infant mortality rate of 102.5 deaths per 1000 live births, much higher than the 46.12 predicted by its level of female illiteracy. There are factors other than female illiteracy in these five countries which would need to be investigated to explain their rate of infant mortality.

Exhibit 8.33 is the requested residual plot. It displays the same information as in the casewise diagnostics but plots all the standardized residuals against their standardized predicted values. From this plot we can see if there is any pattern in the scatter of points which would indicate that the assumption of linearity has been violated. This assumption of regression is based on there being a linear relationship between the residuals and the predicted values and that the variance

Casewise Diagnostics[a]

Case Number	COUNTRY	Std. Residual	INFMOR Infant mortality rate (per thous. live births)	Predicted Value	Residual
87	Lao PDR	2.436	102.56	46.1198	56.4402
89	Lesotho	2.556	93.48	34.2612	59.2188
94	Madagascar	2.834	115.74	50.0726	65.6674
98	Mali	2.120	165.98	116.8622	49.1178
147	Swaziland	2.252	112.08	59.8866	52.1934

[a] Dependent Variable: INFMOR Infant mortality rate (per thous. live biths)

Exhibit 8.32   *Casewise diagnostics for* ILLITF *and* INFMOR

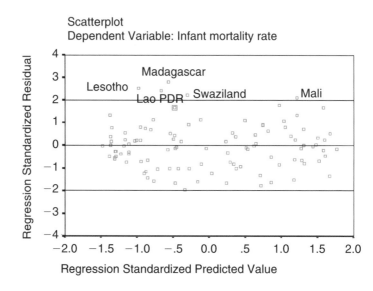

Exhibit 8.33   *Residual plot for* ILLITF *and* INFMOR
Source: World Bank, 1992

of the residuals is the same for each predicted value. There is no obvious pattern to the scatter of points and we conclude that the assumption of linearity has not been violated. Reference lines have been drawn on the plot at two standard deviations above the mean and two below, so that it is clear which countries fall outside these boundaries and are outliers.

In Exhibit 8.34 the regression line is superimposed upon the scatterplot of

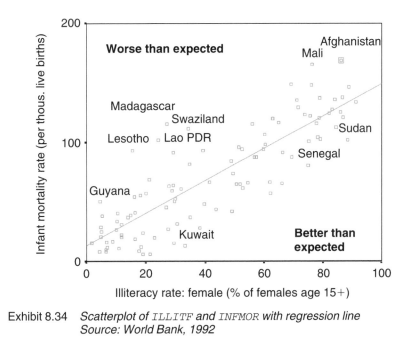

Exhibit 8.34   *Scatterplot of* ILLITF *and* INFMOR *with regression line*
              Source: World Bank, 1992

infant mortality and female illiteracy. Those countries that lie below the
regression line, including Kuwait, Senegal and Sudan, have a lower infant
mortality than would be expected from their respective female illiteracy rates
using the regression equation. They are doing better than expected. However,
those countries that lie above the regression line, including Guyana, Afghanistan, Lesotho, Madagascar and Malawi, have a higher infant mortality than
expected. Notice that those countries previously identified as outliers lie furthest
away from the fitted regression line. In this example there are no outliers below
the regression line.

TRANSFORMATIONS IN REGRESSION: AN EXAMPLE IN SPSS

In the following example you will see how to use SPSS to explore the SID
data to 'explain' differing life expectancies in the countries of the world. Why
is it that life expectancy is higher in some countries than in others? This
example will also demonstrate that even if the scatterplot shows a curved
relationship you can still use simple liner regression techniques to describe the
relationship.

CREATING A SCATTERPLOT

Using LIFEX (life expectancy) as the dependent variable and GNP (gross national product) as the independent variable, we first create a scatterplot. Select **Graphs|Scatter** ... to obtain the scatterplot shown in Exhibit 8.35. Clearly, there is a relationship, but it is a curvilinear relationship.

TRANSFORMING THE VARIABLE GNP

The next step is to transform the variable GNP to LOGGNP (transformations are discussed in Chapter 7). Select **Transform|Compute** ... to see the dialog box in Exhibit 8.36, where the target variable is LOGGNP and the numeric expression is lg10(GNP).

REPEATING THE SCATTERPLOT

Then we need to repeat the scatterplot but this time using LOGGNP as the independent variable to get the scatterplot in Exhibit 8.37. It appears that the

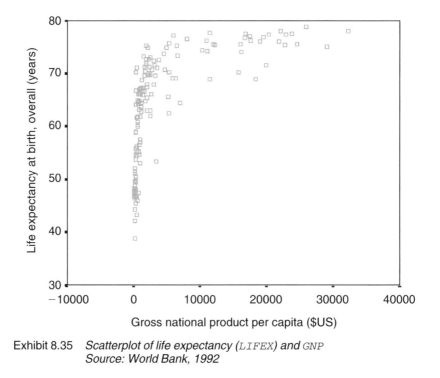

Exhibit 8.35   *Scatterplot of life expectancy (LIFEX) and GNP*
Source: World Bank, 1992

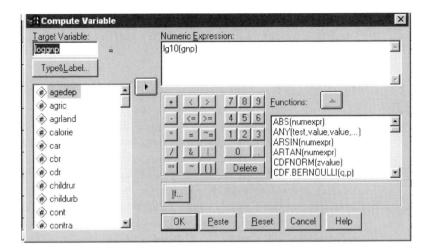

Exhibit 8.36   *Transformation in SPSS:* **Compute Variable** *dialog box*

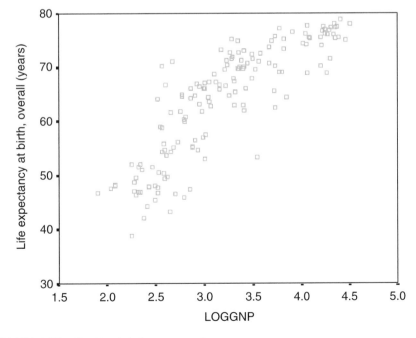

Exhibit 8.37   *Scatterplot of* LIFEX *and* LOGGNP
Source: World Bank, 1992

relationship is more linear using the transformed variable. The model we are now investigating is that life expectancy is dependent on the log of GNP.

PERFORMING THE REGRESSION AND CREATING RESIDUAL PLOTS

Now we carry out the simple regression analysis by selecting **Statistics|Regression ▸|Linear** ... (see Exhibit 8.38). After selecting LIFEX as the dependent variable and LOGGNP as the independent variable, click on **Plots** ... in order to define a residual plot. In this dialog box, select *ZRESID (standardized residuals) as the Y variable and *ZPRED (standardized predicted values) as the X variable. Also select **Statistics** from Exhibit 8.38 and click on **Casewise diagnostics** and change the **Outliers outside** box to 2 **standard deviations**. (Refer back to Exhibit 8.28 and Exhibit 8.29.)

EXAMINING THE OUTPUT

Exhibit 8.39 is the Model Summary output for the regression. From this output we see that $r^2 = 0.725$. In other words, 72.5 per cent of the variation in life expectancy can be explained by log GNP.

Exhibit 8.40 shows the coefficients output from which we can deduce the regression equation to be

$$\text{Life expectancy} = 20.84 + 13.4 \log \text{GNP} + \varepsilon \qquad (8.32)$$

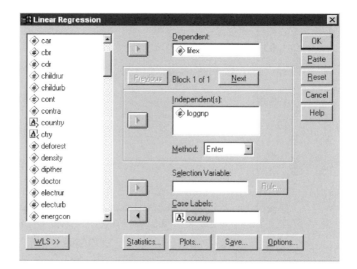

Exhibit 8.38 **Linear Regression** *dialog box with* LIFEX *and* LOGGNP

Model Summary[b]

Model	R	R Square	Adjusted R Square	Std. Error of the Estimate
1	.852[a]	.725	.723	5.4831

a Predictors: (Constant), LOGGNP
b Dependent Variable: LIFEX Life expectancy at birth, overall (years)

Exhibit 8.39   *Model Summary for* LIFEX *and* LOGGNP

Coefficients[a]

Model		Unstandardized Coefficients		Standardized Coefficients	t	Sig.
		B	Std. Error	Beta		
1	(Constant)	20.839	2.205		9.453	.000
	LOGGNP	13.409	.670	.852	20.022	.000

a Dependent Variable: LIFEX Life expectancy at birth, overall (years)

Exhibit 8.40   *Coefficients for the regression of* LOGGNP *against* LIFEX

Thus, for a country with a GNP of $100 per capita we can use the regression model to predict life expectancy as follows. First we transform our value for GNP:

$$\log GNP = \log (100) = 2,\tag{8.33}$$

And then we can substitute into the equation

$$\text{Life expectancy} = 20.84 + 13.4 \ (2) = 47.64 \text{ years}\tag{8.34}$$

So a country with this low value for GNP of $100 per capita is predicted to have an average life expectancy of just over 47 years.

PLOTTING THE REGRESSION LINE

In order to add the regression line to the scatterplot, double-click on the plot in the **Output Viewer**. This will open the **Chart Editor**. Here you can make changes to your chart. We are going to add the regression line and get SPSS to print the value of r^2 next to the plot. To do this select **Chart|Options** ... (to see Exhibit 8.41). Here, in the **Fit Line** box we can select **Total**. In addition, if we click on **Fit Options** ..., we can get SPSS to print the value of r^2 in the legend next to the plot (see Exhibit 8.42). The resulting plot should look like that in

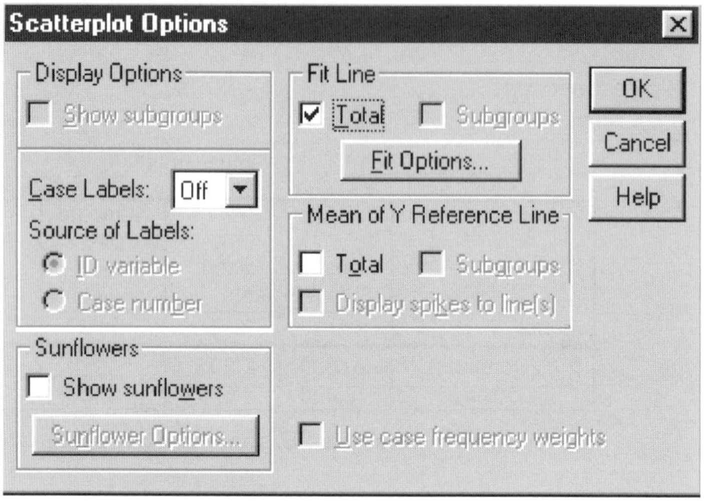

Exhibit 8.41   ***Scatterplot Options*** *dialog box*

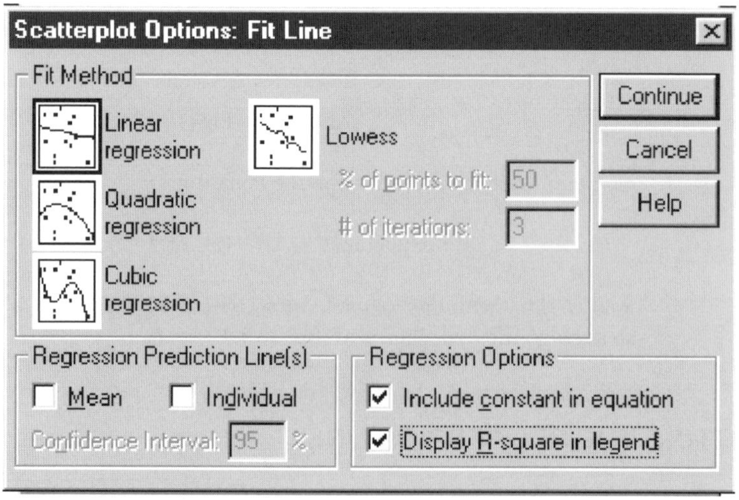

Exhibit 8.42   ***Fit Line*** *options dialog box*

Exhibit 8.43. Notice that the regression line provides a good summary of the scatter of data points. It fits well.

IDENTIFYING THE OUTLIERS

Outliers are those cases (countries) that *do not fit the model* – countries with life expectancies that do not seem to be dependent on the GNP or are not dependent to the same extent as most of the countries. These cases have residuals (the deviation between the fitted value and the actual value for life expectancy) which, when standardized, are greater than +2.0 or less than −2.0. You can identify the cases that are defined as outliers in the regression casewise diagnostics seen in Exhibit 8.44.

Angola has a negative residual greater than −2. Its life expectancy is 45.88, yet the predicted life expectancy based on the regression equation and using GNP as a predictor variable is 58.19. China, São Tomé and Sri Lanka, however, have positive residuals and life expectancies greater than expected based on the regression equation. All these countries *do not fit* the model of life expectancy based on GNP.

Exhibit 8.45 shows a residual plot with the outliers marked above and below

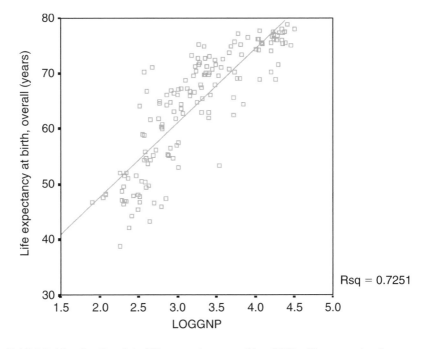

Exhibit 8.43   *Scatterplot of life expectancy and log GNP with regression line*
            Source: World Bank, 1992

Casewise Diagnostics[a]

Case Number	COUNTRY	Std. Residual	LIFEX Life expectancy at birth, overall (years)	Predicted Value	Residual
4	Angola	−2.244	45.88	58.1866	−12.3061
32	China	2.715	70.16	55.2752	14.8886
56	Gabon	−2.725	53.37	68.3101	−14.9398
64	Guinea	−2.370	43.29	56.2843	−12.9969
65	Guinea-Bissau	−2.235	38.82	51.0793	−12.2545
131	São Tomé and Princi	2.003	66.71	55.7292	10.9815
133	Senegal	−2.143	47.32	59.0706	−11.7497
141	Sri Lanka	2.637	71.13	56.6683	14.4590

[a] Dependent Variable: LIFEX Life expectancy at birth, overall (years)

Exhibit 8.44   *Casewise Diagnostics from regression analysis in SPSS*

Scatterplot
Dependent Variable: Life expectancy at birth

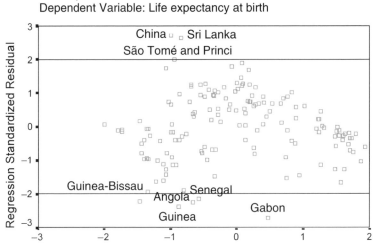

Regression Standardized Predicted Value

Exhibit 8.45   *Residual plot for LIFEX and LOGGNP*
            Source: World Bank, 1992

the reference lines at 2.0 and −2.0 standard deviations. Once again, we can identify those countries that have high residual values and therefore do not fit the model. Why they do not fit and what makes these countries different is a matter for further analysis.

SUMMARY

This chapter has introduced bivariate analysis for continuous variables. Correlation analysis provides measures that indicate whether two variables are associated in some way – whether, as one variable varies, it is accompanied by variation in the other variable. Correlation does not imply any causation or time-ordering between the variables, simply that they covary. Regression analysis, however, does provide a tool where one variable can be identified as the dependent variable, the variable of analytic interest and the one whose variation we wish to 'explain'. And, in simple regression, we can identify one other variable as an independent variable whose predictive powers we wish to test on our dependent variable.

So correlation and regression are bivariate techniques for continuous variables measured on an interval-level scale. The next chapter explores techniques of bivariate analysis appropriate for categorical variables measured on the nominal or ordinal scales.

EXERCISES

1. Repeat the regression analysis example in the text using LOGGNP as the independent variable and LIFEX as the dependent variable.
2. Repeat the regression analysis as in Exercise 1, using LIFEX as the dependent variable, but this time choose DOCTOR (population per physician) as the independent variable. The following list provides an *aide-mémoire* for the procedure.
   (a) Produce a scatterplot.
   (b) Perform any transformations necessary using **Compute**.
   (c) Repeat the scatterplot but use the transformed independent variable.
   (d) Carry out a regression analysis and report r^2 as follows.

Dependent variable	Independent variable	r^2: percentage of variance in the dependent variable explained by the variation in the independent variable
LIFEX	GNP	38.8
LIFEX	log GNP	72.5
LIFEX	DOCTOR	
LIFEX	Transformation of DOCTOR:	

   (e) Write out the regression model equation.
   (f) List the outliers by country.

Country	Life expectancy	Predicted life expectancy

(g)   Which variable is a better predictor of life expectancy?

CATEGORICAL DATA: TABLES

CONTENTS

WHAT'S IN A TABLE

Over the last thirty years, women's involvement in the labour market has increased dramatically in all Western countries. In the UK, the growth in women's employment has primarily been through an increase in part-time work by married women, in contrast to other countries, where a similar proportion of married women are in paid jobs, but more work full-time. This is partly because British employers enjoy several financial advantages in employing part-time rather than full-time labour, and partly because there is a lack of child-care facilities in the UK and this encourages women to work only during the hours their children are at school. In contrast, the great majority of men in the labour force work full-time, at least until they are close to or above retirement age. One of the consequences of their different patterns of employment is the very different prospects men and women have in their old age: men are much more likely to have an occupational pension after they retire, and even when women do have an occupational pension on their own account it is usually much smaller than men's (Arber and Gilbert, 1992).

In this chapter we will explore these aspects of men and women's employment using data from the 1995 General Household Survey. We will continue the theme of the previous chapter by looking at bivariate relationships, but now using tables to display and understand the relationships between two variables. The previous chapter showed how you could investigate relationships between variables measured at the interval level of measurement. When you are interested in the relationship between variables at the categorical or ordinal levels of measurement, tables come into their own. Towards the end of the chapter, we will see how tables can also be used to examine the more complex relationships between three variables.

Exhibit 9.1 is a table confirming that a much greater proportion of women work part-time than men. The figures in the table indicate that 1247 male and 662 female respondents were working full-time, and 118 men and 530 women were working part-time. Overall, there were 1909 (1247 plus 662) full-timers and 648 (118 plus 530) part-timers. Looking at the bottom row of numbers, you can see that there were 1365 men and 1192 women who were working either full- or part-time, and 2557 people altogether. Of course, the table only refers to respondents who were in paid employment; as the footnote to the table states, 2076 people worked less than eight hours a week or were not economically active (retired, keeping house, sick, disabled and so on), unemployed or in a government training scheme and therefore not counted as employed. A few respondents are omitted because there are no data on their hours of work. It is always a good idea to keep a watch on what is not included in a table as well as what is, especially in a case such as this where there is a substantial amount of excluded data.

So does the table suggest that women are much more likely to work part-time than men? We shall look into this in more detail later in the chapter, but it is easy to see that almost all the men are in full-time jobs (1247 of the 1365 men are full-timers, or 91 per cent), but only about half of the women (662 of 1192,

Employment status	Men	Women	All
In full-time work	1247	662	1909
In part-time work	118	530	648
Total	1365	1192	2557

Exhibit 9.1   *Employment status by sex*
Source: ONS, 1995
Note: 'Full-time' work is work for 30 and over hours per week. 'Part-time' work is work for more than 8 and less than 30 hours per week. The 2076 who were not in work or worked less than 8 hours per week are excluded from the table.

or 56 per cent). This confirms that part-time working is largely confined to women.

OBTAINING A TABLE WITH SPSS

To create the table in Exhibit 9.1 using SPSS and the General Household Survey data, we first need to recode the variable WKSTATE into a new variable, TIME, such that those in full-time work are coded 1 and those in part-time work are coded 2.

To do this in SPSS, select **Transform|Recode ▸|Into Different variables** ... as described in Chapter 2. Exhibit 9.2 displays one way of doing this: copying codes 1 and 2 and recoding all other codes as system missing. Value labels can then be added to the new variable, TIME, as described in Chapter 2.

To generate the table in Exhibit 9.1 select **Analyze|Descriptive Statistics ▸|Crosstabs** ... to see the dialog box in Exhibit 9.3. TIME has been selected as the row variable and SEX as the column variable. Clicking on **OK** gives the output in Exhibit 9.4.

THE PARTS OF A TABLE

Before we can look more closely at how to analyse relationships, we need to have some terms to describe the different parts of a table. Although this book will call them simply **tables**, they are also called **crosstabulations** or **contingency tables**. Tables are made up of an array of **cells**, the spaces into which the numbers go. In Exhibit 9.1, the numbers are **counts**, that is, they count the

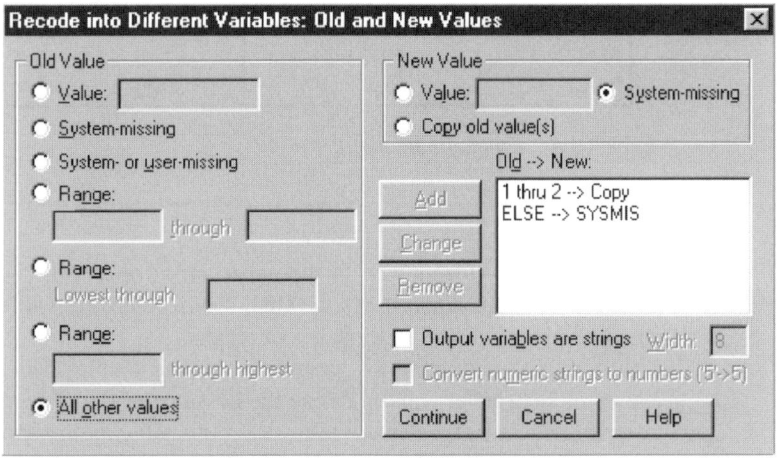

Exhibit 9.2 **Recode** dialog box: WKSTATE recoded into TIME

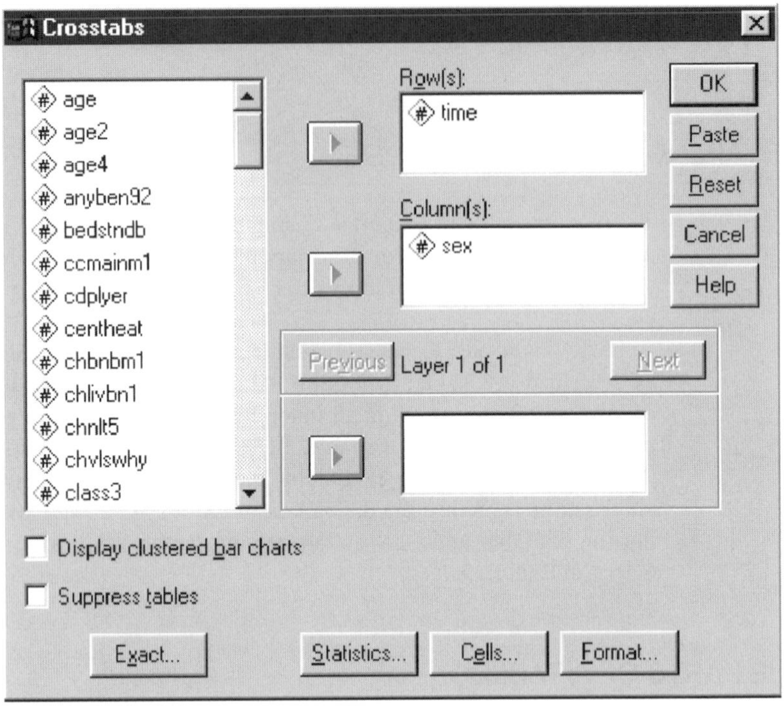

Exhibit 9.3   **Crosstabs** *dialog box*

TIME Employment status * SEX Crosstabulation

Count		SEX SEX		
		1 Male	2 Female	Total
TIME Employment status	1.00 full-time	1247	662	1909
	2.00 part-time	118	530	648
Total		1365	1192	2557

Exhibit 9.4   *Employment status by sex*

number of respondents who fit the particular attributes of each cell (e.g. those who are male full-timers). As we shall see, it is also possible to fill cells with other numbers, such as percentages or means.

Exhibit 9.1 tabulates two variables: sex and employment status. The categories of sex (male, female) define the columns of the table, and the categories of employment status define the rows. In this table, both variables are **dichotomous**, that is, they both have two categories. More complex tables can include variables with more categories. Each column of the table is headed by a label

('Men', 'Women' and 'All'), as is each row. These are **value labels**. The table also includes a **variable label**, 'Employment status' (sex is not explicitly labelled because it is obvious). The value labels for sex are placed in the **heading** of the table, and the labels for employment status are in the table's **stub** (see Exhibit 9.5).

The rightmost column of Exhibit 9.1 shows the counts of the total number of full-timers and part-timers, irrespective of their sex. These are called **marginals** (because the counts are in the margins of the table). Similarly, there are marginals in the bottom row of the table, showing the total number of men and women among the respondents. Finally, the bottom right-hand corner cell displays the **table total** or N, the total number of respondents included in the table. Notice that if you add the counts across one row for men and women, you will obtain the corresponding marginal. For example, 1247 male full-timers and 662 female full-timers sum to 1909, the marginal count for full-timers. The same applies if you add down the columns: for men, 1247 full-timers plus 118 part-timers makes 1365 men altogether. And if you add the marginal counts, either down the rightmost column, or along the bottom row, you will find the total number of respondents (e.g. 1909 full-timers plus 648 part-timers sums to 2557 people altogether).

PRESENTING TABLES

There are a number of conventions for presenting tables neatly and clearly. These are universally followed in books and you should conform to them in your own work as far as possible. However, most statistical packages do not display tables in the conventional style (unless you give them special and complex instructions). There is almost always some formatting needed to extract the information which is relevant and to present it in the clearest possible fashion.

The most important rule is to make sure that the table includes all the information necessary to interpret the data. This information includes:

- The variable and value labels in ordinary English, not 'computerese'. For example, label a variable 'Employment status', not TIME.
- A title for the table that states which variables are tabulated.

Variable label	**Heading**	Row marginal
Stub	a cell	
Value label		530 (a count)	
Column marginal		Table total (N)

Exhibit 9.5   *The parts of a table*

- An indication of the source of the data (e.g. the survey from which it was derived) and the date at which the data were collected. This should either be included in the title or given separately under the table.
- The number of cases or people excluded from the table and who these are.

The second rule of formatting is to present the information as clearly as possible. One tip is to minimize the number of lines ('rules' in printers' jargon). Compare Exhibit 9.1 with Exhibit 9.6 to see why. A good rule of thumb is to use only three horizontal rules: one above and one below the heading of the table, and one above the column marginals.

It is also worth attending to how the figures are placed in the cells of the table. The units digit of the counts in each column should line up, one above the other. As we shall see, tables sometimes contain, not counts, but percentages. In this case, you should consider what is an appropriate number of digits for each percentage. Usually, it is only necessary to include whole numbers (e.g. 37 per cent, not 36.78 per cent); see Chapter 3 on rounding.

COMPLEX TABLES

The tables we have seen so far have just two variables, both of which are dichotomous. It is possible to display much more complex tables, although they become correspondingly difficult to understand. Each variable can have more than two categories and there can be more than two variables. Here are some examples.

Exhibit 9.7 shows the relationship between employment status and sex for

Employment status	Men	Women	All
In full-time work	1247	662	1909
In part-time work	118	530	648
Total	1365	1192	2557

Exhibit 9.6   *The data of Exhibit 9.1 displayed with every cell outlined*

	Age 16 to 44		Age 45 and over		All
Employment status	Men	Women	Men	Women	
In full-time work	797	459	450	203	1909
In part-time work	68	310	50	220	648
Total	865	769	500	423	2557

Exhibit 9.7   *Employment status by sex by age*
Source: ONS, 1995
Note: see Exhibit 9.1 for definitions of full and part-time work.

younger respondents and older respondents separately. Thus there are three variables in this table: employment status, sex and age group. Notice that the table can be sliced in half, the left half table providing information about the younger respondents and the right half about the older ones. These are called **partial** tables.

The respondents tabulated in Exhibit 9.7 are exactly the same as those in Exhibit 9.1, so the marginals for the employment status variable (on the right-hand edge of the tables) are identical. The column totals from the two 'Men' columns in Exhibit 9.7 sum to the column total for men in Exhibit 9.1 and so do the totals for 'Women'. In effect each of the counts in Exhibit 9.1 has been divided into two cells in Exhibit 9.7, one including just the younger respondents and the other the older ones.

Exhibit 9.8 again displays three variables, but in this case the issue of interest is whether respondents went to see their doctor in the previous two weeks, tabulated by sex and age. To show the variation more clearly, there is a finer-grained division of age into four groups. This table does not include any marginals.

This table could be divided into four partial tables, each tabulating doctor consultations by sex for one of the age groups. When SPSS prints tables involving several variables, it does so as a series of partial tables, one after the other.

Exhibit 9.9 is a table of four variables (doctor consultations, visits to the dentist and having own teeth, by sex), but this time each of the three row variables is separately tabulated against sex. It is important to distinguish this kind of table, which is really three independent tables joined together vertically into one, from a table like Exhibit 9.7 in which two of the variables (employment status and sex) are tabulated for each category of the third (age). Observe that the number of men and women (see the rows labelled 'Total') is different for each variable. This is because the number of missing cases resulting from respondents not answering the question differs between the variables. The table shows that a larger proportion of women than men visited the doctor in the two weeks before the survey (313 of 2180 men or 14 per cent, compared with 466 of 2391 women or 19 per cent) and a much smaller proportion of men than women visit the dentist regularly (46 per cent of men and 62 per cent of women go for a regular check-up). Although women are better at going to the dentist, a greater

Consulted doctor in last two weeks	Age							
	Under 30		30 to 44		45 to 59		60 and over	
	Men	Women	Men	Women	Men	Women	Men	Women
yes	40	91	71	118	81	105	126	153
no	477	402	548	565	543	585	535	650

Exhibit 9.8   *Doctor consultations in the last two weeks, by sex and age group*
Source: ONS, 1995

If consulted doctor in the last two weeks (excluding visits to hospital)		Men	Women
	Yes	313	466
	No	1867	1925
	Total	2180	2391
Whether visits dentist regularly			
	Regular checkup	869	1225
	Occasional checkup	258	246
	Having trouble	662	455
	Never go to dentist	107	60
	Total	1896	1986
Whether has own teeth			
	Yes, own teeth	1898	1986
	No teeth	286	408
	Total	2184	2394

Exhibit 9.9   *Medical and dental consultations by sex*
Source: ONS, 1995

percentage no longer have their own teeth (17 per cent of women, compared with 13 per cent of men).

All these tables have counts in their cells. Another way of introducing a third variable is to put the means of a variable into the cells. For example, Exhibit 9.10 shows how the mean number of hours worked in paid employment varies according to the age and sex of the respondent. There are two numbers in each cell. The number in brackets is the count of the respondents who fit into that cell and the number to the left is the mean number of hours worked by those respondents. When presenting tables with cells containing calculated values, such as means or the percentages we shall be using in the next section, you should always include the number of cases that have contributed to the calculation (this is known as the **base**). You will see that the mean number of hours worked by women is only about three-quarters that of men, reflecting the much larger proportion of women who have part-time jobs. The number of hours remains more or less constant for men until near the age of retirement, but declines steadily with age for women.

| **Mean hours usually worked per week** | | | **Age** | | |
	Under 30	30 to 44	45 to 59	60 and over	All
Men	38 (520)	44 (619)	45 (543)	36 (536)	42 (2218)
Women	31 (493)	29 (684)	30 (587)	23 (651)	30 (2415)

Exhibit 9.10   *Mean number of hours worked in paid employment per week by those with a job, by age and sex*
Source: ONS, 1995

RELATIONSHIPS BETWEEN VARIABLES

In Exhibit 9.1, we tabulated employment status by sex and showed that a much greater proportion of women than men work part-time. We can say that employment status is related to sex. The term that is usually used for the relationship between two categorical variables is **association**.

According to Exhibit 9.1, there are 118 part-time male workers in a total of 1365 men. The proportion of men working part-time is therefore 118 of 1365, or about 9 per cent. In contrast, the proportion of women working part-time is 530 of 1192, or about 45 per cent. It is because there is a difference between these two proportions that we conclude that the two variables, employment status and sex, are associated. Exhibit 9.11 shows these percentages in a table.

To indicate that this is a table of percentages, rather than counts, each column marginal is shown as 100 per cent, with the count in brackets underneath. Now we can see clearly the difference between men and women in the proportions working full- and part-time. Comparing the percentages in the first row, while 91 per cent of men work full-time, only 55 per cent of women do. Correspondingly, 9 per cent of men and 45 per cent of women work part-time.

The figures in Exhibit 9.11 can be thought of in terms of proportions, percentages or probabilities. Nine out of 100 men work part-time (a proportion), 9 per cent of men are part-timers (a percentage), and one can also say that the probability that any particular man works part-time is nine in a hundred or 0.09 (a probability). All of these ways of expressing the relative number of part-time working men are equivalent.

PERCENTAGING TABLES

In Exhibit 9.11, we calculated the percentage in each cell by dividing the count by the total at the bottom of each column. These are therefore **column percentages**. It would be possible to calculate percentages by dividing the counts by the totals at the end of the rows to give **row percentages**. Exhibit 9.12 shows that 65 per cent of full-time workers are men, the remaining 35 per cent being women. Eighteen per cent of part-timers are men and 82 per cent are

Employment status	Men	Women	All
In full-time work	91	55	75
In part-time work	9	45	25
Total	100%	100%	100%
	(1365)	(1192)	(2557)

Exhibit 9.11 *Employment status by sex, percentaged*
Source: ONS, 1995
Note: See Exhibit 9.1 for definitions of full and part-time.

Employment status	Men	Women	All
In full-time work	65	35	100% (1909)
In part-time work	18	82	100% (648)

Exhibit 9.12   *Employment status by sex, percentaged by sex*
Source: ONS, 1995
Note: See Exhibit 9.1 for definitions of full and part-time.

women. Note that the percentages for men and women in full-time work differ from those for part-time work, confirming again that the two variables are associated.

Whether you should percentage a table down columns or across rows depends on what you are interested in. In this case, we are primarily interested in the differences between men and women in the likelihood that they will work part-time. Thus, percentaging down columns is the right way for us. But if you were interested in the proportions of men and women in the full-time and the part-time workforce, percentaging across the rows would be the correct thing to do.

Working out which way to percentage is often rather confusing, but there is a useful 'rule of thumb' that can help. One of the variables in a table can often be thought of as influencing the other. For instance, it is certainly the case that sex influences the likelihood that you will work part-time. It is clearly impossible for your employment status to affect whether you are male or female. The variable which is thought of as doing the influencing is known as the **independent** variable, and the other is the **dependent** variable.

If one variable is clearly the independent variable, it is conventional to present the table with that variable as the one that defines the columns. For example, in Exhibit 9.1, sex is the independent variable and therefore this was used as the column variable. Similarly, Exhibit 9.8 was constructed with sex and age, both independent variables, forming the columns and the dependent variable, whether the respondent talked to the doctor in the last two weeks, forming the rows.

Sometimes it is not clear which of the variables is independent and which is dependent, but more usually theoretical assumptions dictate which is which. If one variable comes before the other in time, the former must always be the independent variable. For example, in a table of educational qualification by current income group among those with paid jobs, education must be the independent variable because respondents would have obtained their qualifications some time before the survey, while their income is measured at the time of the survey.

Once the table has been drawn with the independent variable defining the columns, you should percentage down columns. This will enable you to compare percentages across the rows (e.g. compare the proportion of women part-timers with the proportion of men part-timers). The rule of thumb for tables is thus that you should **make the independent variable the column variable** and then **percentage down and compare across**. It should be emphasized that this is only a convention. There may be occasions when you will want to percentage across and compare down.

One exception to this convention is the social mobility table. Traditionally, social mobility tables are constructed the 'wrong way': they tabulate father's social class (the prior, independent variable) as the row variable and the respondent's social class, the dependent variable, as the column variable. Exhibit 9.13 shows a social mobility table of father's social class by respondent's social class, with class being measured in both cases on the Registrar-General's scale derived from the 1991 GHS (Office of Population Consensus and Surveys (OPCS), 1993). This table is percentaged across, as shown by the 100 per cent in the marginal on the right of the table. The percentages show that your best chance of getting into class I occurs if your father was in class I, a 14 per cent probability, compared with a maximum of 7 per cent probability if your father was in any of the other classes. We have used the 1991 GHS for this example because father's social class was not asked in the 1995 survey.

MEASURING ASSOCIATION

One advantage of percentaging a table is that the presence of association between variables is immediately revealed. If you percentage down and compare across and there is a difference between the percentages, there is an association. This is because the proportion of respondents in each category of one variable differs according to the category of the other variable – the definition of

Fathers' social class	Respondents' social class						
	I	II	IIIN	IIIM	IV	V	Total
I	14	36	30	9	8	3	100% (198)
II	7	34	27	14	14	5	100% (796)
IIIN	5	30	35	14	10	6	100% (266)
IIIM	3	20	25	26	17	9	100% (1371)
IV	2	14	23	25	25	12	100% (457)
V	3	9	23	26	24	12	100% (188)
Total	4	24	26	21	17	8	100% (3276)

Exhibit 9.13   *Father's social class by respondent's social class, using the Registrar-General's classification, percentaged by respondents' social class*
Source: OPCS, 1993

association. If there is no difference, the two variables are said to be **independent** (not the same as an 'independent variable').

The difference can give a rough measure of the strength of the association. So, for example, in Exhibit 9.11 the difference is 36 per cent (notice that it does not matter whether you subtract percentages taken from the top row or the bottom row; for a table with just four cells, the answer is always the same whichever you choose).

There is a large number of measures of association, each with its own features. We will mention a few, starting with phi.

PHI AND CRAMÉR'S V

The advantage of measuring association using percentage differences is that percentages are easy and quick to calculate. The disadvantage is that the maximum achievable percentage difference varies from table to table, depending on the row and column marginals in the table, and so it is not easy to compare the percentage differences between tables or to assign an interpretation to any particular amount of difference.[1]

What is needed is a measure of association that can vary in absolute value (that is, in magnitude, disregarding the sign) between 0 and 1, with 0 meaning no association and 1 meaning 'perfect association'. There are several measures with this property, but the most common for tables of two dichotomous categorical variables is called **phi**, the Greek letter written ϕ and pronounced to rhyme with 'pie'. Phi is 0 for tables with no association, and 1 if all the cases are in the top left-hand and bottom right-hand cells. If the cases are all along the other diagonal (the top right and bottom left cells) phi becomes equal to -1, so phi measures not only the strength of association, but also its direction.

The value of phi is obtained by comparing the actual table with the table that would be expected if there were no association between the two variables, but everything else (in particular, the marginal counts) were the same as in the data. The differences in the corresponding cell counts between the two tables (the data and the expected table) are used to calculate the value of phi.

In Exhibit 9.14 the marginal counts are the same as in Exhibit 9.1. In order to

Employment status	Men	Women	All
In full-time work			1909
In part-time work			648
Total	1365	1192	2557

Exhibit 9.14   *Employment status by sex: marginal counts*

[1] For example, the maximum percentage difference that can be attained by moving cases around Exhibit 9.1, while keeping the same marginals to the table, is 54 per cent (achieved by shifting the 118 men part-timers to full-time and 118 women full-timers to part-time). Thus the actual 36 per cent difference is, in fact, quite a large proportion of the maximum achievable percentage difference.

calculate phi we need first to obtain the table of counts to be expected if there were no association between the variables. The task is therefore to find a set of counts for the body of the table which total to these marginals, but which show no association. This table would then be the **expected** table. We know that in a table of no association, the percentage differences are zero. That is, the percentage of full-time working men is equal to the percentage of full-time working women, and must therefore also equal the percentage of full-timers overall, both men and women. The latter we can find from Exhibit 9.14: it is 1909/2557, or 74.65 per cent.

Therefore, in a table showing no association, 74.65 per cent of the 1365 men must be working full-time (that is, 1019 men) and 74.65 per cent of the 1192 women must work full-time (890 women). It only remains to calculate the number of part-timers, by subtracting the number of full-timers from the totals of men and women. We get Exhibit 9.15, in which all the values have been rounded to the nearest whole number. You can check that if you percentage down and compare across the columns of Exhibit 9.15, the percentage differences are zero, as required.

The process of calculating the counts for Exhibit 9.14 involved finding the overall marginal percentage by dividing the row marginal by the table total (N), and then multiplying this percentage by the column marginal. This procedure is easily remembered as 'multiply the marginal counts and divide by the table total'. The result will be the count to go into the expected table.

Now that we have the table that one would expect if there were no association between the two variables, we can compare it with the actual data (Exhibit 9.1). The fact that the cell counts are different in these two tables confirms what we already know: the variables are associated. The differences in the counts give an indication of the amount of association. For instance, the number of full-time men in the data table, Exhibit 9.1, is 1247, the number in the expected table, Exhibit 9.15, is 1019, and the difference is 228. You can do this for all four cells and add up the results to get a summary measure for the table as a whole. Unfortunately, some of the differences are positive and some negative and adding the four together always yields a total of zero.

The way out of this difficulty is to square each of the differences (the square of a number is always positive, regardless of whether that number is positive or negative). However, if there are a large number of respondents in the table, these squared differences will be large, even if the association is weak. To take account of the number of respondents, we divide each of the squared differences by the expected count. The results are then summed. The sum can take any value

Employment status	Men	Women	All
In full-time work	1019	890	1909
In part-time work	346	302	648
Total	1365	1192	2557

Exhibit 9.15   *Employment status by sex, expected counts when there is no association between the variables*

between zero and the number of people in the table, N. To make sure that it always lies between zero and one, we divide it by N. Finally, because we squared the counts to get rid of negative numbers, we take the square root of the answer to obtain the value of phi. Exhibit 9.16 sets out the calculation.

A table showing association tends to have relatively more respondents than the expected table in one pair of diagonally opposite cells and relatively less in the other pair. When there are more cases in the top left-hand and bottom right-hand cells compared with the expected table, phi is positive; and when there are more cases in the other pair of cells, the top right and the bottom left, phi is negative. For Exhibit 9.1, the excess cases compared with the expected table are in the top left and bottom right, so phi is positive.

Phi applies only to two-by-two tables, that is, tables with four cells. Using the formula on larger tables can yield values greater than 1. This defeats the point of using phi, which is designed to have a range between -1 and 1. However, there is an alternative, a similar measure which works correctly for larger tables. This measure, called **Cramér's V** after the statistician who first proposed it, is calculated in just the same way as phi, but instead of dividing by the table total, you divide by the table total multiplied by the smaller of (one less than the number of rows) and (one less than the number of columns). This extra factor ensures that the value of Cramér's V never exceeds 1.

Exhibit 9.17 shows a table with 7 columns and 5 rows derived from the 1993 British Social Attitudes Survey (Social and Community Planning Research (SCPR), 1993). It tabulates the attitude of respondents to the proposal to raise women's retirement age from 60 to 65, by the age of the respondents grouped into ten-year age bands. As with two-by-two tables, the easiest way to appreciate the relationship between these variables is to compare the column percentages. You will see from the marginals that the respondents are somewhat against the idea, with 36 per cent $(6 + 30)$ in favour or strongly in favour of the proposal and 54 per cent $(33 + 21)$ against or strongly against it. But this overall distribution conceals a radical shift of view with age: while 53 per cent of those under 25 are in favour or strongly in favour, only 18 per cent of those in their late fifties are. In short, there is an association between opinion about raising women's retirement age and the age of the respondent.

Employment status	Men		Women		All
In full-time work	$\dfrac{227.92^2}{1019.08}$	$= 50.975$	$\dfrac{-227.92^2}{889.92}$	$= 58.373$	1909
In part-time work	$\dfrac{-227.92^2}{345.92}$	$= 150.172$	$\dfrac{227.92^2}{302.08}$	$= 171.966$	648
Total	1365		1192		2557

Total of all four cells $= 431.49$
Total divided by $N = 431.49/2557 = 0.17$
$\phi = \sqrt{0.17} = 0.41$

Exhibit 9.16   *Calculation of the components of phi*

Attitude	Age							
	18–24	25–34	35–44	45–54	55–59	60–64	65+	All
Strongly in favour	7	7	7	6	2	4	6	6
In favour	46	34	25	26	16	28	31	30
Neither	13	15	12	3	15	9	4	10
Against	27	25	36	36	25	35	42	33
Strongly against	8	20	20	30	42	24	17	21
Total	100%	100%	100%	100%	100%	100%	100%	100%
	(163)	(275)	(310)	(237)	(78)	(85)	(283)	(1431)

Exhibit 9.17   *Attitude to a proposal to raise women's normal retirement age from 60 to 65, by respondent's age*
Source: SCPR, 1993

Cramér's *V* for this table is 0.14, typical for tables of survey results that show a moderate association. You might wonder whether the association is related to gender. Is the association stronger for female respondents? Recalculating the table separately for men and women shows that the answer is no, for the Cramér's *V* for the table of male respondents is 0.18 and for the table of female respondents is 0.16, hardly any different.

It is also worth noticing that while the proportion in favour of the proposal to raise the retirement age declines steadily until age 60, it then rises again to near the average 30 per cent. It seems that those who are already retired or near retirement do not mind the idea that those still in work should stay there for an extra five years, while those in approaching retirement are opposed to the idea of extending the time they have to wait until they retire.

PROPORTIONAL REDUCTION IN ERROR MEASURES: TAU AND GAMMA

In the previous paragraphs, two measures of association based on comparing the data table with a table of no association were introduced: phi and Cramér's *V*. We now describe two further measures of association based on a different principle, that of measuring the **proportional reduction in error**. The first is used when we know which of the two variables in the table is the independent variable and which the dependent variable, and we want to take this into account. The second is best used for tables of ordinal variables.

Once again, we shall use the data of Exhibit 9.1 as an example. Suppose that we wished to predict the employment status of someone about whom we knew nothing except that he or she worked. The best we could do is to use the row marginals and guess that this person has a 75 per cent chance (1909/2557) of being a full-timer.

If we carried out this prediction for all 2557 people in the survey, without knowledge of their sex or status, we would correctly guess the status of the full-timers 75 per cent of the time and incorrectly guess their status 25 per cent of the time. In so doing, 0.25×1909 full-timers would be misclassified as part-timers.

Among the part-timers, we would incorrectly guess that 0.75×648 were full-timers and correctly guess that 0.25×648 were part-timers. The total number of errors in our prediction of the status of the 2557 respondents would therefore be:

$$0.25 \times 1909 + 0.75 \times 648 = 963.25$$

Now suppose that we knew the respondents' sex and carried out the same prediction process for the men and the women separately. Because there is an association between employment status and sex, the predictions will be rather more accurate. The percentages of full- and part-timers among men and women are shown in Exhibit 9.11. The number of misclassifications of men would be the sum of the 9 per cent of the 1247 male full-timers classified as part-timers, and the 91 per cent of the 118 male part-timers classified as full-timers:

$$0.09 \times 1247 + 0.91 \times 118 = 219.6$$

and for women:

$$0.45 \times 662 + 0.55 \times 530 = 589.4$$

The additional information about the respondents' sex has reduced the number of errors of misclassification from 963.25 without any knowledge of their sex to

$$219.61 + 589.4 = 809$$

with knowledge of their sex. The proportional reduction in error is

$$\tau = (963.25 - 809)/963.25 = 0.16$$

This measure of association is called **Goodman and Kruskal's tau**, after the Greek letter τ. As with phi, it has a maximum value of 1 (perfect association) and a minimum of 0 (no association). It differs from phi in that it is **asymmetric** or **directional**. When calculating tau for Exhibit 9.1, we compared the number of misclassifications without any knowledge of the respondents with the number of misclassifications when we knew their sex, the independent variable. It is also possible (although in this instance, not very meaningful) to calculate the value of tau from the proportional decrease in errors when one knows the respondents' employment status. For two by two tables, the values of tau in the two cases are identical, but with tables with more cells, the two versions are usually different. Normally, one should use the version which shows the reduction in error from knowing the independent variable.

All the measures of association we have mentioned so far assume that the variables have been measured at the nominal level. One practical consequence of this is that if the order of the rows or columns in the table is changed (e.g. swapping the columns for men and women in Exhibit 9.1) the numerical values of the measures do not alter.

Exhibit 9.17 tabulated two ordinal variables, attitude to raising women's retirement age, and respondent's age group. Although we calculated the value of Cramér's *V* for the table, this measure does not recognize that the variables are in fact ordinal and treats them as though they were nominal. Doing this is not wrong, but it does ignore the ordering information. It would be better to use a measure devised for the association between ordinal variables. Such is **gamma** (γ), another proportional reduction in error measure.

Like tau, gamma measures the reduction in misclassification once we have knowledge of one of the variables. It is based on the idea of pairs. Suppose that we pick two respondents from the survey. Let us call them Jack and Jill. We find their age group and their attitudes. If Jack's age is greater than Jill's and Jack's attitude is more favourable than Jill's, the pair is said to be **concordant**. If Jack's age is less than Jill's and Jack's attitude is less favourable than Jill's, the pair is also concordant. If neither is the case, the pair is **discordant**. One could in principle compare all possible pairings of the 1431 respondents (there are over one million of them!) and count how many concordant and discordant pairs there are in all. Then gamma is the ratio of the difference in the numbers of concordant and discordant pairs to the sum of the numbers of concordant and discordant pairs. In practice, there is a formula which make it a lot easier to calculate the value of gamma than by considering all possible pairs of respondents, but even this is not worth remembering because SPSS will calculate gamma for you.

OBTAINING PERCENTAGES AND STATISTICS WITH SPSS

To use SPSS to obtain column percentages and statistics from data in cross-tabulations you need to select additional features in the **Crosstabs** dialog box seen in Exhibit 9.3. To include column percentages, select the **Cells** ... button to get the dialog box in Exhibit 9.18. Here column percentages can be selected.

To get SPSS to calculate phi, Goodman and Kruskal's tau, or gamma, select **Statistics** from the **Crosstabs** dialog box in Exhibit 9.3 to obtain the dialog box in Exhibit 9.19. Note that you need to select **Lambda** in order to obtain Goodman and Kruskal's tau (Lambda is yet another measure of association). Exhibit 9.20 displays the output resulting from selecting column percentages. Exhibit 9.21 shows the value of tau for this table, and Exhibit 9.22 the values of phi and Cramér's *V.*

THREE-WAY TABLES

So far we have been concerned only with analysing relationships in tables of two variables. It is also possible to examine more complex relationships, in which three or more variables are interrelated. Exhibit 9.7 tabulated employment status by sex, for both younger and older respondents. The data are reproduced in Exhibit 9.23, but with the counts percentaged down columns.

We can look at each half of the table (that is, each partial table) separately. On

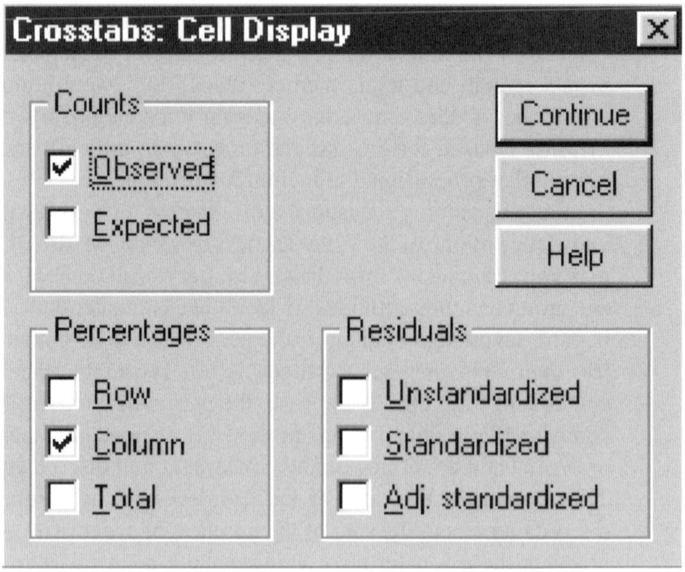

Exhibit 9.18   ***Crosstabs: Cell Display*** *dialog box*

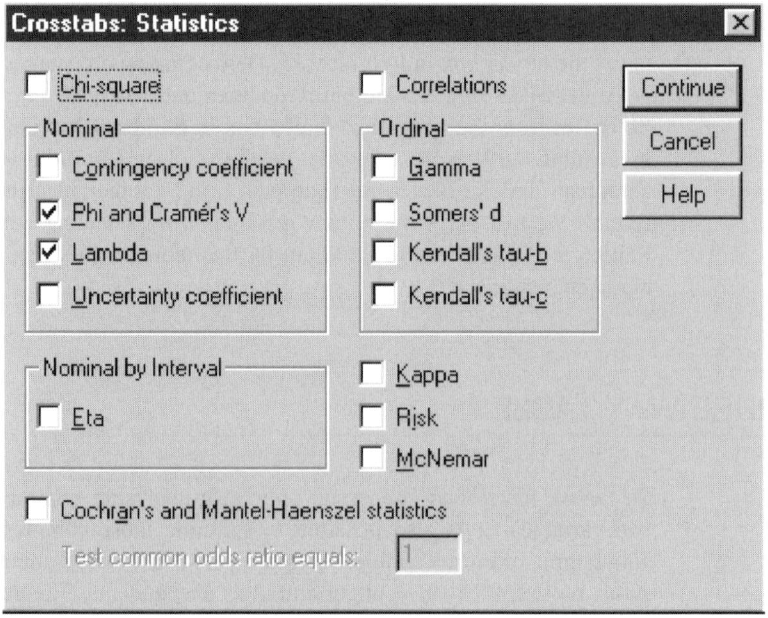

Exhibit 9.19   ***Crosstabs: Statistics*** *dialog box*

TIME Full or part-time * SEX SEX Crosstabulation

			SEX SEX		Total
			1 Male	2 Female	
TIME Full or part-time	1.00 Full-time	Count	1247	662	1909
		% within SEX SEX	91.4%	55.5%	74.7%
	2.00 Part-time	Count	118	530	648
		% within SEX SEX	8.6%	44.5%	25.3%
Total		Count	1365	1192	2557
		% within SEX SEX	100.0%	100.0%	100.0%

Exhibit 9.20   *Crosstab of TIME by SEX with column percentages*

Directional Measures

			Value	Asymp. Std. Error[a]	Approx. T[b]	Approx. Sig.
Nominal by Nominal	Lambda	Symmetric	.224	.010	17.084	.000
		TIME Full or part-time Dependent	.000	.000	.[c]	.[c]
		SEX SEX Dependent	.346	.017	17.084	.000
	Goodman and Kruskal tau	TIME Full or part-time Dependent	.169	.014		.000[d]
		SEX SEX Dependent	.169	.013		.000[d]

[a] Not assuming the null hypothesis.
[b] Using the asymptotic standard error assuming the null hypothesis.
[c] Cannot be computed because the asymptotic standard error equals zero.
[d] Based on chi-square approximation.

Exhibit 9.21   *SPSS output showing the value of Goodman and Kruskal's tau for the data in Exhibit 9.1*

Symmetric Measures

		Value	Approx. Sig.
Nominal by Nominal	Phi	.411	.000
	Cramér's V	.411	.000
N of Valid Cases		2557	

[a] Not assuming the null hypothesis.
[b] Using the asymptotic standard error assuming the null hypothesis.

Exhibit 9.22   *SPSS output showing the value of phi for the data in Exhibit 9.1*

Employment status	Age 16–44 Men	Women	Age 45 and over Men	Women	All
In full-time work	92	60	90	48	75
In part-time work	8	40	10	52	25
Total	100%	100%	100%	100%	100%
	(865)	(769)	(500)	(423)	(2557)

Exhibit 9.23   *Employment status by sex by age, percentaged*
Source: ONS, 1995
Note: see Exhibit 9.1 for definitions of full- and part-time work.

the left-hand side is a two-by-two table of employment status by sex for the younger respondents alone, and on the right-hand side is the table for older people. We can now calculate the percentage differences (32 per cent for the younger and 42 per cent for the older people) or the values of phi (0.38 for the younger, 0.46 for the older) to measure the amount of association in the two partial tables. These are the associations **controlling** for age group, that is, holding the age group constant in each table.

The phi values tell us that the relationship between employment status and sex is stronger among the older people than among the younger ones, although it is substantial in both age groups. The main reason for the difference is that a larger proportion of the younger women are in full-time work (60 per cent) than older women (48 per cent), and so sex makes a bigger impact on the chances of being in full-time work among the older age group.

There are two explanations which could account for this, and the data are not sufficient to distinguish between them. On the one hand, it may be that over the last couple of decades, more and more women of child-bearing age are maintaining full-time involvement in the labour market, rather than moving to part-time work. According to this explanation, the table shows evidence of historical changes, with women born in mid-century behaving in a way that older women, born before the end of World War II, do not. On the other hand, it may be that older women are more likely to take on part-time work than work full-time because there are more opportunities available for part-timers or for other reasons. According to this explanation, the labour market involvement of the women who were aged under 45 at the time of the survey will come to resemble that of the older age group as time passes and they get older. In fact, it is likely that there is some truth in both these explanations and only **longitudinal** data, obtained by following the careers of women over a number of years, would decide between them.

ELABORATION

The process of examining a table of two variables and then controlling for a third variable to see how the overall relationship varies in partial tables is known as **elaboration**, a very useful and powerful way of getting to grips with tabular data.

In the introduction to this chapter, it was noted that women are less likely to have occupational pensions, because of their greater likelihood of being in part-time work and because women tend to be in lower-paid jobs. Membership of a pension scheme is a fringe benefit which is more often available to those who are in full-time work and who are better paid. We can confirm that there is a relationship between being in a pension scheme and sex using the General Household Survey. This includes a variable stating whether the respondent is a member of his or her employer's occupational pension scheme, is not a member of the employer's scheme, or is employed in a workplace where there is no pension scheme (so that the respondent has to rely on either the State pension alone, or a privately financed pension). Using this variable, we can look to see whether being in an employer's pension scheme is associated with the respondent's sex. Exhibit 9.24 confirms that it is ($\phi = -0.1$) although the relationship is fairly weak.

As expected, while 85 per cent of men are in their employer's pension scheme, only 77 per cent of women are. This may be the result of direct discrimination by employers not allowing women to join their scheme, or it could, as we suggested in the previous paragraph, be caused by the fact that women are on average paid less than men. We can find out more about this by elaborating on the basis of income. To simplify the analysis, we shall just use two income bands: below and above the median earnings. Exhibit 9.25 shows the table of scheme membership by sex, controlling for weekly earnings.

Pension scheme membership	Male	Female
Not in employer's scheme	15	23
In employer's scheme	85	77
Total	100% (693)	100% (620)

Exhibit 9.24   *Membership of employer's pension scheme, by sex, for those in employment*
Source: ONS, 1995

	Weekly earnings			
	Below median		Above median	
Pension scheme membership	Male	Female	Male	Female
Not in employer's scheme	23	29	12	13
In employer's scheme	77	71	88	86
Total	100% (197)	100% (357)	100% (496)	100% (263)

Exhibit 9.25   *Membership of employer's pension scheme, by sex and income band, for those in employment*
Source: ONS, 1995

The association between membership and sex in each partial table has almost disappeared (the value of phi is -0.07 for the 'below median' table and -0.02 for the 'above median' table). How can we account for this? Before answering this question, we shall have to return to the idea of causality.

CAUSAL DIAGRAMS

We have previously noted that an independent variable influences or causes changes in a dependent variable. For instance, we treated employment status as a dependent variable, influenced by sex, an independent variable. In Exhibit 9.24, sex is again the independent variable influencing membership of a pension scheme. Causal relationships like this can conveniently be drawn in a diagram using an arrow pointing from the cause (the independent variable) to the effect (dependent variable), as in Exhibit 9.26(a). The arrow means that we are presuming that one's sex affects one's chance of being in a pension scheme (and that membership of a scheme does not affect one's sex).

The arrow represents the social 'mechanism' which links sex and pension membership. Often, we do not have much idea about what the link consists of and it is part of the research to find out more. One avenue of enquiry is whether there are any **intervening** variables. As we have already proposed, earnings may be one such variable. Whether someone is male or female affects their level of earnings, and their level of earnings in turn affects their likelihood of being in a pension scheme (see Exhibit 9.26(b)).

Each of the diagrams (b)–(e) in Exhibit 9.26 represent a different theory about the relationship between the three variables, pension membership, sex and income. Which of the theories is correct is important if one wants to challenge the differences between the opportunities for men and women. If (b) is right, reducing differences in the levels of earnings of men and women will be sufficient to correct the discrepancy in pension scheme membership. If (c) is correct, the apparent relationship between earnings and pension membership is **spurious**. Although the two variables look as though they are related because there is an association between them, in fact the association is due purely to the separate effects of an **antecedent** variable, sex, on each of them. (d) is theoretically impossible since earnings cannot affect sex. If (e) is correct, it is the direct discrimination that is important, while earnings have no effect at all.

We can now return to the results of the elaboration of the original table, Exhibit 9.24. We found that although there was a moderate association between sex and scheme membership overall, when we controlled for earnings the association in each partial table dropped to near zero. This is the typical pattern that arises when one controls an intervening variable. To understand why, consider that, as shown in Exhibit 9.26(b), the only link between sex and scheme membership goes through the earnings variable. In each partial table of Exhibit 9.25, earnings are held constant, in either the low or the high band. These tables

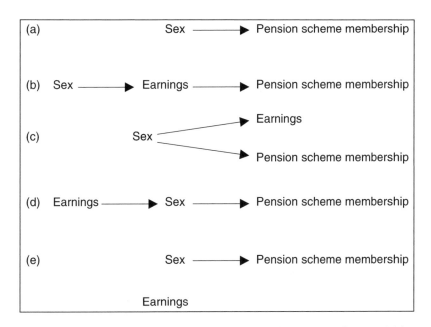

Exhibit 9.26   *Causal diagrams showing possible paths between three variables*

therefore show no association between sex and membership. The only link between those two variables has been controlled and held constant.

If the arrangement of causal links had been any of those shown in Exhibit 9.26(c)–(e), controlling for earnings would have had no effect on the association between sex and scheme membership. That is, both the partial tables of Exhibit 9.25 would show associations comparable in magnitude with the association in the original table, Exhibit 9.24. In order to distinguish between the theories represented by (c) and (e) (remember that (d) has already been rejected as completely implausible), we would need to examine the table of pension membership by earnings, controlling for sex. This table would have low or zero associations in both partial tables if the relationships were those in (c), but relatively strong associations in the partial tables if (e) were correct.

Elaboration is thus a powerful way of testing alternative causal models against tabular data. In summary, the idea is to examine possible reasons for the association between two variables by investigating the influence of a third variable. One of the three variables is controlled by constructing partial tables, one for each category of the variable. If the associations in these partial tables are close to zero, or at least much less than in the original two-variable table, the control variable must be either an intervening variable ((b) or (d) in Exhibit 9.26) or an antecedent variable (c). Distinguishing between antecedent and intervening variables can often be done by considering the causal ordering (in particular, the temporal ordering) of the variables.

SPECIFICATION

As we have seen, introducing a third variable can have the effect of reducing *both* the associations in the partial tables if the control is an antecedent or intervening variable, or it might have no effect on the partial associations if the control variable is unrelated to the other two. It is also possible for the control variable to have a different effect on each of the partial associations, for example, reducing one association and increasing the other. This is known either as **specification** (the third variable helps to specify the amount of association between the other two variables) or as **interaction** (the three variables are said to interact).

An example is shown in Exhibit 9.27. This elaborates Exhibit 9.24 which tabulates pension scheme membership by sex, by controlling for the respondents' occupation (divided into manual and non-manual occupations). The value of phi for the overall table, Exhibit 9.24 is −0.1. However, the phi value for the partial table for non-manual respondents (the left-hand partial table of Exhibit 9.27) is −0.09, while the phi for the manual workers (the right-hand partial table) is −0.16. The association between pension scheme membership and sex is stronger among manual workers than among non-manual workers. That is, the relationship between scheme membership and sex is specified by occupation.

The effect of occupation on the relationship between scheme membership and sex can also be seen by looking at the percentage differences: while the chances of not being in a scheme are 6 per cent worse for women than men in non-manual occupations, the corresponding percentage difference among manual workers is 15 per cent. The table also shows that a third of women in manual occupations are not in a scheme, compared to a fifth of men, and that the majority of non-manual men are in a scheme. In short, the effects of being a women and being a manual worker are additive; each of these factors reduces the likelihood you will be in a scheme, the factors both acting on their own and interacting to result in a cumulative disadvantage.

	Non-manual		Manual	
Pension scheme membership	Male	Female	Male	Female
Not in employer's scheme	13	19	19	34
In employer's scheme	87	81	81	66
Total	100%	100%	100%	100%
	(396)	(489)	(285)	(131)

Exhibit 9.27   *Membership of employer's pension scheme, by sex and occupation, for those in employment*
Source: ONS, 1995

INOCCPEN	POOR	SEX
2	2	2
2	1	2
2	2	1
2	1	2
1	1	1
2	2	1
2	1	1
1	1	1
2	1	1
2	2	1
2	2	1
2	2	1
2	2	1
2	1	2
1	1	1
2	1	1
2	2	2
1	1	1
2	1	1
2	2	2
2	1	2
2	2	1
1	1	2
1	1	2
2	1	2
2	1	2
2	2	1
2	2	2
2	2	1
2	2	1
2	2	1
1	2	2
2	2	1
2	2	1
2	2	1
2	1	2
1	1	2
2	2	2
2	1	2
2	2	1
2	2	1
2	2	2
1	2	2
2	2	2
2	2	2
1	1	2
2	2	1
1	1	1
2	1	2
2	2	2

Exhibit 9.28 *Fifty randomly chosen cases from the General Household Survey: values of whether or not in an occupational pension scheme, whether receiving less or more than median earnings and whether male or female*

SUMMARY

Tables are a very common way of summarizing categorical data in sociological research. It is important that they are presented clearly, using the standard conventions about their arrangement and format.

A table may show that there is association between two variables, that is, that the proportion of respondents in the categories of one variable varies according to the categories of the other variable. Association can be revealed by comparing column percentages and measured using any of several measures of association including phi (for 2×2 tables), Cramér's V (for larger tables), tau (when one variable is dependent on the other) and gamma (when the variables are measured at the ordinal level).

It is also possible to analyse the interaction in tables of three variables using a procedure called elaboration. This involves comparing the associations in each of the partial tables obtained by controlling for one of the three variables.

EXERCISES

1. The data in Exhibit 9.28 are taken from the General Household Survey, and consist of three variables for 50 randomly selected respondents in employment. The three variables are:
    (a) Participation in an occupational pension scheme (1 = not in scheme; 2 = in scheme), INOCCPEN
    (b) Whether receiving less (1) or more (2) than median earnings, POOR
    (c) Whether male (1) or female (2), SEX
    Construct a table to display these data, properly labelled. Then see what conclusions you can draw from the table.
2. Exhibit 12.18 shows the social mobility table that was percentaged to obtain Exhibit 9.13. Using the counts in Exhibit 12.18, a pocket calculator and the rule for calculating expected counts (page 211), calculate the table expected if there were no association between father's social class and respondent's class. Compare the expected counts with the data in Exhibit 12.18 and explain why some cells have larger counts than would be predicted if there were no 'class inheritance'.
3. Using SPSS, crosstabulate MEDINS (whether covered by a private medical insurance scheme) by SEX. Construct a properly labelled table suitable for publication and add a paragraph in which you interpret and comment on the table.

SAMPLING AND INFERENCE 10

Suppose you wanted to find the average income of working women in the UK. Interviewing every working woman would obviously be a huge and expensive task. Fortunately, results for the whole country can be obtained accurately enough for all practical purposes by finding the incomes of just a sample, and then inferring from the sample to the population as a whole. Measuring the income of the working women in the sample gives an estimate of the income of all working women, provided that some basic precautions about how the sample is obtained are satisfied.

The fact that quite small samples can give reasonable estimates about whole populations is one of the discoveries that made surveys and opinion polls possible. Before statisticians had perfected the mathematics that lie behind the process of inference in the 1920s, it was assumed that accurate measures – of poverty, for instance – could only be obtained by exhaustive surveys. Nowadays, however, market research companies regularly obtain commercially useful estimates of the opinions of the 59 million adults in the United Kingdom by interviewing samples numbering between 1000 and 2000 people.

It is quite rare for it to be sensible to conduct a **census**, that is, to obtain data from everyone in the population. By measuring just those in a sample, time and money can be saved that are better used on other aspects of the research, while still obtaining sufficient accuracy for valid conclusions to be drawn. This chapter is about assessing how good an estimate of the characteristics of a whole population can be, using measurements of a sample.

RANDOM AND REPRESENTATIVE SAMPLES

The theory behind statistical inference depends on using a random (or probability) sample to estimate the characteristics of a population. A **random sample** is one in which people are selected to be in the sample at random and every individual has a chance of being included. A random sample is not the same as a **representative sample** (one in which individuals are included in proportion to the number of those in the population like them). For example, if in the population as a whole, 27 per cent of women work full-time, 22 per cent work part-time, and the rest have no paid job, a representative sample of 100 women would be one in which 27 are full-time workers and 22 are part-timers. A random sample of 100 women would be one in which 100 women were picked out of the population entirely at random. There is no guarantee that the randomly selected women would include exactly 27 full-timers, although we might be surprised if the number were very different.

SAMPLING IN SPSS

In the 1995 General Household Survey data set there are 2415 women. Let us treat these women as the population from which to sample. We will first find the percentages of women who work full-time, work part-time and have no paid job in the data set as a whole. To do this using SPSS, refer to Chapter 2, **Select Cases**. The condition for case selection in this example is sex = 2. Make sure that you also select **Unselected Cases Are Deleted**. This is important for the random sampling step below to work correctly (see Exhibit 10.1)

The variable that measures work status is called WKSTATE. As in Chapter 9, we will first recode WKSTATE into a new variable, TIME, which has two categories, full- and part-time working (see Exhibit 9.2). Then, we select **Analyze|Descriptive Statistics ▸|Frequencies** ..., and then select the TIME variable. Exhibit 10.2, taken from the SPSS output, shows that 27.4 per cent of women work full-time and 21.9 per cent work part-time.

Second, we select a sample of 100 women at random from the data set.

In SPSS, select **Data|Select Cases** ...|**Random Sample of Cases** and then click on **Sample** ..., to see the dialog box in Exhibit 10.3. In this dialog box,

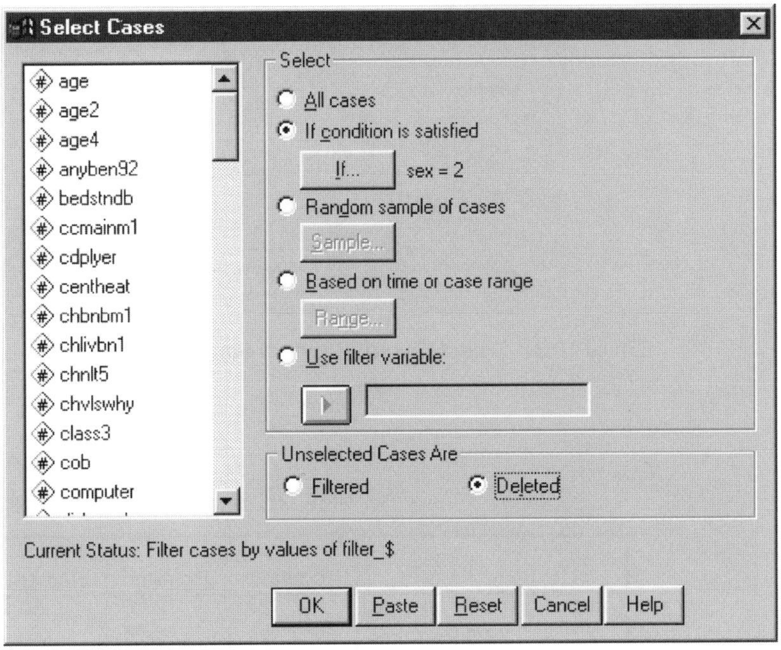

Exhibit 10.1   *Select Cases* dialog box

TIME Full or part-time

		Frequency	Percent	Valid Percent	Cumulative Percent
Valid	1.00 Full-time	662	27.4	55.5	55.5
	2.00 Part-time	530	21.9	44.5	100.0
	Total	1192	49.4	100.0	
Missing	System	1223	50.6		
Total		2415	100.0		

Exhibit 10.2   *The variable* TIME *from the GHS 1995*

select **Exactly** 100 cases from 2415, the number of women in the sample. After pressing **Continue** in this dialog box, we return to the **Select Cases** box (Exhibit 10.1). This time, make sure that **Unselected Cases Are Filtered.**

Once again, we ask SPSS for a display of frequencies for the variable TIME to discover the percentages of full and part-time working women in the sample of 100. Exhibit 10.4 shows the result from this one sample of 100. In the sample, although full-time workers are fairly represented at 27 per cent, compared to the whole data set, part-time workers are over represented at the expense of those not in employment (who are coded as system missing).

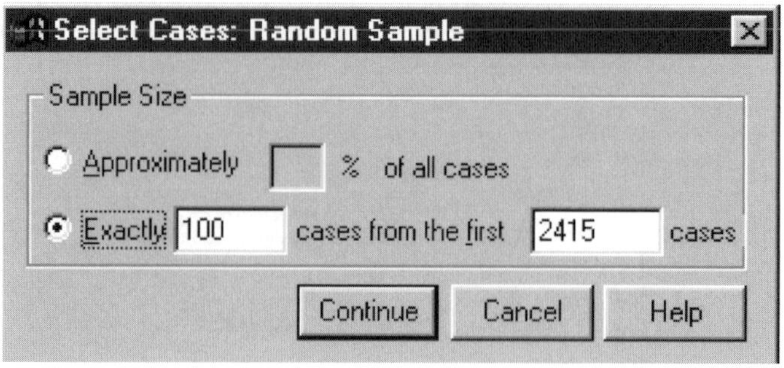

Exhibit 10.3   *Select Cases: Random Sample dialog box*

TIME Full or part-time

		Frequency	Percent	Valid Percent	Cumulative Percent
Valid	1.00 Full-time	27	27.0	50.9	50.9
	2.00 Part-time	26	26.0	49.1	100.0
	Total	53	53.0	100.0	
Missing	System	47	47.0		
Total		100	100.0		

Exhibit 10.4   *The variable TIME for a sample of 100 women*

SAMPLE AND POPULATION MEANS

Although having a representative sample rather than a random sample would be the better option, because it would precisely mirror the characteristics of the population, representative samples are almost always impossible to obtain. This is because the sample needs to be representative not just on one, but on *every* characteristic that could be relevant. Usually we neither know what these relevant characteristics are, nor could we find the right sample members even if we did. Fortunately, a random sample has none of these difficulties and can be used, to make inferences about a population even though there is no guarantee that a random sample is representative. The value of a random sample is that, although one cannot be sure how representative it is, statistical theory will give us an estimate of the chances that it will be seriously unrepresentative. In other words, while we may not be exactly correct in the inferences we make from a random sample, at least we will know how likely it is that we are going to be very wrong.

Although it is unlikely that any particular random sample will be exactly representative of the population, the characteristics of samples will tend, on average, to resemble those of the population. Consider finding the mean weekly gross earnings of working women in the UK. If we draw a random sample of working women and compute the mean weekly income of those in this sample, we might find the mean to be £184. We can use this as an estimate of the mean income of the population. However, we must remember that although the estimate is likely to be close to the actual mean earnings of the population, it will not be exactly equal to the population mean unless the random sample happens by chance to be representative. The difference between the estimate from the sample and the true value in the population is called the **sampling error**.

If we take another random sample, the mean earnings of the women in this second sample might be £187. Taking more and more samples, we would find that the means of these samples cluster around the true, population mean. In fact, if the means from a large number of samples are plotted on a graph (called a **sampling distribution**) such as Exhibit 10.5 they will always form the symmetrical bell-shaped curve known as the **normal distribution** (see Chapter 7). In Exhibit 10.5, the *x* or horizontal axis shows the mean of each sample, and the *y* or vertical axis shows the number of samples with that mean.

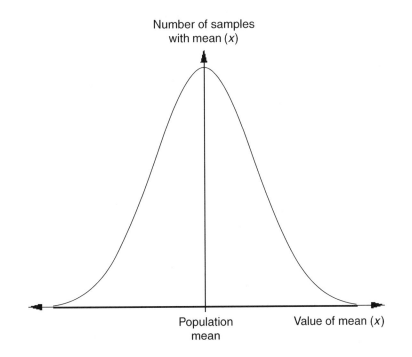

Exhibit 10.5   *The distribution of sample means tends to be normal*

OBTAINING RANDOM NUMBERS

In order to obtain a random sample, we need a numbered list of the population (for example, the electoral roll, or a list of all the pupils in a school) and a set of **random numbers**. Then those people whose numbers are in the list of random numbers are selected to be in the sample. But where do the random numbers come from? They are more difficult to obtain than you might think – the first few numbers that come into your head will certainly not be random. One way of generating random numbers is to use some chance physical event: for example, the National Lottery uses the chance that a particular numbered bouncing ball will escape from a cage. Another way of generating random numbers is to use the times of radioactive decay. But these procedures are obviously inconvenient for social surveys. A practical alternative is to use the random numbers that are printed in books of statistical tables (e.g. Fisher and Yates, 1974).

Nowadays, the usual way is to use a computer to generate random numbers. In fact, computers cannot generate random numbers because they contain no random processes. Instead a 'pseudo-random number generator' is used. This is a complex arithmetic formula that has been shown by statistical tests to yield a sequence of numbers from a given starting value (the **random number seed**) that look as though they were random. The advantage of using a pseudo-random number generator, in addition to its convenience, is that the formula always produces the same sequence for the same seed value, and a different sequence for each different seed. This means that one can carry out repeatable experiments based on random numbers just by using the same seed value.

PLOTTING SEVERAL SAMPLE MEANS USING SPSS

Using the General Household Survey data set as the population, we can draw a number of separate small samples of working women and calculate the mean income of each sample. These means can then be plotted and should result in a graph something like (but not exactly the same as) Exhibit 10.5.

An example of what is obtained is shown in Exhibit 10.6. To produce this we first selected only working women. This was done by selecting **Data|Select cases** ...|**If condition is satisfied|If** ... with the selection condition as sex = 2 and wkstate ≤ 2. The **Unselected Cases** were deleted.

Then 100 women were sampled from this subset, by selecting a random number of cases as in Exhibit 10.4, but choosing **Exactly** 100 cases from 1192.

Then mean weekly earnings were calculated for the sample. This was done by selecting **Analyze|Descriptive Statistics ►|Descriptives**. The variable EARN-INGS, usual gross weekly earnings, was used. This gave the mean earnings of one sample of 100 women. Then 19 further samples were selected and their mean earnings were found in the same way.

Finally, the means from each sample were then re-entered as the values into a

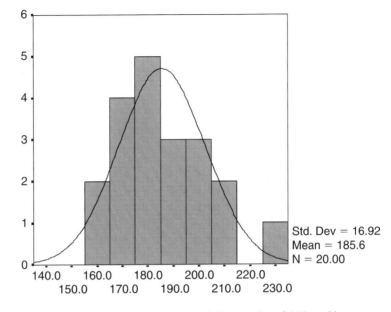

Exhibit 10.6 *Plot of the mean earnings of 20 samples of 100 working women (with a normal curve superimposed)*

new SPSS data window of a new variable and a histogram plotted (Exhibit 10.6).

The graph is not identical to the normal curve in Exhibit 10.5 because the latter is a theoretical curve obtainable only after taking the means of an infinite number of samples. Exhibit 10.6, based on only 20 samples, looks like a 'lumpy' version of the theoretical curve.

THE CENTRAL LIMIT THEOREM

Exhibit 10.6 showed the distribution of sample means obtained from a number of experiments. Each experiment contributed one sample mean. By a fundamental theorem of statistics, called the **central limit theorem**, it can be proved that the distribution of sample means always approximates to the bell-shaped normal distribution, provided that it is based on a sufficient number of samples each large enough in size.

All normal curves are the same basic shape, differing only in the location of their centres (given by the mean) and in their degree of spread (given by the standard deviation). This means that a normal curve can be defined by just two parameters: the mean of the distribution and its standard deviation. The mean of the distribution indicates where the centre of the curve is located (the mean runs through the middle of the bell) and the standard deviation indicates how spread out the curve is.

If we were able to plot an infinite number of sample means, the centre of the curve would be at the population mean. For example, the mean of the distribution of the mean incomes of lots of samples of working women would be approximately equal to the mean income of the population of working women. The standard deviation of the normal curve obtained from means of samples has a special name: the **standard error of the mean**. Suppose that we had drawn a large number of samples of working women, each of size N (e.g. each of 100 women as in the previous section) and had found the average earnings of each sample. The central limit theorem tells us that the mean earnings of the samples are normally distributed and that the mean of the means (that is, the centre of the bell) will be approximately equal to the population mean.

CALCULATING THE STANDARD ERROR OF THE MEAN

The central limit theorem also tells us what the standard error of the mean, $SE(\bar{x})$ is. It is given by the formula

$$SE(\overline{X}) = \frac{\sigma}{\sqrt{N}} \tag{10.1}$$

where σ (sigma) is the standard deviation of the population and n is the number of people in the sample. In practice, it is unlikely that you will know what the standard deviation of the population is, but it can be approximated by using the standard deviation of the sample provided that the sample size, n, is large (more than about 100).

CONFIDENCE INTERVALS

Researchers never actually do draw lots of random samples in the way we have been describing in order to plot a sampling distribution. But knowing that we could do so and that the distribution of means will always tend towards a normal curve is very useful when it comes to making inferences from a single sample. We can use the shape of the sampling distribution to give an estimate of how accurate inferences based on that sample are likely to be. The shape of the curve tells us that sample means are most likely to fall near the middle of the bell (i.e. near the population mean) and rather unlikely to be very far from the middle. As we shall see, we can quantify this using the standard error of the mean.

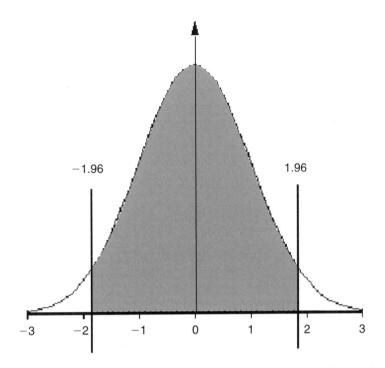

Exhibit 10.7   *The normal distribution with mean 0 and standard deviation 1, with 95 per cent of the area shaded*

For all normal curves, 95 per cent of the area of a normal curve falls between plus or minus 1.96 standard deviations from the mean (see Exhibit 10.7). The value 1.96 comes from the shape of the curve and can be found in statistical tables that describe the normal distribution. When the normal curve is the distribution of sample means, this can be interpreted as saying that 95 per cent of all the means of random samples taken from the same population will fall within the range plus or minus 1.96 standard errors from the population mean. There is thus a 95 per cent chance that the mean of any one sample will fall into the shaded area of Exhibit 10.7. Of course, that also suggests that 5 per cent of the time (100–95 per cent) the random sample will be so unrepresentative that its mean will be more than 1.96 standard errors away from the population mean.

What is rather more interesting from a practical point of view is that, by the same argument, 95 per cent of the time the population mean will fall within plus or minus 1.96 standard errors of a sample mean. So, for example, if we found that the mean income of working women in a particular random sample was £184, we could then go on to infer that there is a 95 per cent chance that the mean income of the population of working women is somewhere between £184 minus 1.96 standard errors and £184 plus 1.96 standard errors. The range from the mean minus 1.96 standard errors to the mean plus 1.96 standard errors is known as the 95 per cent **confidence interval**, since we can say with 95 per cent confidence that the population mean will be within this interval. Thus, one can use the standard error of the mean to find the confidence interval around the mean of a sample and then infer from that one sample that the population mean is very likely to fall within the interval.

PUTTING IT ALL TOGETHER

We can now work through an example of calculating a confidence interval for the mean income of working women in Great Britain. The first step is to select those women in the GHS data set who have some paid employment. Then we can get SPSS to find (using the **Explore** procedure) the number of such women in this sample, N (1054 with valid information about their incomes), the mean income of these women, $\overline{X}$ (£183.94), and the standard deviation of the distribution of these incomes, s (£146.92). Using equation (10.1) and the standard deviation of the sample, s, to estimate the standard deviation of the population, σ, the standard error is:

$$SE(\overline{X}) = \frac{\sigma}{\sqrt{N}} \approx \frac{s}{\sqrt{N}} = \frac{146.92}{\sqrt{1054}} = 4.53 \qquad (10.2)$$

We can conclude that we can be 95 per cent confident that the mean earnings of the population of working women in Great Britain is within the interval from £183.94 − (1.96 × 4.53) = £175.06   to   £183.94 + (1.96 × 4.53) = £192.82. This is illustrated in Exhibit 10.8, which shows the confidence interval surrounding the sample mean.

CONFIDENCE LEVELS

In the previous example, we inferred the population mean income from evidence based on a random sample. We know that different random samples are likely to give us different estimates of the population mean income. But by using a confidence interval we can indicate that, despite the uncertainty of random samples, only in 5 per cent of samples will the population mean be outside the confidence interval, while for 95 per cent of samples the mean will be inside the confidence interval.

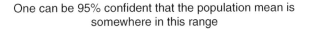

Exhibit 10.8   *A confidence interval*

Although being 95 per cent sure that the population mean is within the confidence interval is usually good enough for most issues of sociological interest, it is possible to use other probability values. For example, 99 per cent and 99.9 per cent are also used, especially in medical statistics where being highly confident of estimates is sometimes very important. The probability of including the population mean within the confidence interval is called the **confidence level** and is something that the researcher has to choose before working out a confidence interval.

In order to be confident that, for example, the population mean is within the confidence interval for 99 per cent of samples, the confidence interval has to be rather wider than it would be for 95 per cent confidence. This is because the proportion of the normal curve that is included in the interval has to be increased from 95 to 99 per cent. As was noted earlier, 95 per cent of the normal curve is included within 1.96 standard deviations of the mean. The corresponding figure for 99 per cent is 2.58. This value can be obtained from the table of the normal distribution in Appendix B. To use the table in Appendix B, first choose the confidence level you want to use, for example 99 per cent. This means that we need to find the interval that covers 99 per cent of the normal curve (see Exhibit 10.9, column A). If the shaded area of the curve includes 99 per cent of the area, 99/2 per cent or 0.495 of the area lies between the mean and the end of the interval. The table in Appendix B (a portion of which is shown in Exhibit 10.9) indicates that the ends of the intervals (z) are located at 2.58 and −2.58.

The confidence interval for the mean income of working women for a confidence level of 99 per cent is therefore from £183.94 − (2.58 × 4.53) = £172.25 to £183.94 + (2.58 × 4.53) = £194.68.

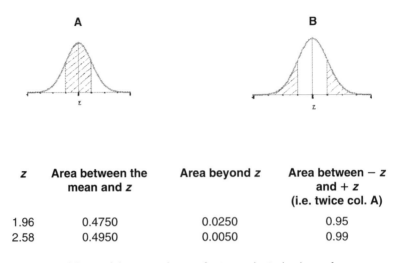

z	Area between the mean and z	Area beyond z	Area between − z and + z (i.e. twice col. A)
1.96	0.4750	0.0250	0.95
2.58	0.4950	0.0050	0.99

Exhibit 10.9   *Views of the normal curve for two selected values of z*

THE STANDARD DEVIATION OF A SAMPLE

In order to work out a confidence interval, we need to know the standard error of the mean. This is given by the central limit theorem as $\sigma/\sqrt{N}$ (see equation (10.2)). Unfortunately, we do not often know the value of the standard deviation, σ. However, it can be calculated: the standard deviation, σ, of some characteristic of a population is the square root of the average of the squared differences between the observations and the population mean:

$$\sigma = \sqrt{\frac{\Sigma(x_i - \mu)^2}{N}} \qquad (10.3)$$

(see also Chapter 5).

However, this equation for σ involves the population mean, which is also not usually known! The way out is to use the sample mean as an estimate of the population mean. However, basing the standard deviation on the sample mean can be shown to yield an underestimate of the standard deviation of the population. This can be corrected by using a formula in which the denominator is not N, but $N - 1$:

$$s = \sqrt{\frac{\Sigma(X_i - \overline{X})^2}{N - 1}} \qquad (10.4)$$

In practice, it does not make much difference whether you use N or $N - 1$ as the denominator when N is greater than 100.

Procedure for confidence intervals around a mean

- A confidence interval around a mean indicates the range within which a population mean is likely to be found.

When to use a confidence interval:

- Confidence intervals are useful when estimating a population mean from statistics about a random sample.

What you need to calculate a confidence interval:

- The size of the sample (N).
- The mean of some characteristic of the sample ($\bar{x}$).
- The sample standard deviation, s, of that characteristic of the sample.
- The points of the normal distribution appropriate to the desired confidence level to be used.
- Select a confidence level (usually 95 per cent).
- Calculate the standard error of the mean from the formula

$$SE(\bar{X}) = \frac{s}{\sqrt{N}}$$

- Calculate the top and bottom points of the interval. For instance, the 95 per cent confidence interval is defined by

$$\bar{X} \pm 1.96 \times SE(\bar{X})$$

Use 2.58 instead of 1.96 for a 99 per cent confidence level.

FACTORS INFLUENCING THE WIDTH OF THE CONFIDENCE INTERVAL

If the distribution of means has a small standard error, the bell-shaped normal curve is narrow. The confidence interval within which 95 per cent of sample means fall is therefore relatively narrow and we can be relatively precise about the value of the population mean. Conversely, if the standard error is large, we will have to be relatively vague about the population mean. The size of the standard error is therefore important in determining the precision of estimates of the population mean.

The formula for standard error, equation (10.1), indicates several interesting things:

1. The standard error depends directly on the size of the standard deviation of the population, σ. The more variability there is in the population, the larger the standard error and therefore the wider the confidence interval.

2. The standard error is inversely proportional to the square root of the sample size, n. Thus, the larger the sample, the smaller is the standard error and the narrower is the confidence interval. In other words, as you would expect, you can be more precise about the population mean if you use a larger sample to estimate it.
3. Because the standard error is inversely proportional to the square root of the sample size, there is a law of diminishing returns for increasing sample size. Multiplying the size of the sample by a factor of 4 only reduces the width of the confidence interval by a factor of 2.
4. The standard error and therefore the confidence interval do not depend on the size of the population, but only on the size of the sample. For example, using a sample of 1000 would achieve exactly the same precision in estimating the mean income of women working in the city of Chester as in estimating the mean income of women working throughout the United Kingdom.
5. The standard error does not depend on the shape of the distribution of the variable whose population mean is to be estimated, but only on its standard deviation. This is because, regardless of the shape of the distribution of the variable in the population, the sampling distribution of the means of random samples always approximates to a normal curve.

The last point, that the means of random samples are normally distributed even if the variable is not, can be illustrated with the distributions of women's earnings.

In a previous section we plotted the distribution of sample means of women's earnings from small random samples taken from the 1995 General Household Survey (Exhibit 10.6). As expected, we found that the distribution approximates to a normal curve.

While the distribution of means follows the normal distribution, the distribution of earnings has a very different shape (Exhibit 10.10): in fact, it is skewed to the right (positively skewed: see Chapter 5), so that the peak is at a relatively low income level and there is a long tail, showing that many women have low incomes and few have high incomes.

This negatively skewed shape for income is typical, not only for women in the UK, but for all groups throughout the world. Different countries, with different economic systems, vary in the degree of skewedness of their income distributions, but in none does the distribution follow the normal curve.

CONFIDENCE INTERVALS FOR A PROPORTION

What proportion of women in the UK have dishwashers? The national proportion can be estimated from a random sample using the same principles as we used to estimate the mean income of working women. As before, we find the proportion of dishwasher users in a sample, and then infer that the proportion in the population is within a confidence interval around the sample proportion. The

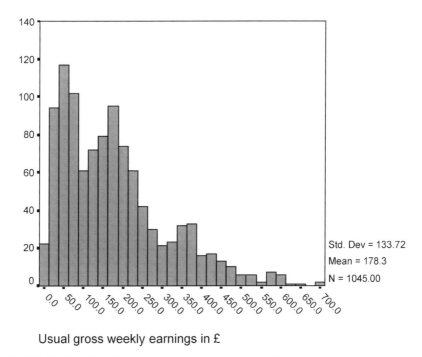

Usual gross weekly earnings in £

Exhibit 10.10   *Usual gross weekly earnings for working women*
                Source: ONS, 1995

only difference is that the standard error is calculated using another formula, appropriate for estimating proportions.

SPSS shows that of the 2415 women in the General Household Survey, 536 own, or are in families that own, a dishwasher. The other 1879 do not have a dishwasher. The proportion who have a dishwasher is therefore the number who have a dishwasher (536) divided by the number in the sample (2415):

$$p = \frac{536}{2415} = 0.222$$

The standard error of the distribution of sample proportions is given by the formula

$$SE(p) = \sqrt{\frac{p(1 - p)}{n}} \qquad (10.5)$$

where p is the proportion who have a dishwasher (and therefore $1 - p$ is the proportion who do not have one). Remember that $p(1 - p)$ means p multiplied by $(1 - p)$; multiplication signs are conventionally omitted in formulae like these. Notice the similarity between this formula and the one for the standard error of the mean (equation (10.1)) – the only difference is that the standard deviation of the population is replaced by $\sqrt{p(1-p)}$.

The standard error for the proportion who have a dishwasher is therefore

$$SE(p) = \sqrt{\frac{p(1-p)}{n}} = \sqrt{\frac{0.222(1-0.222)}{2415}} = 0.0085 \qquad (10.6)$$

and this leads to a 95 per cent confidence interval of

$$0.222 \pm 1.96 \times 0.0085 = 0.222 \pm 0.0166 \text{ i.e. from } 0.2054 \text{ to } 0.2386$$

We can be 95 per cent confident that the proportion of women in the population who have a dishwasher is between 0.2054 and 0.2386 or, expressing it as accurately as we are likely to need, between 21 and 24 per cent. Because we have a large sample of about 2400 women, the confidence interval is narrow and we can be reasonably precise about the inference from the sample to the population.

SUMMARY

- Confidence intervals are used to set bounds to the interval in which population parameters such as the mean or proportion are likely to be found, given a random sample. The great value of confidence intervals is that they give an idea about how accurate the estimate is likely to be. It is much more informative to know, for example, that the unemployment rate is between 10.1 and 10.3 per cent at the 95 per cent confidence level than it is to know that it is 10.2 per cent, for in the latter case we cannot tell how accurately it has been measured.
- Random samples are used because it is very rare that it is sensible to do a census of a whole population. Instead, a random sample is selected and the population parameters are estimated from the random sample.
- The inference from the sample to the population depends on the fact that the mean of the sample is the best estimator of the population mean. By the central limit theorem, the distribution of the means of many independent random samples is normally distributed with mean equal to the population mean and standard deviation (called in this context the standard error given by):

$$SE(\overline{X}) = \frac{\sigma}{\sqrt{N}}$$

- The confidence interval of a statistic is that range within which a population parameter is estimated to fall with a probability at least equal to the specified confidence level (usually 95 per cent).

EXERCISES

1. What is the mean age of mothers at the birth of their first child? Calculate confidence intervals for the 95 per cent and 99 per cent confidence levels.

2. What proportion of women consulted a doctor in the last two weeks? Express the result as a 95 per cent confidence interval. Is the proportion of men who consulted a doctor in the last two weeks different from that for women? Is the difference likely to be a real difference, or does it merely result from basing the proportions on inference from random samples?

3. How large would a sample have to be in order to find the mean weekly earnings of working women to a precision of plus or minus £1? [*Hint*: you will have to use the formulae for confidence intervals and standard errors 'backwards'.]

HYPOTHESIS TESTING

CONTENTS

Despite more than two decades of equal opportunity legislation that makes discrimination on the basis of sex illegal in the United Kingdom, women remain concentrated in occupations with the least chances for promotion and generally lower wages. Men and women tend to be in different jobs (for example, nearly all secretaries are women), women are much more likely to be working in part-time jobs with inferior conditions of employment, and women are more likely to be at the junior rather than the senior levels of career hierarchies (for example, although there are many more women teachers than men, there are more male headteachers than female ones).

Although this is a gloomy picture from the point of view of equal opportunities, it masks substantial changes in the gender composition of the labour force. One area that often receives comment is the increasing number of women taking up jobs that require higher education qualifications: there are more women scientists, engineers, and accountants than there used to be. But does sex discrimination persist even among this highly educated and best paid sector? In this chapter, we shall introduce the idea of testing hypotheses by examining the truth of the proposition that there are now as many highly qualified women as men working as managers and professionals.

Hypothesis testing is an important strategy in social research, although not the only one. In Chapter 6, we described exploratory data analysis, which is appropriate when the intention is to gather information and ideas about areas of social life about which relatively little is known. In contrast, the hypothesis testing strategy requires that you already know quite a lot about the area, enough to construct a hypothesis to test. The advantage of hypothesis testing is that it is often easier to make generalizations from particular research samples to wider populations than with exploratory research.

This chapter depends heavily on ideas about sampling distributions and standard errors that were introduced in Chapter 10. Make sure that you have understood those ideas before starting on this chapter.

HYPOTHESIS TESTING: AN EXAMPLE

In hypothesis testing, we start with a clearly stated proposition, derived from theory or from policy. The proposition, or **research hypothesis**, usually relates two concepts and is specified in a way such that it could be either true or false. In the case of occupational segregation, the research hypothesis might be that 'there are still more highly educated men than women in managerial and professional occupations'. A research hypothesis like this cannot be tested directly, because it consists of relationships between concepts; first, we must find indicators for each of the concepts (see Chapter 1). A reasonable choice of indicators for our research hypothesis is that 'highly educated' men and women are those with educational qualifications higher than A level (e.g. degrees, nursing qualifications, and professional qualifications such as being admitted to membership of the Institute of Chartered Accountants) and 'managerial and professional occupations' are those occupations classified in the standard Socio-Economic Groups (SEGs) 2, 4, 5 and 6, that is, managers in large and small enterprises and employed and self-employed professionals.

This lets us define a **working hypothesis** (also called an **alternative hypothesis**), that 'there are more men than women with higher and professional qualifications in those jobs that are included in SEGs 2, 4, 5 and 6'. The characteristics of such a working hypothesis are that it is precise, testable against data and potentially **falsifiable**. 'Potentially falsifiable' means that one can imagine that it could be false. Whether or not it is actually true or false is something that we shall discover as a result of the hypothesis testing process.

There are standard steps to carry out when testing a hypothesis, and we shall discuss each of them in detail later in this chapter. For the moment, we shall work swiftly through them to give a broad idea of the process. The *first step* we have already begun: define a working hypothesis. We also have to find some data with which to test the hypothesis. The General Household Survey asks a random sample of adults in households about the three matters with which we are concerned – sex, education and occupation – and data from this survey will do fine.

OCCUPATIONAL SEGREGATION IN GREAT BRITAIN

Before we start testing the working hypothesis, it would be helpful to know more about the extent of occupational segregation between men and women. There are two types of segregation, horizontal and vertical. Horizontal segregation occurs when men and women are concentrated in different jobs and vertical segregation when men and women have different pay and promotion prospects.

The GHS includes a variable, SEGEAD, which codes jobs according to their positions on the Registrar-General's classification of SEGs. This distinguishes employers, managers, professionals, non-manual and manual workers and so on. Exhibit 11.1 to Exhibit 11.5 show the distribution of this variable and tabulate it with SEX to indicate the extent of horizontal segregation.

To create these exhibits, open GHS95.SAV. Then obtain a summary of the variable SEGEAD to see the overall distribution of people in the sample between SEG categories by using the **Frequencies** procedure (Exhibit 11.1).

Select only those respondents in managerial or professional occupations (SEG categories 2, 4, 5 and 6) using the selection criterion **ANY(SEGEAD, 2,4,5,6)**; see Exhibit 11.2.

Crosstabulate this variable with SEX to see the extent to which there is an unequal distribution by sex between the SEG categories, asking SPSS for **row per cents** (Exhibit 11.3).

Exhibit 11.3 includes all managers and professionals, regardless of education. Next, select only those with degrees etc. using the variable EDLEV, which records respondents' highest educational qualification. In addition to selecting for managers and professionals, select those who have higher qualifications by adding the selection criterion **EDLEV GE 1 AND EDLEV LE 5** (see Exhibit 11.4). Repeat the crosstabulation for this subsample (Exhibit 11.5).

From Exhibit 11.3 we see that overall there is a greater proportion of men (66.6 per cent) than women (33.4 per cent) in management or professional occupations. Furthermore, we see in Exhibit 11.5 that this difference persists among those with higher qualifications.

The sample from the GHS includes 202 highly educated male professionals and managers, and 101 highly educated female professionals and managers (see Exhibit 11.5). The proportion of men in this subset of the sample is therefore 0.67. However, our interest is not primarily in the sample, but in the wider population. The question we then have to ask is whether we would be likely to have obtained this proportion if, in the population as a whole, there were more highly educated male professionals and managers than highly educated female professionals and managers.

SEGEAD SEG OF ADULTS

		Frequency	Percent	Valid Percent	Cumulative Percent
Valid	1 EMPLOYERS:LARGE	4	.1	.1	.1
	2 MANAGERS:LARGE	321	6.9	7.0	7.1
	3 EMPLOYERS:SMALL	125	2.7	2.7	9.8
	4 MANAGERS:SMALL	181	3.9	4.0	13.8
	5 PROF:SELF EMP	23	.5	.5	14.3
	6 PROF:EMPLOYEE	158	3.4	3.5	17.7
	7 INT NON-MAN ANC	445	9.6	9.7	27.5
	8 INT NON-M FOREMN	172	3.7	3.8	31.2
	9 JUNIOR NON-MAN	799	17.2	17.5	48.7
	10 PERSONAL SERVICE	217	4.7	4.7	53.4
	11 MANUAL:FOREMN/SV	226	4.9	4.9	58.3
	12 SKILLED MANUAL	448	9.7	9.8	68.1
	13 SEMI-SKILLED MANUAL	515	11.1	11.2	79.4
	14 UNSKILLED MANUAL	261	5.6	5.7	85.1
	15 OWN ACC NON-PROF	245	5.3	5.4	90.4
	16 FARMERS:EMP&MGRS	20	.4	.4	90.9
	17 FARMERS:OWN ACC	10	.2	.2	91.1
	18 AGRIC WORKERS	50	1.1	1.1	92.2
	19 ARMED FORCES	16	.3	.3	92.5
	20 FT STUDENT	249	5.4	5.4	98.0
	21 NEVER WORKED	93	2.0	2.0	100.0
	Total	4578	98.8	100.0	
Missing	−9	55	1.2		
Total		4633	100.0		

Exhibit 11.1   *Frequency table of SEGs*
Source: ONS, 1995

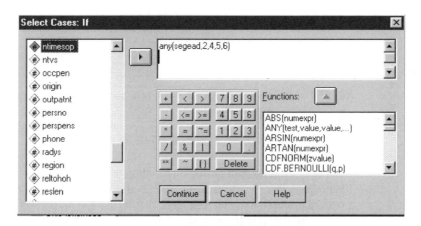

Exhibit 11.2   ***Select Cases: If*** *dialog box selecting managers and professionals*

SEGEAD SEG OF ADULTS * SEX SEX Crosstabulation

			SEX SEX		
			1 Male	2 Female	Total
SEGEAD SEG OF ADULTS	2 MANAGERS:LARGE	Count	205	116	321
		% within SEGEAD SEG OF ADULTS	63.9%	36.1%	100.0%
	4 MANAGERS:SMALL	Count	108	73	181
		% within SEGEAD SEG OF ADULTS	59.7%	40.3%	100.0%
	5 PROF:SELF EMP	Count	18	5	23
		% within SEGEAD SEG OF ADULTS	78.3%	21.7%	100.0%
	6 PROF:EMPLOYEE	Count	124	34	158
		% within SEGEAD SEG OF ADULTS	78.5%	21.5%	100.0%
Total		Count	455	228	683
		% within SEGEAD SEG OF ADULTS	66.6%	33.4%	100.0%

Exhibit 11.3   *Crosstabulation of SEG and sex, for managers and professionals*

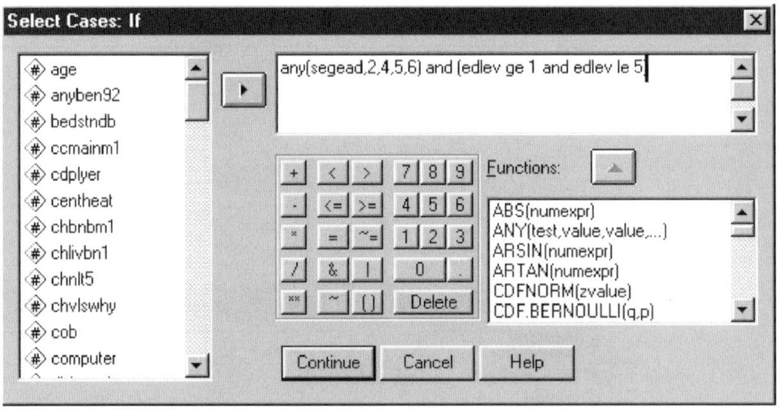

Exhibit 11.4   ***Select Cases: If*** *dialog box, selecting highly educated managers and professionals*

The question would be somewhat simpler to answer if we had started with a hypothesis that stated that there are equal numbers of highly educated men and women professionals and managers, that is, that the proportion of men to women is exactly 0.5. But if you look back to the working hypothesis we are using, it only states that that there are 'more' men than women, not any specific

SEGEAD SEG OF ADULTS * SEX SEX Crosstabulation

			SEX SEX		
			1 Male	2 Female	Total
SEGEAD SEG OF ADULTS	2 MANAGERS:LARGE	Count	81	57	138
		% within SEGEAD SEG OF ADULTS	58.7%	41.3%	100.0%
	4 MANAGERS:SMALL	Count	27	17	44
		% within SEGEAD SEG OF ADULTS	61.4%	38.6%	100.0%
	5 PROF:SELF EMP	Count	10	4	14
		% within SEGEAD SEG OF ADULTS	71.4%	28.6%	100.0%
	6 PROF:EMPLOYEE	Count	84	23	107
		% within SEGEAD SEG OF ADULTS	78.5%	21.5%	100.0%
Total		Count	202	101	303
		% within SEGEAD SEG OF ADULTS	66.7%	33.3%	100.0%

Exhibit 11.5   *Crosstabulation of SEG and sex for highly educated respondents*

proportion. To get round this difficulty, instead of testing the working hypothesis, we test its converse: that there are *equal* numbers of highly educated men and women in managerial and professional jobs. This is called the **null hypothesis** (abbreviated as H_0). Testing the null hypothesis has two major advantages. First, the proportion of men to women is stated specifically by the null hypothesis (it is 0.5). Secondly, it is a lot easier to falsify a hypothesis than it is to prove it. Consider a man accused of a crime. A single piece of evidence, such as an alibi, will be enough to prove his innocence. But a great deal of supporting evidence is required to show beyond all reasonable doubt that he is guilty. The same is true for statistical hypotheses. Thus, what we do is to try to find evidence to reject or **falsify** the null hypothesis. If we can reject the null hypothesis, the working hypothesis can be accepted as the only alternative.

Remembering that the immediate task is now to test the null hypothesis, we can choose a sampling distribution and a significance level, this being the *second step* of hypothesis testing. The distribution in this instance is the sampling distribution of proportions that we encountered previously in Chapter 10. This is a normal curve, with a mean equal to the presumed proportion in the population (p) and a standard deviation given by the standard error of the proportion ($SE(p)$).

The mean of the sampling distribution is easy to determine: the null hypothesis has specified that it is at 0.5 (50 per cent men and 50 per cent women). The standard error is given by

$$SE(p) = \sqrt{\frac{p(1-p)}{n}} \qquad (11.1)$$

where p is the hypothesized proportion in the population and n is the number of people in the sample. The 1995 GHS includes 303 people with higher educational qualifications working in managerial and professional jobs. These people constitute the sample and so n is equal to 303. Hence the standard error is

$$SE(p) = \sqrt{\frac{0.5(1-0.5)}{303}} = 0.0287 \qquad (11.2)$$

We also need to decide on a statistical **level of significance**: how prepared we are to be wrong about the conclusion we come to. We will use the 5 per cent level, indicating that any result so unlikely that it would only occur 5 per cent of the time will be enough to reject the null hypothesis. As we saw in Chapter 10, 95 per cent of the area of a normal curve falls within 1.96 standard deviations of the mean. 1.96 is called the **critical value**. If the null hypothesis is correct, we would expect the sample proportion to be less than 1.96 standard deviations away from the population proportion; alternatively, if it lies outside, it would be safe to reject the null hypothesis. The choice of a significance level and a critical value completes the second step of the testing process.

The *third step* involves computing the **test statistic** for the sample. In this case, the test statistic is known as the z score. The z score is the difference between the proportion of men in the sample ($\hat{p}$) and the hypothesized proportion in the population (p, which we have specified as 0.5), all divided by the standard error:

$$z = \frac{\hat{p} - p}{SE(p)} \qquad (11.3)$$

From the GHS, we find that of the 303 people with higher educational qualifications working in managerial and professional jobs, 202 are men, giving a sample proportion ($\hat{p}$) of $202/303 = 0.67$. In other words, 67 per cent of the 303 people in the sample are men. The z score is therefore equal to

$$z = \frac{\hat{p} - p}{SE(p)} = \frac{0.67 - 0.5}{0.0287} = 5.92 \qquad (11.4)$$

The *final step* in the testing process is to see whether the proportion from the random sample (0.67) is sufficiently far from the proportion assumed by the null hypothesis (0.5) to warrant the rejection of the null hypothesis. This means asking whether the sample proportion is so far from the hypothesized population proportion that one would be likely to get such a sample proportion in less than 5 per cent of samples by chance. This would be the case if the z score were greater than 1.96, or less than -1.96. It is actually equal to 5.92 and so we can safely reject the null hypothesis. This of course means that the working hypothesis, that there are still more highly educated men than women in managerial and professional jobs, can be accepted. We conclude that even among the higher strata of UK society, there is still a long way to go before there are truly equal opportunities for men and women.

In this introduction, we have gone very quickly over the stages of hypothesis testing to give an overview of the process, avoiding many of the issues. The next section discusses these stages in more detail.

THE PROCESS OF HYPOTHESIS TESTING

As we have seen in the example presented in the previous section, hypothesis testing involves working systematically through a sequence of four steps. The logic of testing demands that each of the steps be completed before one can conclude with a definite result. The steps are: make some appropriate assumptions; select a test statistic, sampling distribution and significance level; compute the value of test statistic; and make a decision to accept or reject the hypothesis.

STEP 1: MAKE ASSUMPTIONS

The guiding principle of hypothesis testing is that we make some assumptions about the social world and then see whether the data we possess could plausibly have come from such a world. For example, in the previous section we assumed that there are equal numbers of highly educated male and female professionals and managers. Then we tested data from a sample taken from the GHS to see whether the data could have come from this assumed world (it could not, so we concluded that there is no sex equality). The first step in hypothesis testing is therefore to decide what assumptions we want to make. The main assumption will be in the form of a statement that expresses some relationship between concepts among some defined set of people. This assumption is called the research hypothesis. Because it is easier to disprove a hypothesis than to prove it, it is usual to define a null hypothesis that expresses the inverse of the research hypothesis and then attempt to falsify this null hypothesis.

For example, a researcher might be interested in whether women are more afraid than men of walking down a dark street at night. The research hypothesis would be that women are more afraid than men. The null hypothesis would be that women are no more afraid than men. We would then see whether data about how afraid people say they are could have come from a world in which the null hypothesis is true, that is, from a world in which men and women are equally afraid. If the data showed that the null hypothesis was very unlikely to be true, we would have falsified the null hypothesis and obtained evidence in favour of the original research hypothesis that women are more afraid than men of dark streets.

Supposing that we can reject the null hypothesis that men and women are equally afraid of dark streets, we would accept the research hypothesis that women are *more* afraid than men. Yet, rejecting the null hypothesis says no more than men and women are not equally afraid. It could be that men are more afraid than women. However, the research hypothesis has explicitly stated that women are more afraid than men. For a reason that will become clear in a moment, this is known as a one-sided or **one-tailed test**. Now consider the null hypothesis that women have the same attitude to nuclear weapons as men. There seems to be no obvious reason why the corresponding research hypothesis should state that either men or women are more opposed to nuclear weapons. The research hypothesis should be that the attitudes of men and women are different, not stating the direction of the difference. This is an example of a two-sided or **two-tailed test**. We need to decide before proceeding with hypothesis testing whether the test is to be one- or two-tailed, because this can affect the conclusions that are drawn.

It is also important to be clear about those to whom the research hypothesis (and therefore the null hypothesis) applies. When we consider whether women are more afraid of dark streets than men, are we concerned with men and women in some specific city, in the whole of the country or in the whole of the world? Those to whom the research hypothesis is assumed to apply are known as the relevant **population**, or (rather grandiloquently) the **universe**. Being clear about the relevant population is important because the sample used to test the null hypothesis must be a random sample from this same population. For example, it is no good testing a hypothesis about the fears of men and women in the whole country using a random sample drawn from just one city.

Hypothesis testing, since it is based on inference from random samples, cannot yield conclusions in which one can have absolute confidence. Rather, conclusions are probabilistic, for example, that there is less than one chance in 20 that the distribution of men and women managers in a particular random sample could have come from a population that contained equal numbers of male and female managers. The consequence is that the best that hypothesis testing can achieve is a probabilistic statement: either that it is likely that the null hypothesis can be rejected, or that the evidence fails to warrant the rejection of the null hypothesis. As we shall see, these rather weak and guarded conclusions can nevertheless be useful.

STEP 2: CHOOSE CRITERIA FOR THE TEST

Once one has formulated a null hypothesis, it is necessary to decide on the indicators to be used. For example, we would need some measure of 'being afraid of dark streets': perhaps an answer to an attitude statement or some questions about respondents' actual behaviour. Then, one can collect or find data from an appropriate random sample drawn from the population of interest. The sample must be random, because we shall be using inferential tests that depend on the sample's randomness. It must be a sample from the relevant population because we shall be wanting to infer from the sample to that population.

Next, we need to select a test statistic: a statistic whose sampling distribution is known. As we saw in the previous chapter, a random sample is not guaranteed to be representative of the population from which it was drawn. However, we can estimate how likely it is that a sample will deviate from representativeness by reference to a sampling distribution (Chapter 10). In general, we calculate a test statistic from the data (the z score in the earlier example) and then use the sampling distribution of that test statistic to find the probability that the obtained value of the test statistic could have come from a population in which the null hypothesis is true.

There are a number of test statistics commonly used, each appropriate for different situations and different types of hypothesis. The second half of this chapter reviews several of them. For the moment, we shall focus only on the z score. This is the test statistic that is used when either the sample is large (more than about 100 respondents) or the distribution of data is known to be normally distributed. As a consequence of the central limit theorem (Chapter 10) we know that the sampling distribution of z is the normal curve with a mean of 0 and a standard deviation of 1.

In the next step of the hypothesis testing process, the test statistic (computed from the sample data) will be compared with the sampling distribution. This distribution shows the likelihood of getting any particular value of the test statistic on the assumption that the null hypothesis is true. If the value of the test statistic is so far from the mean of the distribution that the probability of getting such a value is very small, we will conclude that the null hypothesis must be rejected. What is meant by 'very small' is determined by our choice of the level of significance.

Another way of saying the same thing is that there are two reasons why the value of a test statistic might be far from that predicted by the null hypothesis. One reason is that the null hypothesis is wrong. The other reason is that, by chance, the sample is very unrepresentative. In either case, the result would be the same, a test statistic at an extreme of the sampling distribution. We cannot tell which of the two reasons is correct. However, if the chance of getting such a test statistic value is very small, less than the significance level, we conclude that it is the null hypothesis which is at fault, because the chances of getting such an unrepresentative sample are so small.

Suppose that we decide on a 5 per cent significance level. Provided that the null hypothesis is true, 95 per cent of samples will have values of the test statistic that are within 1.96 standard deviations of the sampling distribution mean (the logic here is the same as with confidence intervals). Therefore, we need to find whether the sample we have has a test statistic greater than 1.96 (or less than -1.96). If it does, we use this as evidence to reject the null hypothesis. The extreme ends of the sampling distribution are known as its **tails**, and the area including both tails is called the **critical region** (Exhibit 11.6). We reject the null hypothesis if the value of the test statistic falls into the critical region.

It is important to remember that with a 5 per cent significance level, on average five samples in every 100 will have a test statistic in the critical region even if the null hypothesis is true. This is because, by random chance, these 5 per cent of samples are very unrepresentative of the population. So the results of testing a hypothesis can only be probable rather than certain. We cannot be

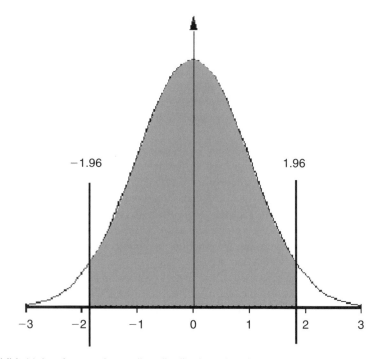

Exhibit 11.6   *A normal sampling distribution, showing the critical region for a 5 per cent significance level (the unshaded tails)*

completely sure that we are correct in rejecting the null hypothesis, only that it is probable that it is false.

The 5 per cent level of significance is the one that is most commonly used in sociological research, but other levels are possible. For example, one could use the 1 per cent level. Then, to reject the null hypothesis, it would be necessary to obtain a test statistic that was so far from the sampling distribution's mean that it would only occur one in 100 times when the null hypothesis is true. At first sight this appears to be a better significance level to use, because we stand less chance of incorrectly rejecting the null hypothesis. However, reducing the significance level from 5 to 1 per cent also means that there is more chance that the null hypothesis will be accepted when it is in fact false.

The possibility that we reject the null hypothesis although it is actually true is known as a **type I error**. The converse, the possibility that we accept the null hypothesis although it is actually false, is a **type II error** (see Exhibit 11.7). The aim is to minimize both type I and type II errors, but because they are the converse of each other, anything we do to reduce the type I error will increase the type II error and vice versa. The 5 per cent significance level gives a reasonable compromise between type I and type II errors.

Your decision	H_0 is actually...	
	False	True
Reject H_0	Correct decision	Type I error
Fail to reject H_0	Type II error	Correct decision

Exhibit 11.7   *Type I and type II errors*

STEP 3: COMPUTE THE VALUE OF THE TEST STATISTIC

Steps 1 and 2 have mainly been about making decisions about what kind of test to apply. In step 3, we proceed to apply these decisions to the calculation of the test statistic.

Whenever a hypothesis is tested, there is some summary statistic describing an attribute in the sample that is the focus of interest. For instance, in the example at the beginning of this chapter, the summary statistic was the proportion of men among highly educated managers and professionals. In order to test hypotheses based on this summary statistic, we need to find the statistic's sampling distribution. This is usually not known, so the statistic is transformed to a suitable test statistic whose sampling distribution is known. There are three test statistics that are in common use in sociological research: the z score, the t statistic and chi square. Each has its own specific use and its own sampling distribution. In this section, we will discuss only the first two, leaving chi-square to the end of the chapter.

The z score should only be used if some basic requirements about the data are met. These requirements are:

- The measurements are at the interval or ratio level.
- The observations are independent, that is, the value for each person does not depend on those of others in the sample. For instance, the age of each respondent is independent of the ages of the others. But it is quite likely that the friendship choices of respondents are not independent – if respondent A is a friend of respondent B, then B is likely to say that A is a friend and so the observations are not independent.
- The values are normally distributed in the population. While this can be true of some characteristics (e.g. IQ), it is much more often not the case (e.g. income is far from normally distributed). However, violation of this requirement is usually only serious if the sample size is small.
- The sample was selected using simple random sampling. Other random sampling designs are also possible, but correction factors have to be applied to the test statistics, a topic that is dealt with in advanced textbooks (e.g. Moser and Kalton, 1971; Kish, 1965).

Provided that these requirements are met, or sufficiently well met, you can proceed to calculate a test statistic.

THE NORMAL DISTRIBUTION AND Z SCORES

In the case of the example at the beginning of the chapter, the proportion of men to women was transformed to a z score by subtracting the hypothesized population proportion and dividing by the standard error. This gave a test statistic whose distribution is approximately normal with mean 0 and standard deviation 1 (standard normal).

A z score is an appropriate test statistic when the summary statistic on which the hypothesis is based is a proportion. It is also the appropriate test statistic when the hypothesis concerns the mean and the sample size is large, or when the standard deviation of the attribute in the population is known. For example, if a mean is being tested on the basis of a sample including more than 100 people, the z score is the correct test statistic to use. If the hypothesis concerned respondents' scores on the General Health Questionnaire (GHQ), a measure of general health (Bowling, 1991) for which the standard deviation in the population is known from previous studies, and the number of people in the sample was only 20, a z score would again be the appropriate test statistic to use. In other circumstances, the appropriate sampling distribution is not the normal, but one called Student's t distribution.

STUDENT'S t DISTRIBUTION AND THE t TEST STATISTIC

To calculate the standard error of a mean, you need to know the standard deviation of the population (equation (10.1)). Usually, however, this is not known and must therefore be estimated from the characteristics of the sample. While this is an acceptable thing to do, it does introduce a further source of uncertainty, for a sample may be as unrepresentative in its standard deviation as in its mean. The additional uncertainty is minimal if the sample is 'large', that is, if there are more than about 100 people. But with smaller samples, the test needs to be made more conservative, so that the null hypothesis is not rejected too easily. Instead of the normal distribution, a family of curves called Student's t distribution is used. These are 'flatter' than normal curves and have a greater proportion of their area in the tails (Exhibit 11.8). 'Student' was the pen-name of a statistician called William Gossett who discovered the effect of small sample sizes on the sampling distribution when working as a consultant for Guinness, the brewery, in the early twentieth century.

There is a slightly different Student's t distribution for every sample size, but as the sample size increases, the distributions become closer and closer to the shape of the normal distribution. The curves for sample sizes above 100 are indistinguishable from the normal curve (which is why the normal distribution can be used for large samples). Below 100, the shapes of the t distribution are tabulated in statistics texts according to the sample size minus one, a value called the **degrees of freedom** of the sample. Just as with the normal distribu-

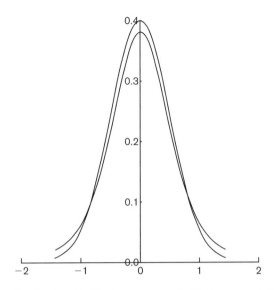

Exhibit 11.8   *Student's* t *distribution compared with the normal distribution (the
lower and wider curve is the* t *distribution for 5 degrees of freedom;
the other curve is the standard normal distribution)*

tion, the figures of interest are the critical values: the number of standard
deviations from the mean which includes 95 per cent of the area of the curve (or
99 per cent, depending on whether a 5 per cent or a 1 per cent significance level
is being used). For a normal curve and a two-tailed test, the critical value is
1.96. For a sample of 20, the critical value of the *t* distribution is 2.09 (this is the
value of the *t* distribution for a 5 per cent significance level and 19 degrees of
freedom). Thus, with a small sample of 20, if the standard error has to be
calculated from the sample itself, the value of the test statistic has to be slightly
larger than would be the case for a large sample in order to reject the null
hypothesis (greater than 2.09, rather than 1.96).

The *t* statistic is not used for hypotheses which consider proportions, because
the standard error of a proportion can be calculated directly from the population
proportions (equation (10.6)). There is no need to estimate standard deviations
from samples, and so no need to use the *t* distribution.

CALCULATING THE TEST STATISTIC AND THE CRITICAL VALUE

The only difference between the *z* score and the *t* statistic is the sampling
distribution against which the value is compared. The formula for the test
statistic itself is the same for both: it is the difference between the sample value
and hypothesized population value, divided by the standard error:

$$z = \frac{\overline{X} - \mu}{SE(\overline{x})} \text{ or } t = \frac{\overline{X} - \mu}{SE(\overline{x})} \tag{11.5}$$

This is the value that has to be compared with the critical value to see whether it lies within the critical region. The critical value is obtained from tables of the sampling distribution or calculated by computer program. The critical value depends on two factors as well as the sampling distribution: the level of significance and whether the test is one- or two-tailed.

To see why it matters whether the test is one- or two-tailed, consider a null hypothesis that the proportion of homosexuals in the population is 4 per cent. As was noted earlier, if the research hypothesis is that the population proportion is not equal to 4 per cent, we have a two-tailed test because the test checks both whether the mean is below and whether it is above 4 per cent. On the other hand, if the research hypothesis states that the proportion is less than 4 per cent, because we know for sure that the proportion is not more than 4 per cent, we have a one-tailed test. The important difference between one- and two-tailed tests is the areas of the sampling distribution that form the critical region. Exhibit 11.6 illustrates a normal sampling distribution for a two-tailed test at the 5 per cent significance level. The unshaded area, representing the critical region, occupies 5 per cent of the total area under the curve and is distributed equally on both sides of the mean. Exhibit 11.9 shows the curve with the critical region marked for a one-tailed test at the 5 per cent significance level. The critical region is all on one side of the mean, but still occupies 5 per cent of the total area. The edge of the critical region (the critical value) is at 1.645.

STEP 4: MAKE A DECISION

After all this preparatory work, the last step is relatively easy. Steps 1 and 2 defined a null hypothesis, a test statistic and a sampling distribution. In step 3, the test statistic was calculated and the critical value found. All that remains is to compare the value of the test statistic with the critical value to see whether it falls within the critical region (e.g. the unshaded portions of Exhibit 11.6 or Exhibit 11.9).

If the test statistic does fall into the critical region, the conclusion is that the null hypothesis can be rejected (remembering that there is a five in 100 chance of error about this conclusion for a 5 per cent significance level). Since either the null hypothesis or the research hypothesis must be true, rejecting the null hypothesis is equivalent to accepting the research hypothesis. Alternatively, if the test statistic does not get into the critical region, the null hypothesis cannot be rejected. The research hypothesis might still be true, but we have not found sufficient evidence to tell one way or the other.

ONE-SAMPLE AND TWO-SAMPLE TESTS

In all the examples we have met so far, the hypotheses have compared the sample statistic with a specified population parameter. For instance, we com-

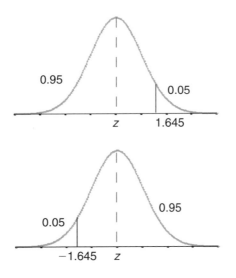

Exhibit 11.9   *One-tailed distributions*

pared the sample proportion of men in managerial and professional occupations with 0.5. Such tests are known as **one-sample** tests. Although the process of hypothesis testing is easier to follow with one-sample tests, in sociological research it is much more common to compare statistics from two samples. For example, we might be interested in whether the number of times men have visited their doctor in the last few weeks is different from the number of times women have done so, or whether the income of employed single men is higher than that of employed single women. In these examples, there are two independent samples (one of men and the other of women) and a summary statistic can be calculated for each (the mean number of times the doctor has been visited, or the mean income). The question is, are any differences in the means from the two samples just due to the fact that we are dealing with random samples that may not be representative, or are the differences in the means due to some real differences in the populations (of men and women) from which they were drawn?

It is fairly easy to extend the procedures we have been describing to the case of such **two-sample** tests. The general logic of hypothesis testing remains the same, as do the test statistics (the z score and the t statistic) and their sampling distributions. The main difference lies in the formulae used to calculate the standard errors.

If there are two samples, each with a mean (e.g. the mean incomes of men and women), the matter of interest is the size of the difference between the means. The research hypothesis is that there is a difference in incomes; the null hypothesis is that the mean incomes are the same, that is, the difference between the mean incomes of men and women is zero. The standard error is called the **standard error of the difference** and is given by the formula:

$$SE(\overline{X}_1 - \overline{X}_2) = \sqrt{\sigma^2 \left(\frac{1}{N_1} + \frac{1}{N_2} \right)} \qquad (11.6)$$

This is similar to the one-sample standard error of the mean (equation 10.1), but it includes the sizes of both samples, N_1 and N_2 (e.g. the number of men in the male sample and the number of women in the female sample).

For a hypothesis involving a difference in proportions, for example, that the proportion of chronically ill women is greater than the proportion of chronically ill men, the standard error of the difference of proportions is given by:

$$SE(p_1 - p_2) = \sqrt{pq \left(\frac{1}{N_1} + \frac{1}{N_2} \right)} \qquad (11.7)$$

This is the formula to use when the null hypothesis states that the two-samples are drawn from the same population of which proportion p has the attribute (e.g. being chronically ill) and proportion q is without the attribute (and therefore $q = 1 - p$).

Once the standard error has been calculated, the z score or t statistic can be found using variations on the ordinary formulae. For example, if the average income of the men in a sample is $\overline{X}_1$ and the average income of the women in the sample is $\overline{X}_2$, the z score for the difference of these means is

$$z = \frac{\overline{X}_1 - \overline{X}_2}{SE(\overline{X}_1 - \overline{X}_2)} \qquad (11.8)$$

ESTIMATING THE STANDARD DEVIATION FOR TWO-SAMPLE DIFFERENCES IN MEANS

Equation 11.6 provides the standard error of the difference, an essential ingredient in testing a hypothesis about sample means. However, in practice this equation is not very useful, because it is based on the population standard deviation, σ, and it is rare that this is known (the same does not apply to hypotheses involving differences in proportions, because the standard deviation is calculated from the population proportions and these are usually specified in the hypothesis). We have already encountered exactly this problem with the one-sample case and there the solution was to estimate the population standard deviation from the sample standard deviation. To take account of the extra uncertainty, the test statistic was compared to the t distribution rather than the normal distribution.

The same idea can be followed for the two-sample case, but with an additional complication arising from having two samples and thus two estimates of the population standard deviation. If both samples are from the same population, the two samples can be combined for the purpose of estimating the population standard deviation. The resulting estimate is known as the pooled standard deviation and the *t* test using this estimate is called a **pooled variance *t* test**. If the two samples come from different populations having different standard deviations, the two samples cannot be pooled to estimate the population standard deviation and another formula must be used instead to estimate the standard deviation. This estimate can then be used in the **separate variance *t* test**. However, for large samples (*N* larger than 1000), this and the pooled variance *t* test give almost identical results.

Procedure for choosing a test statistic and sampling distribution

When to use a test statistic:

- When you want to test a hypothesis about the value of some summary statistic (e.g. mean or proportion) describing an attribute of a population (age, gender etc.).

What you need to know to choose a test statistic and sampling distribution:

- The type of summary statistic to be used.
- The size of the sample (*N*).
- Whether the test is a comparison of two-samples, or a comparison of one sample with the population.
- Whether the standard deviation of the attribute in the population (σ) is known.

The procedure:

1. Calculate the standard error.
   (a) If the summary statistic is a mean:
      (i) if the standard deviation of the attribute in the population is known, for the one-sample case, the standard error of the mean is

$$SE(\overline{X}) = \frac{\sigma}{\sqrt{N}}$$

for the two-sample case, the standard error of the difference of two means is

$$SE(\overline{X}_1 - \overline{X}_2) = \sqrt{\sigma^2 \left(\frac{1}{N_1} + \frac{1}{N_2} \right)}$$

      (ii) if the standard deviation of the attribute is not known, for the one-sample case use

$$SE(\overline{X}) \approx \frac{s}{\sqrt{N}}$$

for the two-sample case use

$$SE(\overline{X}_1 - \overline{X}_2) \approx \sqrt{s^2\left(\frac{1}{N_1} + \frac{1}{N_2}\right)}$$

(this formula only applies if the standard deviations of the attribute in the two populations from which the samples were drawn are the same – if not, a more complicated formula for the 'pooled variance' must be used).

(b) If the summary statistic is a proportion:
for the one-sample case, the standard error of a proportion is

$$SE(p) = \sqrt{\frac{p(1 - p)}{N}}$$

for the two-sample case:

$$SE(p_1 - p_2) = \sqrt{pq\left(\frac{1}{N_1} + \frac{1}{N_2}\right)}$$

2. Choose a test statistic.

(a) If the number in the sample (or samples) is greater than 100 or the standard deviation of the attribute in the population is known, use the z score and the normal sampling distribution. For the one-sample case

$$z = \frac{\overline{X} - \mu}{SE(\overline{X})}$$

or, for proportions, use $\hat{p} - p$. For the two-sample case, use $\overline{X}_1 - \overline{X}_2$ in the numerator.

(b) If the number in the sample(s) is less than or equal to 100 and the standard deviation of the attribute in the population is not known (and therefore had to be estimated to calculate the standard error) use Student's t distribution:

$$t = \frac{\overline{X} - \mu}{SE(\overline{X})}$$

TESTING HYPOTHESES ABOUT CATEGORICAL VARIABLES

The z score and Student's t are the test statistics to use when the hypothesis concerns a variable measured at the interval or ratio level, such as income or the proportions of men and women. A different test statistic, known as **chi square** (χ^2, pronounced 'ky square'), is used for hypotheses involving categorical variables. For example, a random sample of people living within ten miles of a chemical incinerator in North-West England was surveyed by sending out a postal questionnaire (Twigger, 1995). However, the response rate was poor, despite reminder letters, at only about 37 per cent. Of the 1899 questionnaires sent out, only 711 were eventually returned. The researchers were worried whether the poor response rate had introduced a bias: perhaps those who did reply were different in some way from those who did not.

A straightforward (but not foolproof) test for such bias is to compare the characteristics of the sample who did reply with the characteristics of the population, known from Census returns. The researchers chose to do this with respect to the respondents' sex and age. The sex distribution of the respondents and the distribution that should have been obtained if the sample had followed the Census exactly, are shown in Exhibit 11.10. The top row of the table shows the **observed** counts, how many people of each sex were among the respondents. The bottom row shows the **expected** counts, how many men and women would be expected if the response had been exactly proportional to the distribution in the 1991 census. The figures in the two rows differ, but this is not surprising as the top row is based on a random sample. The critical question is, do the figures differ by more than might be expected by chance?

In this example, we have a categorical variable, sex, and need to test the null hypothesis that the distribution of men and women does not differ from that shown in the Census. The χ^2 statistic is calculated by squaring the difference between each expected count and the corresponding observed count, dividing by the expected count and summing these results over all the categories. Thus the χ^2 test statistic measures by how much the observed counts differ from the expected ones. If the observed counts are O_i and the expected counts are E_i, the χ^2 test statistic is given by the formula

$$\chi^2 = \sum \frac{(O_i - E_i)^2}{E_i} \qquad (11.9)$$

The meaning of a particular value of the test statistic will differ depending on the number of categories in the variable (2 in this case: men and women). This is taken into account by the **degrees of freedom**, which for this example is one less than the number of categories, that is, $2 - 1 = 1$.

The sampling distribution for the test statistic is called the chi-square distribution (see Appendix B). There is a slightly different chi-square distribution for each different number of degrees of freedom. In the same way as a z score was assessed by comparing it to the critical value of the normal distribu-

	Male	Female	Total
Respondents to survey	365	338	703
Survey percentage	51.9	48.1	100%
Census percentage	52.4	47.5	100%
Expected number	368	334	702

Exhibit 11.10 *Sex distribution of the survey sample and comparable data from the 1991 Census*

tion, so the χ^2 test statistic is compared with the critical value of the appropriate chi-square distribution. At the 5 per cent level with 1 degree of freedom, the critical value is 3.84. Thus the null hypothesis that the sample is not biased with respect to employment status can be rejected if the value of the test statistic is larger than 3.84. Applying equation 11.9 to the data in Exhibit 11.10 gives a value for the test statistic of 0.074. The null hypothesis cannot be rejected, providing some reassurance that the low response rate had not biased the sample.

The researchers also compared the distribution of age with the Census. Exhibit 11.11 shows the proportions in each of seven age categories with the corresponding Census proportions. Once again, we can apply Equation 11.9, using the top row as the observed counts and the bottom row as the expected counts. The χ^2 test statistic for this table is 46.4. Because the age variable is divided into seven categories, there are $7 - 1 = 6$ degrees of freedom. At the 5 per cent level, the critical value from chi-square tables is 10.64. Since the test statistic is much larger than the critical value, we must reject the null hypothesis and conclude that the age distribution in the sample is significantly different from that of the local population. In fact, it seems that survey respondents in the 25–44 age bracket are somewhat less likely to reply to the survey than are other age groups. This sample bias may have affected the results of the study.

In the above example, we compared the distribution of one categorical variable with its 'expected' distribution obtained from the Census. A more frequent use of the chi-square statistic is to compare a crosstabulation of two variables with the table that would be expected if the null hypothesis were true. As before, the aim of the test is to see whether any difference between the actual and expected tables could be due to chance, or whether it is more likely to be the result of some real effect. To illustrate this, let us look again at the table which formed the focus of Chapter 9, displayed again as Exhibit 11.12. This table has been obtained from a random sample of 2557 respondents taken from the population of Great Britain. As we demonstrated in Chapter 9, the table shows a relationship between gender and employment status: there is a moderate association such that men are more likely to be in full-time work than women. However, while this result is certainly true just for the respondents included in the table, we would probably be more interested in whether it is true for Great Britain as a whole. Are we safe in inferring from this sample to the country as a whole? The chi-square statistic can help in answering this question.

Age	18–24	25–34	35–44	45–54	55–64	65–74	75+	Total
Respondents	97	112	121	155	95	87	29	696
Row percentage	14%	16%	17%	22%	14%	13%	4%	100%
Census percentage	14%	21%	20%	15%	13%	10%	7%	100%
Expected count	99.8	145.0	140.9	102.6	89.4	72.7	45.5	695.9

Exhibit 11.11 *Age distribution of the survey sample and comparable data from the 1991 Census*

Employment status	Men	Women	All
In full-time work	1247	662	1909
In part-time work	118	530	648
Total	1365	1192	2557

Exhibit 11.12   *Employment status by sex*
Source: ONS, 1995
Note: 'Full-time' work is work for 30 and over hours per week.
'Part-time' work is work for more than 8 and less than 30 hours per
week. The 2076 who were not in work or worked less than 8 hours
per week are excluded from the table.

We need to follow the general procedure outlined at the beginning of this chapter. First, we formulate a research hypothesis. This hypothesis is that there is indeed an association between employment status and gender in Great Britain. The corresponding null hypothesis is that there is no association. The second step is to choose a test statistic, which in this case will be the chi-square test. We shall use the conventional 5 per cent level of significance. The third step is to compute the value of test statistic. For this, we shall need some expected values (E) to plug into Equation 11.9. These expected values are those that would be obtained if the null hypothesis were true: that is, if there were no association between the variables. These values have already been calculated in Chapter 9 as part of the procedure for computing the value of the phi coefficient of association and are shown in Exhibit 11.13 (a copy of Exhibit 9.15). You may want to go back to Chapter 9 if you are not clear about how the numbers in Exhibit 9.11 were obtained.

Applying equation 11.9 gives, for the top left cell,

$$\frac{(1247 - 1019.08)^2}{1019.08} = 50.975$$

for the top right cell,

$$\frac{(662 - 889.92)^2}{889.92} = 58.373$$

Employment status	Men	Women	All
In full-time work	1019	890	1909
In part-time work	346	302	648
Total	1365	1192	2557

Exhibit 11.13   *Employment status by sex, expected count when there is no*
association between the variables

for the bottom left cell,

$$\frac{(118 - 345.92)^2}{345.92} = 150.72$$

for the bottom right cell,

$$\frac{(530 - 302.08)^2}{302.08} = 171.966$$

so

$$\chi^2 = 431.49$$

We also need to know the number of degrees of freedom. This can be calculated using a rule of thumb: multiply one less than the number of rows in the table by one less than the number of columns. So a two by two table such as Exhibit 11.12 has $(2 - 1) \times (2 - 1) = 1$ degree of freedom.

THE MEANING OF DEGREES OF FREEDOM

Degrees of freedom measure the number of parameters which are not constrained by the structure of the table. In constructing the table of no association, Exhibit 11.13, we needed to ensure that the number of respondents included in the table (2557) was the same as in the observed table, Exhibit 11.12, and that the number of men and women, and full- and part-timers were the same as in Exhibit 11.12 Fixing all these numbers has the effect of constraining the counts in any three cells of the table (for otherwise the marginals would not be correct), leaving one count which is 'free' and which is determined by the fact that the table is required to show no association. There is therefore one degree of freedom. Another way of looking at the same thing is that as soon as one count has been calculated (for example, by multiplying the corresponding marginals and dividing by the table total, see Chapter 9), the other three follow immediately by subtraction from the marginals.

If the table has more than four cells, there are more counts which are 'free' and the number of degrees of freedom is greater than one. For example, a table of two variables, both having three categories, will have $(3 - 1) \times (3 - 1) = 4$ degrees of freedom.

To recap, for Exhibit 11.12 there is one degree of freedom. We now need to use a chi-square table (Appendix B) to determine the critical value for a 5 per cent significance level and 1 degree of freedom. It is 3.84.

This brings us to the fourth step of the general inference procedure: making a decision. Because 431.7, the chi-square test statistic, is greater than 3.84, the critical value, we can conclude that there is statistically significant difference between the observed and expected tables and that the chance of the null hypothesis being true is less than 5 per cent (in fact it is very much less than 5 per cent, 431.7 being very much greater than 3.84). This is strong evidence in favour of accepting the research hypothesis. We can reasonably infer from our finding that because there is an association between employment status and gender in the sample, the same is true of the population of Great Britain as a whole.

Because the formulae for phi and chi-square are similar (in fact, phi squared is equal to χ^2/N), and both are applied to tables, it is easy to get them confused. Remember that phi is a measure of association which will tell you about the strength and direction of the relationship *in the table*, while chi-square will tell you whether that relationship is likely to be found *in the population* as a whole.

In this example, we have traced through the calculation of chi square step by step. In practice, SPSS will compute the value of chi-square, the degrees of freedom and the probability level whenever you ask it to display a crosstabulation. You do not need tables of the chi-square distribution because SPSS determines the critical significance level for the value of the test statistic it has found.

OBTAINING χ^2 USING SPSS

To get SPSS to give a value and significance for chi square we need to select an additional feature in the **Crosstabs** dialog box.

Crosstabulation in SPSS is described at length in Chapter 9, but, to remind you, select **Analyze|Descriptive Statistics▸|Crosstabs** …. To obtain the cross-tabulation seen in Exhibit 11.12 we selected the recoded variable TIME (derived from WKSTATE) as the row or dependent variable, and SEX as the column or independent variable. Then we selected the **Statistics** dialog box to see Exhibit 11.14. Notice that the **Chi-square** box has been selected. The output from this procedure is seen in Exhibit 11.15.

The chi-square value that we are interested in is the Pearson chi-square value, 431.49. The observed significance is reported in the column headed **Asymp. Sig. (2 sided)** and is very low. In fact, it is so low that it is reported as **.000** which actually means that it is less than 0.0005. The conventional way to quote this result is that $p < 0.05$. The rule is that if the value is less than 0.05, then you can reject the null hypothesis that the two variables are independent.

Another way of looking at this is that a significance value of .000 means that the likelihood of getting a value for chi square as large as 431 by chance is very, very low. Remember that the value for chi square is derived from the difference between the observed data and the data expected *if there is no relationship*. Therefore the larger the difference and, consequently, the larger the value for chi square, the less likely it is that the two variables are unrelated or independent. However, there is always a possibility that even if the observed data are very different from your expected data, they could have occurred by chance. It is this chance that is reported as the significance value. So a

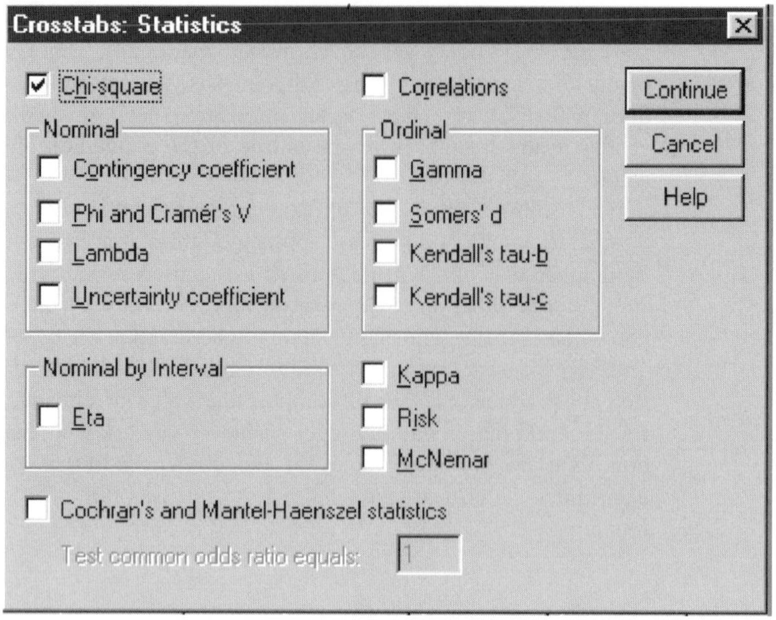

Exhibit 11.14   ***Crosstabs: Statistics*** *dialog box*

Chi-Square Tests

	Value	df	Asymp. Sig. (2-sided)	Exact Sig. (2-sided)	Exact Sig. (1-sided)
Pearson Chi-Square	431.490[b]	1	.000		
Continuity Correction[a]	429.599	1	.000		
Likelihood Ratio	453.760	1	.000		
Fisher's Exact Test				.000	.000
Linear-by-Linear Association	431.322	1	.000		
N of Valid Cases	2557				

[a] Computed only for a 2 × 2 table
[b] 0 cells (.0%) have expected count less than 5. The minimum expected count is 302.08

Exhibit 11.15   *Chi-square tests SPSS output*

significance value of 0.04 means that, despite rejecting the null hypothesis in support of the research hypothesis that there is a relationship between our two variables, there is a 4% chance that the data (and relationship) could have occurred by chance.

SUMMARY

Hypothesis testing is a useful research strategy for situations where you already have a fairly good understanding, sufficient to allow you to formulate a research hypothesis linking two or more relevant concepts. From the research hypothesis, you develop a working hypothesis, expressed in terms of indicators, and then its inverse, the null hypothesis. It is the latter that is tested against data obtained from a random sample of the appropriate population. Hypothesis testing involves four steps: first, make assumptions about the situation that is being researched; second, choose the population, define the sample, select a test statistic, a sampling distribution and a significance level; third, calculate the test statistic and, if necessary, its degrees of freedom; and finally, compare the value of the test statistic with the critical value of the sampling distribution and decide whether to accept or reject the research hypothesis.

The z score is used as a test statistic when the hypothesis concerns the mean of a variable measured at the interval or ratio level and the number of people in the sample is large. Student's t is used when the sample is small. The z score is also used for hypotheses involving proportions. Chi square is the test statistic to use for hypotheses involving categorical variables, for example, when testing hypotheses about tables.

EXERCISES

Exercise

The following exercises are based on the 1995 GHS data set.

1. Using the variable SOCLASE, test the hypothesis that social class IIIN (skilled non-manual) includes more women than men. If you find the hypothesis confirmed, explain why there are more women than men.
2. Test the hypothesis that the mean earnings of men and women are different. (Should this be a one- or a two-tailed test?)
3. Are the 'geeks' who invest first in audio technology also likely to be the first to buy a home computer? Begin to investigate this by constructing a table of COMPUTER by CDPLYER, and drawing conclusions from the values of phi and chi-square. (You would need data obtained from a panel study, visiting the same respondents on at least two different occasions, to obtain a definite answer to this question. Explain why.)

MODELLING DATA

12

CONTENTS

Much of this book has been concerned with descriptive statistics, although in the previous two chapters we turned to seeing how one can make inferences to a wider population. In this chapter we take statistical analysis one stage further, to see how models of the social world can be developed and tested that aim not only to describe but also to understand social relationships

A **model** is like a theory in that it proposes relationships between concepts. Usually, statistical models are expressed in a mathematical form, typically as equations, so that the relationships can be defined quite precisely. You will already have encountered one example of a model in Chapter 8 (equation (8.26)).

No model can ever take account of all the complexities of the social world. In order to be tractable and useful, a model needs to be a simplification of reality. For example, a model which accounted for respondents' income in terms of variables such as education, sex and job experience may succeed in explaining a great deal, but nobody would assume that education, sex and experience exhaust the factors which affect a person's income. The model focuses on those factors which it is hoped are the most important and the most theoretically interesting.

The objective of model building is to find a model that is powerful in explaining the phenomenon of interest, but that is also as simple as possible and that fits the data. Once a model has been formulated it can be tested using one of the many statistical techniques that determine whether a model conforms to a given set of data. Because of measurement error, the effects of random sampling from a population and the omission of some of the less important factors, a useful model will never fit the data exactly. Statistical techniques therefore also provide criteria for deciding whether a model's fit is as good as could be expected given these various sources of error.

There are two approaches to modelling. If you already have a well-worked-out model, you can use the data to confirm (or reject) it according to how well it fits the data. This is known as **confirmatory** analysis. Alternatively, if you are less sure of your model and the model does not fit well, you can modify it to try to find one that fits better. This is called an **exploratory** approach. Of course, if you have amended the model to make the fit as good as possible, you can no longer use that same data set to give the model a rigorous test. You need to follow your exploratory work with a confirmatory analysis on a different data set, perhaps using a different sample from the same population.

In the following sections, we shall illustrate the process of modelling through explanations of two of the most powerful statistical modelling techniques, multiple regression and loglinear analysis. We only have space to provide an introduction here. To use them to their full potential you will need to consult more advanced texts. Some suggestions can be found in the Further Reading section at the end of the chapter. There are a number of other modelling techniques that are appropriate to specific kinds of model, and the final section will briefly review these.

MULTIPLE REGRESSION

In Chapter 8, on bivariate analysis, we described the regression equation which related one dependent and one independent variable (this might be a good time to look back over that chapter, because this one will draw on many of the ideas first presented there). Although it was not described in that way, the bivariate regression equation is an example of a statistical model. In fact, it is one of the simplest such models. In this section we shall be seeing how it can be developed in order to build models which include not just one independent variable, but several.

The general regression equation introduced in Chapter 8 is

$$Y = a + bX + \varepsilon \tag{12.1}$$

This equation says that the value of the dependent variable (Y) can be predicted by the value of the independent variable (X) multiplied by a coefficient (b), plus a constant (a). An 'error' component (ε) is then added which records the extent to which the value of the dependent variable is not in fact accurately predicted by the independent variable. As we saw in Chapter 8, another way of putting this is that the variance of Y is explained by the variance of X and by a random component uncorrelated with X. Both X and Y must be variables measured at the interval level because calculating the regression equation involves doing arithmetic on the values of the variables, an operation which is only appropriate for interval-level variables.

The random component, ε, represents the effect of all the other factors in the world which have an influence on the dependent variable, Y, other than the one independent variable in the equation, X. For example, we might have a model which suggested that a country's infant mortality rate depends in part on the rate of illiteracy among women (uneducated women are less likely to know how to keep themselves and their babies healthy). Using the SID data, we find that 73 per cent of the variance in infant mortality is explained by the proportion of women who are illiterate, and the two variables are related by the regression equation:

$$Y = 13.1 + 1.36X + \varepsilon \qquad (12.2)$$

Of course, it is likely that there are also many other variables which affect the infant mortality rate. A more refined model could also include some of these. For example, it is possible that infant mortality is also influenced by the degree to which the country has been urbanized. We might suppose that infant mortality would be lower in urban environments than in predominantly rural ones. This can be investigated by adding a further variable, the percentage of the population living in urban areas. The model would then include two independent variables, X_1 and X_2, standing for female illiteracy rate and urbanization respectively:

$$Y = a + b_1 X_1 + b_2 X_2 + \varepsilon \qquad (12.3)$$

If we fitted this model, we would expect that the proportion of variance explained would increase to reflect the additional explanatory power of the second independent variable. This is in fact the case. The improved model is:

$$Y = 46.9 + 1.10X_1 - 0.50X_2 + \varepsilon \qquad (12.4)$$

which has an R^2 (the proportion of variance explained) of 77 per cent, a modest increase of 4 per cent over the original model of Equation 12.2.

There are several points to make about this new model. First, the prediction of a country's infant mortality rate is now found from considering both the level of female illiteracy and the extent of urbanization. Secondly, both equations (12.2) and (12.3) include an 'error' term, ε, to represent the variance left unexplained by the independent variables. The unexplained variance in the second equation is less than in the first, because we have explained more of the variation in the dependent variable. This can be seen from the increase in the value of R^2 from 73 per cent to 77 per cent. Thirdly, each b parameter indicates the effect of one independent variable on the dependent variable, holding the other independent variable constant. Notice that the value of b_1, the coefficient for female illiteracy, has changed slightly as a result of introducing urbanization as an additional independent variable.

Suppose that we had two countries with exactly the same level of female illiteracy, but one country was 10 per cent more urbanized than the other (that is, the value of the urbanization variable was 0.1 greater for one country than the other). Then Equation 12.3 would predict that the infant mortality rate for the second country would be

$$0.50 \times 0.1 = 0.05$$

lower than in the first (lower because the b_2 coefficient for variable X_2 is -0.5, i.e. negative).

As we saw in Chapter 9 when considering crosstabulations, holding one variable constant in this way and examining the effect of another variable is often called 'controlling' for the first variable. The b coefficients are properly called **partial regression coefficients**, 'partial' because they are the coefficients obtained when controlling for the other independent variables.

We can extend the model by including any number of additional independent variables, each of which may have some influence on the dependent variable. The principle is exactly the same, regardless of whether we use one, two or more independent variables. However, including too many independent variables brings with it disadvantages which increase as the number of variables grows. First, a model with many variables is inevitably a very complicated model and therefore difficult to interpret and understand. Secondly, the additional variables may not actually contribute to explaining much of the variance; we shall shortly see how one can assess the importance of each of the variables in a multiple regression. Thirdly, as the number of variables increases, so the number of cases (i.e. the size of the sample) has to be greater in order to obtain results that can be used to infer reliably to the population as a whole. In practice, regression equations with more than five or six independent variables are not often useful.

When we introduced regression in Chapter 8, we did so by drawing a regression line on a scatterplot that showed points for each of the cases in the data. Exhibit 8.26 displayed the scatterplot for the two variables, infant mortality and female illiteracy. If we now wanted to include the urbanization variable, the points would each have to represent three values (a country's infant mortality rate, female illiteracy and urbanization) and the only way to do this is to display them in three-dimensional space, rather than on a flat, two-dimensional plot. Exhibit 12.1 shows a three-dimensional plot of infant mortality, illiteracy rate and urbanization created by SPSS.

In three dimensions, what was a regression line for a bivariate analysis becomes a **regression plane**. Imagine a cloud of points in space and a flat plane drawn through them. For the two-variable regression illustrated in Exhibit 8.26, the regression coefficient, b, is proportional to the angle of the line. With three variables, there are two partial regression coefficients, one for each independent variable, which are related to the angles of the regression plane relative to each of the independent variables' axes.

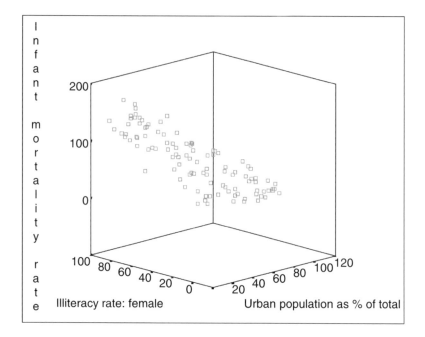

Exhibit 12.1   *Three-dimensional plot of infant mortality, illiteracy rate and urban*
population
Source: World Bank, 1992

While it is just about possible to imagine a cloud of points in three-dimensional space, if there are more than two independent variables, we would need four or more dimensions in which to draw the points. Although a geometrical representation of the regression becomes impossible with more than two independent variables, the principles and the methods of calculation remain the same, no matter how many variables there are in the equation.

ASSESSING THE IMPORTANCE OF THE INDEPENDENT VARIABLES

Earlier in this section, we first fitted a model which predicted the countries' infant mortality rates from their rates of female illiteracy and then added a second independent variable, the countries' degree of urbanization. The second model explained slightly more of the variance in infant mortality, as shown by R^2 increasing from 73 per cent to 77 per cent. Since the increase in R^2 is so small, we might want to ask whether the two independent variables are both needed in the equation and if so what their relative importance is.

First, consider whether they are both needed. The usual way to answer this is to test the hypotheses that the regression coefficients, b_1 and b_2, are significantly different from zero. (If either b is not significantly different from zero, the corresponding variable has no significant effect on the dependent variable and can be omitted from the model.) These hypotheses can be tested using a t test (see Chapter 11), comparing the coefficient divided by its standard error with Student's t distribution with degrees of freedom two less than the number of cases.[1] In the SID data set there are 105 countries with data on all three variables. The t ratio for female illiteracy is 11.78 and for urbanization is -4.67, both with 103 degrees of freedom (column 5 of Exhibit 12.2). The probability that values as high as these would be obtained if the null hypothesis were true is very small, and so in both cases we can safely reject the hypothesis that the regression coefficient is zero.

Even if both variables make statistically significant contributions, one may be much more important than the other. A way to assess their relative importance is to compare the absolute magnitudes of the b coefficients (1.10 for female illiteracy and 0.50 for urbanization – column 2 of Exhibit 12.2). From these it looks as though female illiteracy may be more important (1.10 is larger than 0.50). However, this may be a consequence of there being more variance in the data on female illiteracy than urbanization. This can be dealt with by standardizing all the variables in the regression to the same mean and variance by calculating z scores (see Chapter 7) and recalculating the parameters. The regression coefficients of such a standardized regression model are called **beta** (β) coefficients and for the model of Equation 12.3 are 0.69 for female illiteracy and -0.27 for urbanization (column 4 of Exhibit 12.2), confirming that female illiteracy is more important than urbanization in explaining infant mortality rates. The ratio of the beta coefficients is not much different from the ratio of the b coefficients because in this example the standard deviations of the two variables are not very different.

Coefficients[a]

Model		Unstandardized Coefficients		Standardized Coefficients			Correlations		
		B	Std. Error	Beta	t	Sig.	Zero-order	Partial	Part
1	(Constant)	46.939	8.176		5.741	.000			
	ILLITF Illiteracy rate: female (% of females age 15+)	1.103	.094	.689	11.780	.000	.852	.759	.554
	URBPOP Urban population as % of total	−.504	.108	−.273	−4.673	.000	−.684	−.420	−.220

[a] Dependent Variable: INFMOR Infant mortality rate (per thous. live births)

Exhibit 12.2   *SPSS coefficients for the multiple regression of infant mortality against female illiteracy and per cent urban population*

[1] Strictly speaking, it is inappropriate to carry out inferential tests on these data, since they describe a population (all the countries of the world). Although some countries are not represented, this is because of missing data, not because we have a random sample. However, the t test is a useful criterion, even if its results cannot be interpreted in terms of inferential statistics.

Beta coefficients will tell you how much each independent variable contributes to the predicted value of the dependent variable. Another way of considering importance is to ask how much less variation in the dependent variable would be explained if each independent variable was removed from the model. For our example, this would mean finding the reduction in R^2 for the model with female illiteracy as the sole independent variable, expressed as a proportion of the R^2 of the model with both independent variables, and the corresponding proportional reduction in R^2 for a model with just urbanization compared with the full model. These proportional reductions in R^2 are called **partial correlation coefficients** and can be thought of as the correlations between the dependent and the independent variables, controlling for the effect of any other independent variables in the model. For Equation 12.3, the partial correlation coefficients are 0.76 for female illiteracy and -0.42 for urbanization (column 8 of Exhibit 12.2); again we find the same story, female illiteracy makes more difference than urbanization.

SELECTING A MODEL

It has probably already occurred to you that there must be other important determinants of infant mortality beyond the rate of female illiteracy and the degree of urbanization of a country. Although just using those two variables accounts for 77 per cent of the variance in infant mortality rates, it seems very likely that the level of economic development (measured, for example, by the gross national product), the availability of medical facilities, the average size of families and a host of other factors will also have some explanatory power. The SID data set allows us to explore the influence of some but not all of these. Unfortunately, if we add all the possible variables into the regression equation, we will have a model which is very complicated and difficult to interpret. It may also include variables that, while contributing a little to the explained variance, are nevertheless not very important compared with others in the model. Moreover, the standard errors of the coefficients in a complex model will be higher than for a relatively simple model.

For these reasons, it is a good idea to use a modelling strategy which aims to minimize the number of variables in the final regression equation. There are two basic ways of doing this. The first is to start with a model with just one independent variable (the most important one, using one of the criteria suggested above), and then add the next most important variable and so on until the model fit does not improve significantly with the addition of further variables. This method is called **forward selection**. Alternatively, you can start with a model including all the likely variables and successively eliminate them, starting with the least important, until the removal of a variable makes the fit decrease significantly. This is called **backward elimination**. In either case, the test of whether the fit has significantly improved (or got significantly worse, for backward elimination) is based on an assessment of the change in the model's R^2 as a result of adding (or removing) a variable. A third procedure, called

stepwise selection, alternates between forward and backward fitting, adding the next most important variable and then considering all the variables now in the equation to see whether any should be removed. The following section uses SPSS to find a model predicting infant mortality from four independent variables using stepwise selection.

STEPWISE REGRESSION USING SPSS

The following example uses stepwise multiple regression to find a model to explain variations in infant mortality rates among countries of the world.

For the first part of this example we use the SPSS regression procedure to regress infant mortality (INFMOR) against the following independent variables: female illiteracy rate (ILLITF), population growth (POPGROW), energy consumption (ENERGCON) and population per doctor (DOCTOR).

First, we open the SID data set as usual. We then use the **Matrix** option in the **Graphs|Scatter**... procedure to create several plots at once in order to decide whether any transformations are necessary. Exhibit 12.3 is a matrix scatterplot of INFMOR, ILLITF, POPGROW, ENERGCON and DOCTOR.

If you look down the first column of the matrix scatterplot in Exhibit 12.3 you

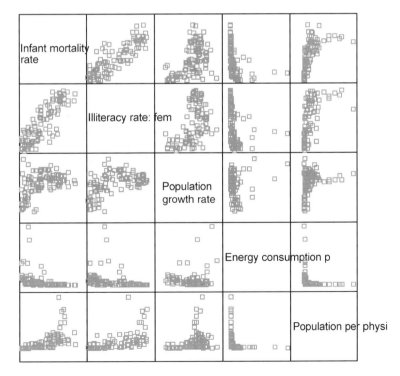

Exhibit 12.3   *Matrix scatterplot of the untransformed variables*

will see that `ILLITF` and `POPGROW` demonstrate a fairly linear scatter of data points. In comparison, `ENERGCON` and `DOCTOR` show a curvilinear relationship with `INFMOR`. This indicates that it would be desirable to transform these variables to make the relationship more linear, as described in Chapter 8. We shall try the log transformation for each variable using the **Compute** command in SPSS. Repeating the matrix scatterplot gives Exhibit 12.4. It appears that log population per doctor (`LOGDOC`) and log energy consumption (`LOGENG`), now have relationships with `INFMOR` that are nearly linear.

We are now ready to enter the variables into the regression by selecting **Analyze|Regression ▶|Linear** .... Exhibit 12.5 shows `INFMOR` as the dependent variable with `ILLITF`, `POPGROW`, `LOGENG` and `LOGDOC` entered as the independent variables. In order to perform a stepwise regression, we need to select **Stepwise** from the **Method:** drop-down list.

Examination of the model summary (Exhibit 12.6) and the coefficients (Exhibit 12.7) reveals that the most powerful predictor of infant mortality rate is female illiteracy, followed by energy consumption and then population growth. Population per doctors was excluded from the model.

The final model, model 3, can be represented by the equation

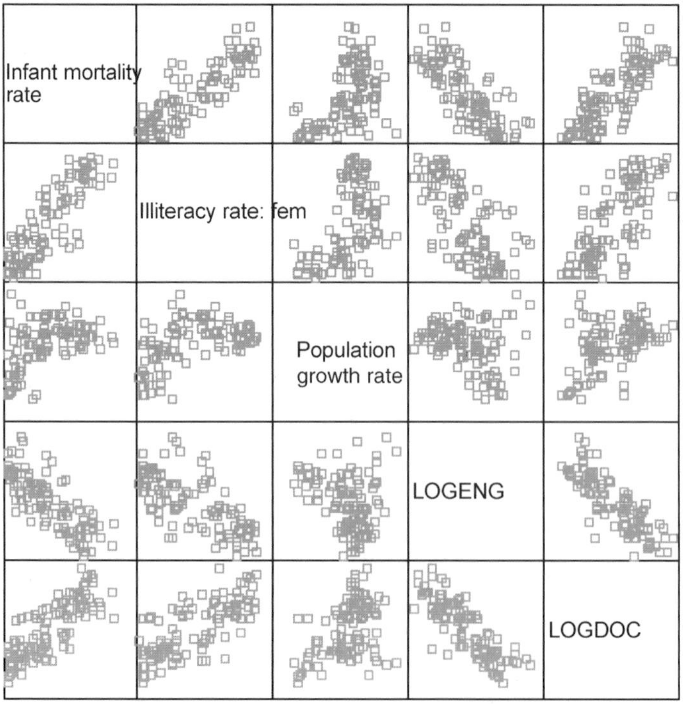

Exhibit 12.4   *Matrix scatterplot of the transformed variables*

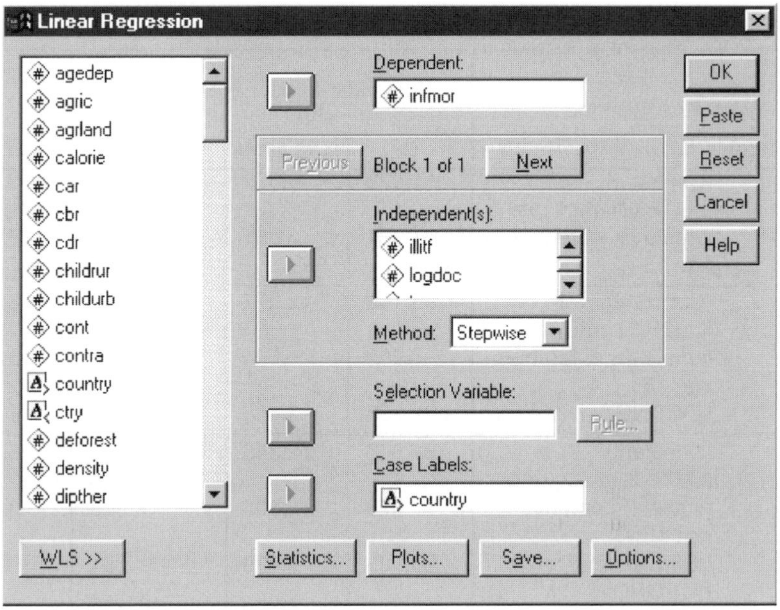

Exhibit 12.5   *Linear Regression* dialog box for stepwise multiple regression

Model Summary[d]

Model	R	R Square	Adjusted R Square	Std. Error of the Estimate
1	.862[a]	.743	.741	22.5201
2	.903[b]	.815	.811	19.2028
3	.907[c]	.823	.818	18.8686

[a] Predictors: (Constant), ILLITF Illiteracy rate: female
(% of females age 15+)

[b] Predictors: (Constant), ILLITF Illiteracy rate: female
(% of females age 15+), LOGENG

[c] Predictors: (Constant), ILLITF Illiteracy rate: female
(% of females age 15+), LOGENG, POPGROW
Population growth rate

[d] Dependent Variable: INFMOR Infant mortality rate
(per thous. live births)

Exhibit 12.6   *Model Summary of the stepwise regression*

Coefficients[a]

Model		Unstandardized Coefficients		Standardized Coefficients		
		B	Std. Error	Beta	t	Sig.
1	(Constant)	11.678	4.096		2.851	.005
	ILLITF Illiteracy rate female (% of females age 15+)	1.384	.081	.862	17.174	.000
2	(Constant)	86.100	12.377		6.957	.000
	ILLITF Illiteracy rate female (% of females age 15+)	.982	.094	.612	10.457	.000
	LOGENG	−22.988	3.668	−.367	−6.268	.000
3	(Constant)	81.508	12.348		6.601	.000
	ILLITF Illiteracy rate female (% of females age 15+)	.879	.104	.548	8.454	.000
	LOGENG	−23.903	3.629	−.381	−6.587	.000
	POPGROW Population growth rate	4.751	2.213	.106	2.147	.034

[a] Dependent Variable. INFMOR Infant mortality rate (per thous. live births)

Exhibit 12.7   *Coefficients of the stepwise regression*

$$\text{INFMOR} = 81.5 + 0.879\text{ILLITF} - 23.9\text{LOGENG} + 4.75\text{POPGROW} + \varepsilon$$

$$(12.5)$$

In this model ILLITF and POPGROW have a positive relationship with INFMOR; the greater the female illiteracy and the greater the population growth, the greater the infant mortality. However, LOGENG, transformed energy consumption is shown to have a negative relationship with infant mortality; the lower the energy consumption, the greater the infant mortality.

ASSUMPTIONS AND HOW TO CHECK THEM

While multiple regression is a very powerful method of model building, it has dangers. In particular, it will always provide some results, even if they are meaningless because the data violate the assumptions on which regression is based. It is therefore always important to be aware of these assumptions and to check that they are satisfied. The most important assumptions are as follows:

- The dependent variable is normally distributed for any particular set of values of the independent variables. This implies that the dependent variable must be continuous and measured at the interval level (see Chapter 1) and that the error term (ε) is also normally distributed, with constant variance.

- All the relevant independent variables have been included in the model.
- The relationship between the dependent variable and the independent variables is linear, i.e. the equation is a sum of terms.
- The variables have been accurately measured.

The best way to check whether these assumptions are met is to examine the **residuals** (see Chapter 8) that are left when a model is fitted to the data. A residual is the difference between an actual, measured value of the dependent variable and the value predicted from the right-hand side of the regression equation. If the assumptions are satisfied, we expect these residuals to be normally distributed and there to be no relationship between the predicted values of the dependent variable and their corresponding residuals.

Rather than use the values of the residuals themselves, it is helpful to standardize them so that they have a mean of 0 and a standard deviation of 1. Whether the residuals are normally distributed can be checked by getting SPSS to draw a normal probability plot. This plots the cumulative distribution of the (standardized) residuals against the expected normal distribution. The points for the residuals should be along a straight line; if they are not, the deviation shows how their distribution differs from normality. Another plot will show whether there is a relationship between the residuals and the predicted values of the dependent variable; the points should be scattered all over the plot with no clear pattern.

To see what the residuals look like when an inappropriate model is tried, consider the results of regressing infant mortality rate against the gross national product per head and the population growth rate as independent variables. R^2 is 0.51, but the residual plots show that the assumptions of multiple regression are being violated. Exhibit 12.8, a normal probability plot, clearly shows that the points do deviate from the expected normal distribution. Exhibit 12.9, a plot of the residuals against the dependent variable, shows a curvilinear pattern of points, suggesting that the error term in the regression does not have constant variance. The problems can be corrected by applying a log transformation to the dependent variable and to one of the independent variables, GNP per head (see Chapter 8). The resulting model has a much improved fit (R^2 is 0.86) and the residual plot no longer shows a pattern (Exhibit 12.10).

OUTLIERS

Transforming the data by taking the logarithm of the dependent variable has yielded a model which fits the data quite well and where the regression assumptions seem to be adequately satisfied. Nevertheless, the residual plot (Exhibit 12.10) shows that some countries have large residuals and the model fits them rather poorly. It may be that these countries are in some way 'special' and need to be considered separately, outside the model. It is possible that an

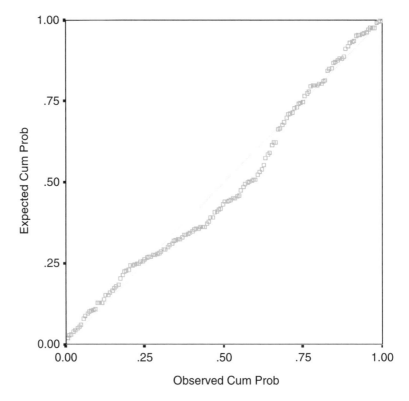

Exhibit 12.8   *Normal probability plot from regressing infant mortality rate against
GNP per head and the population growth rate*

important variable which influences the infant mortality rates of these countries
has been omitted from the analysis. Or it may be that these data points are wrong
as a result of errors in data collection. In any event, such **outliers** always deserve
some attention.

Outliers can have an undue effect on the magnitude of regression coefficients.
If an outlier is both distant from the regression line and has an unusually large
value on an independent variable (referred to as its **leverage**), it will have a
major influence on the slope of the regression line and the slope may change
substantially if the outlier is omitted from the data set. The degree to which an
outlier does have an influence on the model coefficients can be assessed by a
measure called **Cook's distance**. The country with the largest Cook's distance is
Kuwait, with a distance of 0.13, compared with the mean over all countries of
0.007. Exhibit 12.11 shows the scatterplot created by plotting Cook's distance
against logged infant mortality. The values for Cook's distances can be saved
with the regression by selecting **Save...** from the **Linear Regression** dialog box
(Exhibit 12.5) and then selecting **Cook's** from the **Distance** box.

One way of finding out more precisely what influence an outlier has is to
repeat the regression, but omitting the outlier. This will yield different values R^2

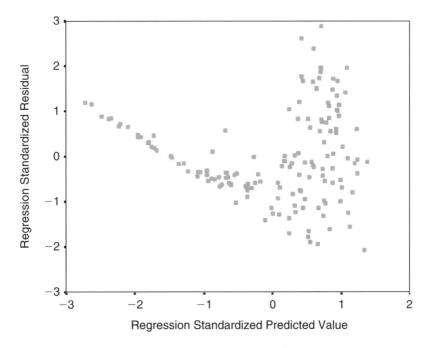

Exhibit 12.9   *Plot of residuals from regressing infant mortality rate against GNP per head and the population growth rate*

and the regression coefficients will be substantially different if the case is influential. In fact, omitting Kuwait causes R^2 to increase from 0.862 to 0.865, the coefficient for population growth rate to change from 0.132 to 0.14 and the coefficient for log GNP per head to change from -0.457 to -0.446. All this suggests that the processes that affect infant mortality in Kuwait are quite different from those in the rest of the world and it should therefore not be included in the regression.

DUMMY VARIABLES

The regression equations we have considered so far have involved only variables measured at the interval level. This is because regression requires that the values of the variables be subjected to arithmetic operations (for example, each independent variable is multiplied by its regression coefficient, b), and arithmetic can only legitimately be done on interval-level variables. Unfortunately, this is a significant constraint in much sociological analysis, particularly when using data about individuals.

There is, however, a 'trick' which can be used to introduce categorical-level variables as independent variables in a regression equation. This trick depends

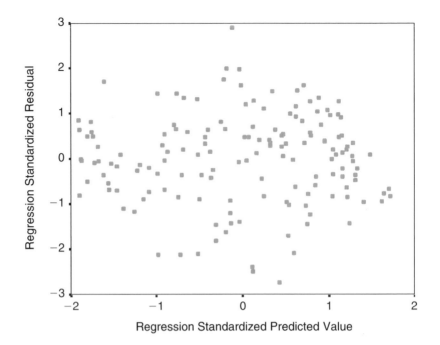

Exhibit 12.10   *Plot of residuals from regressing logged infant mortality rate against logged GNP per head and the population growth rate*

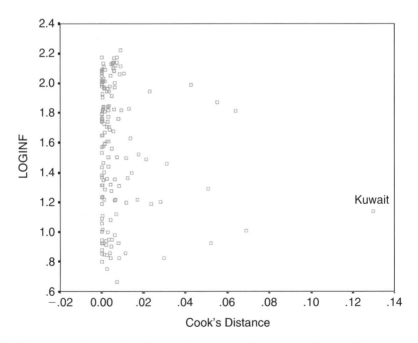

Exhibit 12.11   *Scatterplot of logged infant mortality rate and Cook's distances*

on the fact that a variable with just two values such as sex, even if measured at the categorical level, can be coded with 0 and 1 (e.g. 0 for men and 1 for women) and can then be treated as though it were interval in a regression equation. For example, let us see the effect of sex on respondents' income, using the General Household Survey. We can construct a regression model with usual gross earnings as the dependent variable, age and number of hours worked per week (both interval level-variables) as two of the dependent variables, and sex (recoded to 0 for men and 1 for women) as the third variable. The b coefficient for sex will then indicate the predicted extra income resulting simply from being female, controlling for age and hours of work.

Unfortunately, the model fits rather badly ($R^2 = 0.163$). The normal probability plot indicates that this is because the residuals are not normally distributed (Exhibit 12.12). A log transformation of the usual gross weekly earnings variable might improve matters. That this is so is shown in Exhibit 12.13, another normal probability plot, but now with the log of earnings (LOGEARN). A model with log usual gross earnings as the dependent variable and age, working hours per week (WORKHRS) and sex as the dependent variables has an R^2 of 0.396 (Exhibit 12.14). The b coefficient for sex is -0.104 (Exhibit

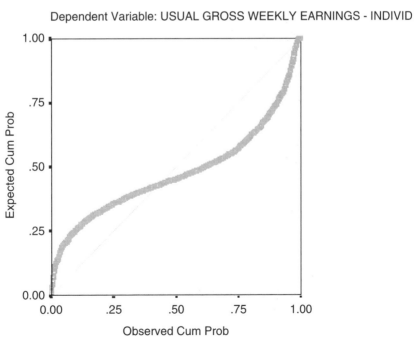

Exhibit 12.12   *Normal probability plot for regressing usual weekly earnings against age, hours of work and sex*
Source: ONS, 1995

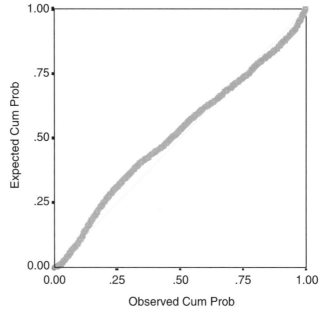

Exhibit 12.13   *Normal probability plot from regressing the logarithm of usual gross weekly earnings against age, hours of work and sex*
Source: ONS, 1995

Model Summary[d]

Model	R	R Square	Adjusted R Square	Std. Error of the Estimate
1	.616[a]	.380	.379	.3361
2	.627[b]	.393	.392	.3326
3	.629[c]	.396	.395	.3318

[a] Predictors: (Constant), WORKHRS HOURS USUALLY WORKED PER WEEK

[b] Predictors: (Constant), WORKHRS HOURS USUALLY WORKED PER WEEK, DSEX

[c] Predictors: (Constant), WORKHRS HOURS USUALLY WORKED PER WEEK, DSEX, AGE AGE

[d] Dependent Variable: LOGEARN

Exhibit 12.14   *Model Summary from regressing the logarithm of usual weekly earnings against age, hours of work and sex*

12.15), negative because women earn less than men. Since the dependent variable is logged, this represents the reduction in *log* earnings that results from being female rather than male. To make this more meaningful, we need to convert back, taking antilogs. The result is that women in 1995 earned just 79 per cent of male earnings, after having taken into account their age and working hours (0.79 is the antilog of -0.104 since $10^{-0.104} \approx 0.79$).

If a categorical variable has more than two categories, it can be entered into a regression model using a set of variables, each of which has just two values. These are called **dummy variables**. For example, we could take into account the effect of educational qualifications by adding a set of dummy variables representing different levels of qualification. Supposing that we considered that four grades of qualification were enough. One dummy variable would be coded 1 for those respondents who had a degree or equivalent qualification, everyone else being coded 0. A second dummy variable would be coded 1 for those with A-level or equivalent qualifications and 0 for everyone else. A third variable would be coded 1 for those with O-level/GCSE qualifications and 0 for everyone else. Respondents with no qualifications would have a zero on all three dummy variables (see Exhibit 12.16). One less dummy variable is needed than there are categories in the original nominal variable.

The regression equation now has six independent variables: hours of work per week, age, sex, and whether qualified to degree, A-level or O-level standard. The regression coefficients for the dummy variables (Exhibit 12.17) are 0.317, 0.177, 9.33E-02 (9.33E-02 is used by SPSS to mean 9.33×10^{-2} or 0.0933) respectively, which when transformed out of logs, means that earnings are increased by a factor of 2.1 if one has a degree, by 1.5 for A levels and by 1.2 for O levels, compared with having no qualifications (and controlling for the other independent variables in the model). The introduction of these education dummy variables makes almost no difference to the coefficient measuring the effect of sex.

Coefficients[a]

Model	Unstandardized Coefficients		Standardized Coefficients		
	B	Std. Error	Beta	*t*	Sig.
1 (Constant)	1.660	.034		49.481	.000
DSEX	−.104	.016	−.122	−6.601	.000
AGE	1.974E-03	.001	.057	3.428	.001
HOURS USUALLY WORK/WEEK	1.626E-02	.001	.566	30.707	.000

[a] Dependent Variable: LOGEARN

Exhibit 12.15   *Coefficients from regressing the logarithm of usual weekly earnings against age, hours of work and sex*

Procedure for developing a multiple regression model

Multiple regression is a technique for developing and testing a model relating one dependent and several independent variables.

When to use multiple regression:

- Multiple regression is appropriate when the dependent variable is continuous and measured at the interval level, and the independent variables are continuous and interval, or are dichotomies. The dependent variable should be approximately normally distributed with constant variance for all fixed values of the independent variables, and the values of the dependent variable should be independent of each other.

What you need for a multiple regression:

- Measurements of the dependent and independent variables for every respondent. To make inferences to a population, the respondents should be a random sample of that population.

The procedure:

- Choose a dependent variable (measured at the interval level) and one or more independent variables. Ensure that all the independent variables which your theory anticipates are important are included.
- If any of the independent variables are not at the interval level, construct dummy variables for them.
- Construct scatterplots for the dependent variable against each of the independent variables separately and check that the relationship between them looks roughly linear (i.e. follows a straight line). If not, consider whether the variables need to be transformed.
- Run the multiple regression (using stepwise selection unless you have a very firm theory about which variables are necessary). Request a normal probability plot and check that the residuals are normally distributed. Request a plot of the residuals against the dependent variable and check that there are no evident patterns in the distribution of the residuals (if there are, consider alternative transformations of the variables, and whether an important variable has been omitted from the analysis).
- Examine the residual plot for the presence of outliers (e.g. points more than 2 standard deviations from the mean). If there are outliers, request a 'casewise' display of them (and associated statistics such as Cook's distance) and try to account for why these cases are outliers.
- Check that all the independent variables in the equation have partial regression coefficients significantly different from 0 (this will always be the case if you used stepwise selection).
- Note the proportion of variance explained (R^2) and the regression coefficients.

Variable:	DEGREE	A LEVEL	O LEVEL
Respondent with a degree	1	0	0
Respondent with one or more A levels, but no degree	0	1	0
Respondent with one or more O levels or GCSE, but no A levels	0	0	1
Respondent with no qualifications	0	0	0

Exhibit 12.16 *Dummy variable coding for four respondents with differing educational qualifications*

Coefficients[a]

	Unstandardized Coefficients		Standardized Coefficients		
Model	B	Std. Error	Beta	t	Sig.
1 (Constant)	1.476	.038		39.083	.000
DSEX	−.104	.015	−.122	−7.030	.000
AGE	4.081E-03	.001	.119	6.838	.000
HOURS USUALLY WORKED/WEEK	1.519E-02	.001	.528	30.368	.000
DEGREE	.317	.019	.329	16.423	.000
ALEVEL	.177	.024	.144	7.478	.000
OLEVEL	9.331E-02	.019	.103	4.903	.000

[a] Dependent Variable: LOGEARN

Exhibit 12.17 *Coefficients from regressing the logarithm of usual weekly earnings against age, hours of work, sex and educational level*

LOGLINEAR ANALYSIS

Multiple regression is best suited for modelling interval-level variables, although categorical-level independent variables can be accommodated with dummy variables. Although regression cannot be used when the dependent variable is categorical, **loglinear analysis** can come to the rescue. This is a technique for modelling relationships between several categorical variables.

Consider the table shown in Exhibit 12.18. This crosstabulates respondents' social class with the social class of their fathers (in both cases, using the Register-General's classification based on occupation and employment status). The data are the same as Exhibit 9.13, although that table shows row percentages and this one shows the counts. As might be expected, there is a clear association between the two variables, with a strong tendency overall for respondents to occupy a social class that is the same as or similar to that of their

Father's class	Respondent's social class						
	I	II	IIIN	IIIM	IV	V	Total
I	28	71	60	17	16	6	198
II	56	267	211	114	111	37	796
IIIN	14	79	92	38	27	16	266
IIIM	36	278	344	356	238	119	1371
IV	10	62	103	113	115	54	457
V	5	16	43	49	46	29	188
Total	149	773	853	687	553	261	3276

Exhibit 12.18   *Social mobility table showing inter-generational mobility from fathers' to respondents' class, from the 1991 General Household Survey*
Source: OPCS, 1993

fathers. This is a pattern to be found in all Western countries to a greater or lesser extent and is known as status persistence or class immobility (see Goldthorpe, 1980, and Marshall, 1988, for extended treatments of social mobility).

The degree of social mobility revealed by these data can be assessed by finding the table that would result if there were perfect social mobility, that is, if the class destination of every respondent were completely unrelated to the social class of their father. Consider respondents whose fathers were managers or professionals in class I. If there were perfect mobility, the chances of them finding themselves in any particular class would be proportional to the number of people overall in each class. For instance, the chance of being in class IIIM would be 687/3276. Under perfect mobility, the number of people expected in the cell for class I fathers and class IIIM respondents would be this proportion multiplied by the number of people with fathers in class I (198). Hence the expected number in cell (I,IIIM) would be

$$\frac{687 \times 198}{3276} = 42$$

This calculation is exactly the same as that used to compute the expected frequencies for a hypothesis of no association (see Chapter 11): each cell of the perfect mobility table is found by multiplying the two corresponding marginal totals and dividing by the table total. Exhibit 12.19 shows the expected cell frequencies for no association between the two variables. This is the table we would expect if there were perfect mobility; the differences between this table and the data represent the extent to which British society is not perfectly mobile.

To check whether the differences between the data and model tables are due to chance, we can use a chi-square test of the null hypothesis of no difference (see Chapter 11). The χ^2 test statistic is equal to 321 with 25 degrees of freedom, yielding a significance level very close to zero. The null hypothesis can be rejected: social mobility was far from perfect in Great Britain in 1991.

Father's			Respondent's social class				
class	I	II	IIIN	IIIM	IV	V	Total
I	9	47	52	42	33	16	198
II	36	188	207	167	134	63	796
IIIN	12	63	69	56	45	21	266
IIIM	62	324	357	288	231	109	1371
IV	21	108	119	96	77	36	457
V	9	44	49	39	32	15	188
Total	149	773	853	687	553	261	3276

Exhibit 12.19   *Expected frequencies (rounded to the nearest whole number) under the hypothesis of no association (perfect mobility), fitted to the mobility table in Exhibit 12.18*

MODELLING MOBILITY

In order to study mobility patterns in greater depth, we can construct a loglinear model for these data which treats the cell counts as the dependent variable, that is, the values to be predicted by the model. The loglinear equation predicts these cell counts from knowledge of the distribution of respondents on each individual variable (that is, from the two marginals), plus a term which represents the association in the table. In fact it is not the cell counts themselves that are predicted, but the logarithm of the counts. The equation is similar to a regression equation in that it is linear, consisting of the summation of a set of predictors. Hence the technique is called loglinear analysis.

Using m_{11} to mean the cell count in row 1 and column 1 (for father's class I and respondent's class I), the loglinear equation can be written:

$$\log m_{11} = \lambda + \lambda_1^F + \lambda_1^C + \lambda_{11}^{FC} \tag{12.6}$$

where the λs (another Greek letter, pronounced 'lambda') are respectively a constant term (the same for all cells), a term representing the effect of the father's class marginal, a term representing the respondent's class marginal and a term representing the association. Similar equations can be written for all the other cells in the table. In each case, the left-hand side (the ms) are the cell counts predicted by the model.

Because the equation includes terms representing the fathers' and the respondents' class marginals and an association term, it will always predict the data table cell counts exactly. However, if we use an equation which omits the association term we will get the set of predicted frequencies that would be obtained if there were no association between the variables (but the same marginal distributions of the two variables as in the data).

This model table is exactly the same table as the table of expected frequencies under the hypothesis of no association (Exhibit 12.19) and of course might have been calculated much more straightforwardly using the formula of cross-multiplying the marginals and dividing by the table total. So far, loglinear modelling may seem to have done nothing but complicate a fairly simple analysis. Nevertheless, there are two advantages to the loglinear approach. First, equation 12.6 represents an explicit model that can be applied to the data. Secondly, precisely the same logic can be applied to tables cross-classifying three, four or even more variables, while the simple method of calculating expected counts applies only to tables of two variables.

Multivariate Models

To see how this works, let us see the effect of introducing 'generation' into the analysis of mobility. While the respondents' social class variable describes their class at the moment of the survey, 1991, the father's social class variable measures the fathers' class when the respondents were aged 16, which may have occurred at varying dates between 1909 and 1991, depending on the age of the respondent. For simplicity, let us divide the sample into two parts: respondents aged 16–39, and those aged 40 and over. For younger respondents (aged below 40), their fathers' social class will be determined by their fathers' occupation sometime during the period 1968–1991. Older respondents (40 and over) will have stated what their father's occupation was on a date sometime before 1967, and possibly as early as 1909. Since the class structure has changed markedly over the century, the relationship between fathers' class and respondents' class among those whose fathers were in employment before 1967 might be quite different from the relationship among those whose fathers were employed after 1967.

   This can be studied through modelling the three-way table of fathers' class by respondents' class by 'generation'. The appropriate loglinear model is similar to Equation 12.6, but with extra parts to recognize the fact that there are now three variables. The full or **saturated** model for the table of the three variables, fathers' class (F), respondents' class (C) and generation (G) is:

$$\log m = \lambda + \lambda^F + \lambda^C + \lambda^G + \lambda^{FC} + \lambda^{FG} + \lambda^{CG} + \lambda^{FCG} \qquad (12.7)$$

The subscripts that indicate particular cells of the table have been omitted here. The terms represent, respectively, a constant for the whole table, the effects of the three marginals, the three associations (one for each pair of variables) and, finally, the interaction between the three variables. The **interaction** term measures the extent to which the association between two variables (say, the association between fathers' class and respondents' class) varies between levels of the third variable (generation).

   To test the hypothesis that the degree of mobility has changed between the generations, we can examine the null hypothesis that there is *no* difference in the association between father's and respondent's class across the generations, that is, that there is no interaction. This null hypothesis can be tested by fitting a reduced model which omits the interaction term, calculating the predicted cell counts and comparing the resulting model table with the data table (note the similarity of the logic here with the previous analysis of the two-variable table of fathers' and respondents' class). The chi-square value is 29.4 with 25 degrees of freedom, giving a significance of 24.6 per cent. This is well above the criterion level of 5 per cent, indicating that we can accept the hypothesis that there is no interaction detectable in the data: mobility chances have not changed significantly between the generations.

MODEL SELECTION

The respondents in Exhibit 12.19 include both men and women, but the two analyses carried out so far have not distinguished between the sexes. It would be reasonable to suppose that patterns of mobility differed between men and women, not only because women's mobility chances are likely to be different from those of men, but also because the marginal distribution of women between the social classes is very different from that for men (note that the GHS data only contains data about fathers' social class, so that an analysis of mobility between mothers and daughters (or sons) is not possible).

We can investigate the effect of gender by including sex as a fourth variable in the analysis. The method is the same as before, except that we now have a four-way cross-classification and there are yet further terms in the loglinear model. Because it is no longer so obvious precisely which hypothesis should be tested (should the model include an association between fathers' class and respondents' sex, for instance?), it would be appropriate to use a method of model selection. SPSS provides backward elimination. It starts with a saturated model, the one with all possible terms included, and gradually deletes terms until the minimal model that fits the data according to a chi-square criterion is found. The result is a model which includes the following relationships:

- the association between fathers' and respondents' social class;
- the association between fathers' social class and generation;
- the interaction between respondents' social class, generation and sex.

The most interesting point about this model is the relationships that are found *not* to be statistically significant and that are therefore not included. In particular, there is no interaction between fathers' class, respondents' class and sex in the model. This suggests that, contrary to what we presumed, once one has controlled for other relationships, there is no significant difference between the inter-generational mobility of men and women. The interaction term that is in the model (between respondents' social class, generation and sex) means that there is a significant change between generations in the distribution of men and women between the social classes.

There is a lot more that one can do with loglinear analysis than there is space here to illustrate, but this example of social mobility has hinted at some of the possibilities for multivariate analyses of cross tabulations. Further details can be found in Gilbert (1993b).

LOGLINEAR MODELLING IN SPSS

This example uses the 1991 GHS data because father' social class was not recorded in 1995. First, AGE is recoded into those between 16 and under 40 and those over 40, into new variable GEN, and SOCLASE recoded so that those in the armed forces (code 7) are excluded from the analysis by recoding to system missing (**SYSMIS**). See Chapter 2 on how to recode in SPSS. The **Crosstabs** procedure is used to print the four-dimensional table of father's class by social class by generation by sex. In Exhibit 12.20, GEN is the first layer (1 of 2) and SEX is entered as the second layer (2 of 2). See whether you can draw any interesting conclusions from inspection of this table (Exhibit 12.21). It is so complicated that discovering any pattern to the counts is very hard.

The loglinear backward selection procedure is used to find the best model to fit this table. Select **Analyze|Loglinear ▶|Model selection** ... to see the dialog box in Exhibit 12.22. FSOCCLSE, GEN, SEX, SOCLASE are selected as

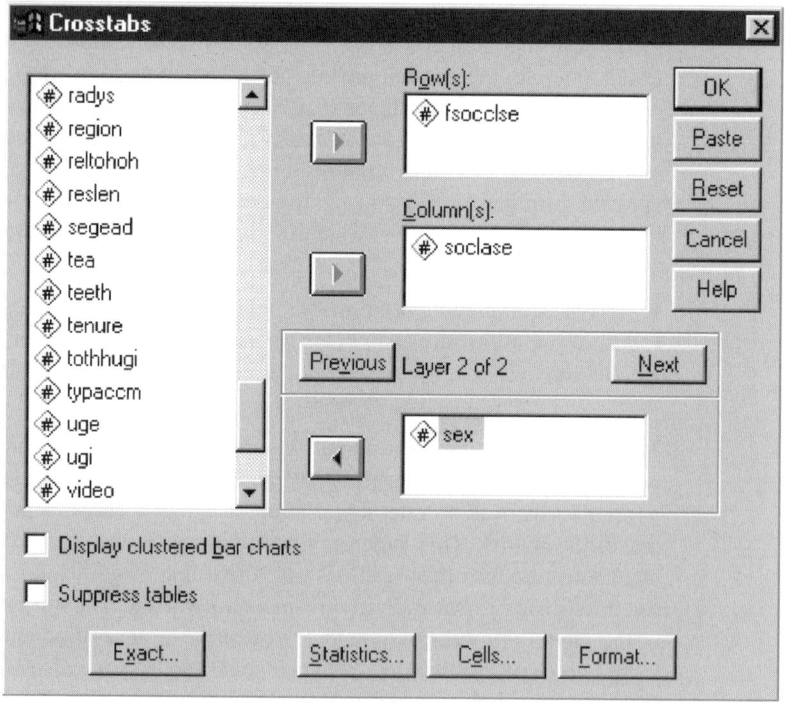

Exhibit 12.20   ***Crosstabs*** *dialog box used to create a four-dimensional table using layers*

FSOCCLSE FATHER'S SOCIAL CLASS * SOCLASE SOCIAL CLASS * GEN * SEX SEX Crosstabulation

Count

SEX	GEN			SOCLASE SOCIAL CLASS						
				CLASS I	CLASS II	CLASS IIIN	CLASS IIIM	CLASS IV	CLASS V	Total
MALE	1.00	FATHER'S SOCIAL CLASS	CLASS I	9	19	12	13	4	3	60
			CLASS II	24	70	41	66	35	14	250
			CLASS IIIN	4	17	11	21	10	6	69
			CLASS IIIM	14	66	44	145	64	29	362
			CLASS IV	5	15	12	45	39	15	131
			CLASS V	2	6	1	22	14	5	50
		Total		58	193	121	312	166	72	922
	1.00	FATHER'S SOCIAL CLASS	CLASS I	13	12	2	2	1	1	31
			CLASS II	22	61	22	35	10	2	152
			CLASS IIIN	8	27	6	11		1	53
			CLASS IIIM	16	90	25	142	33	12	318
			CLASS IV	3	22	9	49	14	9	106
			CLASS V	2	5	4	18	8	6	43
		Total		64	217	68	257	66	31	703
FEMALE	1.00	FATHER'S SOCIAL CLASS	CLASS I	6	21	30	2	10	1	70
			CLASS II	8	80	102	8	42	11	251
			CLASS IIIN	2	14	44	4	13	4	81
			CLASS IIIM	4	65	152	44	86	42	393
			CLASS IV	1	12	41	11	34	9	108
			CLASS V	1	5	23	5	8	9	51
		Total		22	197	392	74	193	76	954
	1.00	FATHER'S SOCIAL CLASS	CLASS I		19	16		1	1	37
			CLASS II	2	56	46	5	24	10	143
			CLASS IIIN		21	31	2	4	5	63
			CLASS IIIM	2	57	123	25	55	36	298
			CLASS IV	1	13	41	8	28	21	112
			CLASS V			15	4	16	9	44
		Total		5	166	272	44	128	82	697

Exhibit 12.21   *Four-dimensional table of father's social class by own social class by generation by sex*
Source: OPCS, 1993

Factor(s): and **Define Range** ... is used to define the ranges of each of these variables as shown.

Output from loglinear modelling is in the form of a long textual report. SPSS first lists the expected cell values and then goes through a model selection procedure. In Exhibit 12.23 we see step 1. A model consisting of four three-way interactions is tested and then each interaction term is removed in turn to examine the effect on the model. While removal of the first three terms does not have a significant effect on the model (the significance levels shown in the **Prob** column are greater than 0.05), removal of GEN*SEX*SOCLASE has a significant effect and is therefore considered necessary.

By step 5 in the output (Exhibit 12.24), the three non-significant terms have been removed and in this final step, one three-way and two two-way terms are

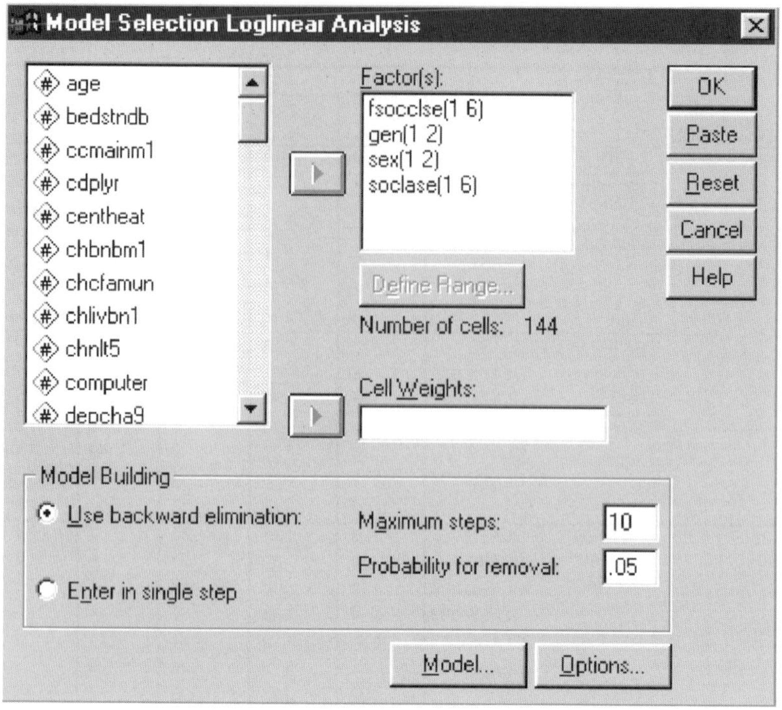

Model Selection Loglinear Analysis   ☒

age
bedstndb
ccmainm1
cdplyr
centheat
chbnbm1
chcfamun
chlivbn1
chnlt5
computer
depcha9

Factor(s):

fsocclse(1 6)
gen(1 2)
sex(1 2)
soclase(1 6)

Define Range...

Number of cells: 144

Cell Weights:

OK

Paste

Reset

Cancel

Help

Model Building

◉ Use backward elimination: Maximum steps: 10

○ Enter in single step   Probability for removal: .05

Model...   Options...

Exhibit 12.22   ***Loglinear Analysis*** *dialog box*

```
Step 1

   The best model has generating class

        FSOCCLSE*GEN*SEX
        FSOCCLSE*GEN*SOCLASE
        FSOCCLSE*SEX*SOCLASE
        GEN*SEX*SOCLASE

   Likelihood ratio chi square = 29.22194   DF = 25   P =   .255

- - - - - - - - - - - - - - - - - - - - - - - - - - - - - - -

If Deleted Simple Effect is          DF      L.R. Chisq
                                             Change        Prob    Iter

FSOCCLSE*GEN*SEX                      5       4.696         .4540 4
FSOCCLSE*GEN*SOCLASE                  25      33.464        .1199 5
FSOCCLSE*SEX*SOCLASE                  25      28.737        .2750 5
GEN*SEX*SOCLASE                       5       41.577        .0000 5
```

Exhibit 12.23   *Extract from loglinear analysis output*

```
Step 5

  The best model has generating class

        GEN*SEX*SOCLASE
        FSOCCLSE*GEN
        FSOCCLSE*SOCLASE

Likelihood ratio chi square = 96.98318      DF = 85  P
=  .176




* * *  H I E R A R C H I C A L    L O G    L I N E A R
* * * *

Step 5
If Deleted Simple Effect is          DF      L.R.
                                             Chisq
                                             Change       Prob    Iter

    GEN*SEX*SOCLASE                   5      38.844      .0000 5
    FSOCCLSE*GEN                      5      38.237      .0000 2
    FSOCCLSE*SOCLASE                 25     330.978      .0000 2

```

Exhibit 12.24   *Loglinear analysis output (continued)*

being tested for removal. Removal of any of these terms affects the model and so none of them can be dropped.

As Exhibit 12.25 shows, the final model is the one described earlier, containing the association between fathers' and respondents' social class; the association between fathers' social class and generation; the interaction between respondents' social class, generation and sex.

```
Step 6

  The best model has generating class

        GEN*SEX*SOCLASE
        FSOCCLSE*GEN
        FSOCCLSE*SOCLASE

Likelihood ratio chi square =  96.98318    DF = 85  P =  .176
```

Exhibit 12.25   *Loglinear analysis (continued)*

OTHER MODELLING TECHNIQUES

The two modelling techniques that we have described, multiple regression and loglinear analysis, are appropriately applied to quite different situations: regression when there is a dependent variable and this variable is measured at the interval level, and loglinear analysis for categorical-level variables. Other techniques have been developed for situations where the data have other characteristics.

One way of distinguishing the various techniques is according to the level of measurement of the dependent variable. As we have seen, multiple regression suits data when all the variables are measured at the interval level. A similar technique, **analysis of variance** (often abbreviated to ANOVA), works best when the dependent variable is interval and there are one or more categorical dependent variables (ANOVA can be easier to use than regression with many dummy variables). If both the dependent variable and the independent variables are categorical, loglinear analysis is the technique of choice. If the dependent variable is categorical, but the independent variables are interval or a mixture of interval and categorical, one should choose **logistic regression**, which is in some ways a hybrid of loglinear analysis and multiple regression.

Another class of modelling techniques is concerned with identifying the structure of relationships between variables. Instead of starting with a model, as we did with the examples of regression and loglinear analysis, these techniques start with the data from which a model is derived. **Factor analysis** is the best known of these techniques. It assumes that there are a small number of 'latent' and unmeasurable variables which cause the measured variation in the observed variables. The task of the analysis is to recover the latent variables (the 'factors') from the variables in the data.

Cluster analysis is a technique with similar aims. It groups variables (or cases, depending on how you choose to do the analysis) into clusters according to their similarity (e.g. the correlations between variables, or the similarity of attributes of cases). **Multidimensional scaling** positions points representing cases in space according to their similarity to each other, with similar cases close together and dissimilar cases far apart.

While there are many more attributes of multivariate techniques that could be used to classify them, the final one we shall mention is the number of dependent variables. Multiple regression models have just one dependent variable. However, it can be extended to solve structural equation models, in which the dependent variable of one equation also features as an independent variable in other equations. There are versions of other techniques that can handle problems where there are several dependent variables, such as **multiple analysis of variance** (MANOVA) and **discriminant analysis**.

Although this may seem like a bewildering number of techniques to choose among and learn about, in fact they are all based on three families of ideas, known as the general linear model (regression, analysis of variance, discriminant analysis and factor analysis), the generalized linear model (loglinear analysis and logistic regression) and similarity models (cluster and multidimensional scaling analysis). You will need to refer to advanced textbooks (see Further Reading) to gain a good understanding of any of these techniques, but the foundations will have been laid in the material in this book and especially in this chapter.

FURTHER READING

Agresti, A. (1996) *An Introduction to Categorical Data Analysis*. New York: Wiley.

Draper, N. and Smith, H. (1981) *Applied Regression Analysis* (2nd edition). New York: Wiley.

Gilbert, N. (1993) *Analyzing Tabular Data*. London: UCL Press.

Hutchinson, G.D. and Sofroniou, N. (1999) *The Multivariate Social Scientist*. London: Sage.

Kim, J. and Mueller, C.W. (1979) *Factor Analysis: Statistical Methods and Practical Issues*. Newbury Park, CA: Sage.

Lindsey, J.K. (1995) *Introductory Statistics: a Modelling Approach*. Oxford: Clarendon Press.

Menard, S. (1995) *Applied Logistic Regression Analysis*. Quantitative Applications in the Social Sciences, 106. Thousand Oaks, CA: Sage.

APPENDIX A
ACCESS TO DATA

All data sets can be accessed via the World Wide Web at the following address:

http://www.soc.surrey.ac.uk/uss/

Main data sets

General Household Survey (GHS) 1995 subset

GHS95.sav: 4633 cases and 70 variables

Variable Name	Position	Label
AGE	37	AGE
ANYBEN92	25	RECEIPT OF ANY BENEFIT BY HOH/PARTNER
BEDSTNDB	14	BEDROOM STANDARD EXC COOKING BEDROOMS
CCMAINM1	44	MAIN CONTRACEPTIVE METHODS
CDPLYER	12	COMPACT DISC PLAYER
CENTHEAT	4	CENTRAL HEATING INSTALLED
CHBNBM1	45	AGE OF MOTHER WHEN HAD 1ST CHILD
CHLIVBN1	46	NO. OF LIVEBORN CHILDREN
CHNLT5	32	WHETHER CHILDREN UNDER 5 IN FAMILY UNIT
COB	40	COUNTRY OF BIRTH
COMPUTER	13	HOME COMPUTER
DISHWASH	9	DISH WASHER
DNTSTWHN	68	WHETHER VISITS DENTIST REGULARLY
DOCTALK	62	CONSULTED DOCTOR IN LAST 2WKS (EXC.HOSP)
DPCHOA8	34	NO. OF OWN DEPENDENT CHILDREN
DRIER	8	TUMBLE DRIER
EARNINGS	70	USUAL GROSS WEEKLY EARNINGS – INDIVIDUAL
ECSTAA	47	ECONOMIC STATUS LAST WEEK
EDLEV	53	HIGHEST EDUCATIONAL QUALIFICATION
EDLEVHH2	15	EDUCATION LEVEL OF HOH
FAMUNIT	30	FAMILY UNIT NO.
FREEZER	6	DEEP OR FRIDGE FREEZER
FUT	31	FAMILY UNIT TYPE
GEIND92	51	GROSS WEEKLY EARNINGS GROUPED – INDIVIDL
GENHLTH	61	HEALTH ON THE WHOLE IN LAST 12 MONTHS
GID92	52	GROSS WEEKLY INCOME GROUPED – INDIVIDUAL
HCNOW	29	IF HHLD CONTAINS CARER
HHTYPF1	16	HOUSEHOLD TYPE F
HOHECSTA	17	ECONOMIC STATUS OF HOH LAST WEEK
HOHFTPTE	18	WHETHER HOH WORKS FULL TIME OR PART TIME

Variable Name	Position	Label
HOHSCLE	19	SOCIAL CLASS OF HOH
HOHSEX	20	HOH SEX
HOHX	21	USUAL GROSS WEEKLY INCOME OF HOH
INPATNT	65	HOSPITAL INPATIENT STAY IN LAST YEAR
JOBTIME	59	TIME IN PRESENT JOB
LONGILL	55	IF LIMIT OR NON-LIMIT LONG-STANDING ILL
MARSTAT	38	MARITAL STATUS
MEDINS	69	COVERED BY PRIVATE MEDICAL INSURANCE
MICROWVE	10	MICROWAVE
NADULTS	2	NO. OF ADULTS IN HOUSEHOLD
NDEPCHLD	23	NO. OF DEPENDENT CHILDREN
NEMPEST	49	NO. OF EMPLOYEES AT AN ESTABLISHMENT
NOCARS	22	NO. OF CARS
NPERSONS	1	TOTAL NO. OF PERSONS IN HOUSEHOLD
NSTAYS	66	NO. OF SEPARATE STAYS AS INPATIENT
NTIMESOP	64	NO. OF OUTPATIENT VISITS IN 3 MONTHS
NTVS	24	NO. OF TELEVISIONS
OCCPEN	50	EMPLOYEE-MEMBER OF EMPLS PENSION SCH
ORIGIN	39	ETHNIC ORIGIN
OUTPATNT	63	HOSPITAL OUTPATIENT ATTENDANCE: LAST 3MT
PERSNO	33	PERSON NO.
PERSPENS	60	WHETHER HAS PERSONAL PENSION SCHEME
PHONE	11	TELEPHONE
RADYS	56	NO. OF DAYS RESTR ACTIVITY IN LAST 2 WKS
REGION	27	REGION
RELTOHOH	35	RELATIONSHIP TO HOH
RESLEN	41	LENGTH OF RESIDENCE
SEGEAD	42	SEG OF ADULTS
SEX	36	SEX
SOCLASE	43	SOCIAL CLASS
TEA	54	TERMINAL AGE OF EDUCATION
TEETH	67	WHETHER HAS OWN TEETH
TENURE	28	TENURE
THHY	26	USUAL GROSS WEEKLY INCOME OF HOUSEHOLD
TYPACCM	3	ACCOMMODATION TYPE
VIDEO	5	VIDEO
WASHMACH	7	WASHING MACHINE
WKSTATE	48	IF WORKS FULL OR PART TIME(& ECON STAT)
WORKHRS	58	HOURS USUALLY WORKED PER WEEK

Note that further information about this data set, including the questionnaire, can be seen in the GHS publication, *Living in Britain* (ONS, 1995).

Subsets taken from the GHS95 file

GHS95_16case.sav: 16 cases and 5 variables

General Household Survey (GHS) 1991 subset

GHS91.sav: 4790 cases and 63 variables

Variable Name	Position	Label
AGE	32	AGE
BEDSTNDB	13	BEDROOM STANDARD EXC COOKING BEDROOMS
CCMAINM1	38	MAIN CONTRACEPTIVE METHODS
CDPLYR	11	COMPACT DISC PLAYER
CENTHEAT	63	WHETHER HAS CENTRAL HEATING IN HOME
CHBNBM1	39	AGE OF MOTHER WHEN HAD 1ST CHILD
CHCFAMUN	29	CHILDCARE USED BY FAMILY UNIT
CHLIVBN1	40	NO. OF LIVEBORN CHILDREN
CHNLT5	27	WHETHER CHILDREN UNDER 5 IN FU
COMPUTER	12	HOME COMPUTER
DEPCHA9	28	NO. OF DEPENDANT CHILDREN IN FAMILY UNIT
DISHWASH	8	DISH WASHER
DNTSTWHN	62	DENTAL CHECK-UP
DOCTALK	60	CONSULTED DOCTOR IN LAST 2WKS (EXC. HOSP)
DRIER	7	TUMBLE DRIER
ECSTAA	41	ECONOMIC STATUS LAST WEEK
EDLEV	42	HIGHEST EDUCATIONAL QUALIFICATION
EDLEVHOH	14	EDUCATIONAL LEVEL OF HOH
EYEHELP	43	IF WEARS GLASSES OR LENSES
FREEZER	5	DEEP OR FRIDGE FREEZER
FSOCCLSE	35	FATHER'S SOCIAL CLASS
GENHLTH	59	HEALTH ON THE WHOLE IN LAST 12 MONTHS
HHTYPF1	15	HOUSEHOLD TYPE F
HOHECSTA	16	ECONOMIC STATUS OF HOH LAST WEEK
HOHSCLE	17	SOCIAL CLASS OF HOH
HOHSEX	18	SEX OF HEAD OF HOUSEHOLD
HOHUGI	19	USUAL GROSS WEEKLY INCOME OF HOH
JOBPENUG	44	USUAL GROSS INCOME FROM PENSIONS
JOBTIME	58	TIME IN PRESENT JOB
LIFECYCL	45	STAGE OF LIFE CYCLE – WOMEN
LONGILL	46	IF LIMIT OR NON-LIMIT LONG-STANDING ILL
MARSTAT	33	MARITAL STATUS
MICROWVE	9	MICROWAVE
NADULTS	2	NO. OF ADULTS IN HOUSEHOLD
NDEPCHLD	21	NO. OF DEPENDENT CHILDREN IN HHLD
NEMPEST	47	NO. OF EMPLOYEES AT AN ESTABLISHMENT
NOCARS	20	NO. OF CARS OWNED
NPERSONS	1	TOTAL NO. OF PERSONS IN HOUSEHOLD
NSTYSY	48	NO. OF INPATIENT STAYS LAST YEAR
NTIMSOP	49	NO. OF OUTPATIENT VISITS IN 3 MONTHS
NTVS	22	NUMBER OF TVS
OCCPEN	50	EMPLOYEE-NUMBER OF EMPLS PENSION SCH
ORIGIN	51	ORIGIN
PHONE	10	TELEPHONE
PPROOMB	23	PERSONS PER ROOM EXC. SMALL KITCHENS
RADYS	52	NO. DAYS RESTRICTED ACTIVITY – LAST 2 WKS
REGION	24	REGION 2
RELTOHOH	30	RELATIONSHIP TO HOH
RESLEN	34	LENGTH OF RESIDENCE

Variable Name	Position	Label
SEGEAD	36	SEG OF ADULTS
SEX	31	SEX
SOCLASE	37	SOCIAL CLASS
TEA	53	TERMINAL AGE OF EDUCATION
TEETH	61	NATURAL TEETH
TENURE	25	TENURE
TOTHHUGI	26	USUAL GROSS WEEKLY INCOME OF HHLD(PENCE)
TYPACCM	3	ACCOMMODATION TYPE
UGE	54	USUAL GROSS WEEKLY EARNINGS
UGI	55	USUAL GROSS WEEKLY INCOME
VIDEO	4	VIDEO
WASHMACH	6	WASHING MACHINE
WKSTATE	56	IF WORKS FULL/PART TIME & ECON STATUS
WORKHRS	57	HOURS USUALLY WORKED PER WEEK

Socioeconomic Indicators of Development (SID)

SID.sav: 171 cases (countries) and 97 variables

Variable Name	Position	Label
AGEDEP	9	Age dependency ratio
AGRIC	63	Share of agriculture in GDP (%)
AGRLAND	40	Agricultural land as per cent of total land area
CALORIE	64	Daily calorie supply per capita
CAR	75	Population per passenger car
CBR	18	Crude birth rate (per thous. population)
CDR	23	Crude death rate (per thous. population)
CHILDRUR	22	Child (0–4) : woman (15–49) ratio, rural
CHILDURB	21	Child (0–4) : woman (15–49) ratio, urban
CONT	2	Continent
CONTRA	20	Contraceptive prevalence (% of females 15–49)
COUNTRY	3	
CTRY	1	Abbreviated country name
DEFOREST	43	Net deforestation rate (annual %)
DENSITY	39	Population density (population per sq km)
DIPTHER	85	Immunized: diphtheria (under 12 months) % age grp
DOCTOR	80	Population per physician
ELECTRUR	73	Households with electricity, rural
ELECTURB	72	Households with electricity, urban
ENERGCON	71	Energy consumption per capita (kg of oil equiv)
ENERGEX	70	Expenditure as % of GDP, energy
EXEDUC	87	Expenditure as % of GDP, education
EXPMED	79	Expenditure as % of GDP, medical care
F15.64RU	33	Females (15–64) per 100 males, rural
F15.64UR	32	Females (15–64) per 100 males, urban
FEMRURAL	12	Females (total) per 100 males, rural
FEMURBAN	11	Females (total) per 100 males, urban
FERT	19	Total fertility rate (births per woman)
FOODAID	61	Food aid, cereals (metric tonnes)
FOODPROD	62	Food production per capita (1979-81=100)

Variable Name	Position	Label
GDPFOOD	57	Expenditure as % of GDP, all foods
GDPPROT	59	Expenditure as % of GDP, proteins
GDPSTAP	58	Expenditure as % of GDP, staples
GNP	47	Gross national product per capita ($US)
GRADE4	95	Pupils reaching grade 4 (% of cohort), total
H2OSAFET	44	Access to safe water (% of total pop)
H2OSAFEU	45	Access to safe water (% of urban pop)
H2PSAFER	46	Access to safe water (% of rural pop)
HLTHCARE	83	Access to health care as % of total population
HOSPBED	82	Population per hospital bed
HOUSE	66	Expenditure as % of GDP, housing
ILLIT	97	Illiteracy rate: overall (% of pop age 15+)
ILLITF	98	Illiteracy rate: female (% of females age 15+)
IMPCER	60	Food imports, cereals (metric tonnes)
INCBOT20	51	Share of household income to bottom 20%
INCBOT40	50	Share of household income to bottom 40%
INCTOP10	48	Share of household income to top 10%
INCTOP20	49	Share of household income to top 20%
INFMOR	24	Infant mortality rate (per thous. live births)
INVHOUSE	69	Fixed investment as % GDP, housing
INVTRANS	76	Fixed investment as % of GDP, transport & equip
LABFORCE	28	Total labor force
LANDAREA	38	Tot land area (sq km – incl. land & inland water)
LFAGR	29	Labor force in agriculture as % of total
LFEDUC	36	Tot labor force, educ attain (sch yrs completd)
LFFEM	31	Female labor force as % of total
LFIND	30	Labor force in industry as % of total
LFMEDUC	37	Male labor force, educ attain (sch yrs completd)
LFPART	34	Labor force participation rate, overall
LFPARTF	35	Labor force participation rate, female
LIFEX	26	Life expectancy at birth, overall (years)
LIFEXF	27	Life expectancy at birth, female (years)
MALNUTR	56	Prevalence of malnutr. (under 5), % of age grp
MEASLES	84	Immunized: measles (under 12 mth) % age grp
NURSE	81	Population per nurse
ORALREHY	86	Oral rehydration therapy use (under 5) % age grp
PAPER	99	Newspaper circulation per 1000 population
PERSONT	67	Persons per household, total
PERSONUR	68	Persons per household, urban
POP14	7	Population age 0–14, as % of total
POP15.64	8	Population age 15–64, as % of total
POP2000	16	Projected population, year 2000
POPAGR	41	Population per sq km of agricultural land
POPGROW	13	Population growth rate
POVINRUR	53	Absolute poverty income ($US per person), rural
POVINURB	52	Absolute poverty income ($US per person), urban
POVRUR	55	Population in absolute poverty (% rural)
POVURB	54	Population in absolute poverty (% urban)
PRIMARYF	89	Gross enroll. ratio, prim., fem (% schl age grp)
PRIMARYT	88	Gross enroll. ratio, prim, tot (% schl age grp)
PRIMTEA	93	Pupil-teacher ratio: primary
PROTEIN	65	Daily protein supply per capita (grams)
REPEAT	96	Repeater rate, primary (% of total enrollment)

Variable Name	Position	Label
ROADS	77	Road length (km)
SCIENG	92	Science & engr students (as % of tot tertiary)
SECONDF	91	Gross enroll. ratio, sec., fem (% schl age grp)
SECONDT	90	Gross enroll. ratio, sec., tot (% schl age grp)
SECONTEA	94	Pupil-teacher ratio: secondary
STATPOP	17	Stationary population
TELEPHON	78	Population per telephone
TOTPOP	6	Total population
TRANSEX	74	Expenditure as % of GDP, transport & commun
U5INFMOR	25	Under 5 mortality rate (per thous. live births)
URBPOP	10	Urban population as % of total
URBPOPDF	15	Urban
URBPOPGR	14	Urban population growth rate
WOODS	42	Forests and woodland area (sq km)

Further information about this dataset can be found in World Bank (1992).

Subsets taken from the SID data set

EU.sav	15 European Union countries and 10 population variables used in Chapter 4.

Other data sets

MARKS.sav	10 cases and 2 variables (sociology marks and psychology marks) used in Chapters 2 and 5.
REGRESS.sav	5 cases and 2 variables (marks gained and study hours) used in Chapter 7.

APPENDIX B: STATISTICAL TABLES

The Normal Distribution

A	B
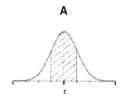	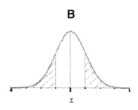

z	Area between the Mean and z Area in Exhibit A	Area beyond z Area in Exhibit B	z	Area between the Mean and z Area in Exhibit A	Area beyond z Area in Exhibit B
0.00	0.0000	0.5000	0.25	0.0987	0.4013
0.01	0.0040	0.4960	0.26	0.1026	0.3974
0.02	0.0080	0.4920	0.27	0.1064	0.3936
0.03	0.0120	0.4880	0.28	0.1103	0.3897
0.04	0.0160	0.4840	0.29	0.1141	0.3859
0.05	0.0199	0.4801	0.30	0.1179	0.3821
0.06	0.0239	0.4761			
0.07	0.0279	0.4721	0.31	0.1217	0.3783
0.08	0.0319	0.4681	0.32	0.1255	0.3745
0.09	0.0359	0.4641	0.33	0.1293	0.3707
0.10	0.0398	0.4602	0.34	0.1331	0.3669
			0.35	0.1368	0.3632
0.11	0.0438	0.4562	0.36	0.1406	0.3594
0.12	0.0478	0.4522	0.37	0.1443	0.3557
0.13	0.0517	0.4483	0.38	0.1480	0.3520
0.14	0.0557	0.4443	0.39	0.1517	0.3483
0.15	0.0596	0.4404	0.40	0.1554	0.3446
0.16	0.0636	0.4364			
0.17	0.0675	0.4325	0.41	0.1591	0.3409
0.18	0.0714	0.4286	0.42	0.1628	0.3372
0.19	0.0753	0.4247	0.43	0.1664	0.3336
0.20	0.0793	0.4207	0.44	0.1700	0.3300
			0.45	0.1736	0.3264
0.21	0.0832	0.4168	0.46	0.1772	0.3228
0.22	0.0871	0.4129	0.47	0.1808	0.3192
0.23	0.0910	0.4090	0.48	0.1844	0.3156
0.24	0.0948	0.4052	0.49	0.1879	0.3121

z	Area between the Mean and z Area in Exhibit A	Area beyond z Area in Exhibit B	z	Area between the Mean and z Area in Exhibit A	Area beyond z Area in Exhibit B
0.50	0.1915	0.3085	0.93	0.3238	0.1762
			0.94	0.3264	0.1736
0.51	0.1950	0.3050	0.95	0.3289	0.1711
0.52	0.1985	0.3015	0.96	0.3315	0.1685
0.53	0.2019	0.2981	0.97	0.3340	0.1660
0.54	0.2054	0.2946	0.98	0.3365	0.1635
0.55	0.2088	0.2912	0.99	0.3389	0.1611
0.56	0.2123	0.2877	1.00	0.3413	0.1587
0.57	0.2157	0.2843			
0.58	0.2190	0.2810	1.01	0.3438	0.1562
0.59	0.2224	0.2776	1.02	0.3461	0.1539
0.60	0.2257	0.2743	1.03	0.3485	0.1515
			1.04	0.3508	0.1492
0.61	0.2291	0.2709	1.05	0.3531	0.1469
0.62	0.2324	0.2676	1.06	0.3554	0.1446
0.63	0.2357	0.2643	1.07	0.3577	0.1423
0.64	0.2389	0.2611	1.08	0.3599	0.1401
0.65	0.2422	0.2578	1.09	0.3621	0.1379
0.66	0.2454	0.2546	1.10	0.3643	0.1357
0.67	0.2486	0.2514			
0.68	0.2517	0.2483	1.11	0.3665	0.1335
0.69	0.2549	0.2451	1.12	0.3686	0.1314
0.70	0.2580	0.2420	1.13	0.3708	0.1292
			1.14	0.3729	0.1271
0.71	0.2611	0.2389	1.15	0.3749	0.1251
0.72	0.2642	0.2358	1.16	0.3770	0.1230
0.73	0.2673	0.2327	1.17	0.3790	0.1210
0.74	0.2704	0.2296	1.18	0.3810	0.1190
0.75	0.2734	0.2266	1.19	0.3830	0.1170
0.76	0.2764	0.2236	1.20	0.3849	0.1151
0.77	0.2794	0.2206			
0.78	0.2823	0.2177	1.21	0.3869	0.1131
0.79	0.2852	0.2148	1.22	0.3888	0.1112
0.80	0.2881	0.2119	1.23	0.3907	0.1093
			1.24	0.3925	0.1075
0.81	0.2910	0.2090	1.25	0.3944	0.1056
0.82	0.2939	0.2061	1.26	0.3962	0.1038
0.83	0.2967	0.2033	1.27	0.3980	0.1020
0.84	0.2995	0.2005	1.28	0.3997	0.1003
0.85	0.3023	0.1977	1.29	0.4015	0.0985
0.86	0.3051	0.1949	1.30	0.4032	0.0968
0.87	0.3078	0.1922			
0.88	0.3106	0.1894	1.31	0.4049	0.0951
0.89	0.3133	0.1867	1.32	0.4066	0.0934
0.90	0.3159	0.1841	1.33	0.4082	0.0918
			1.34	0.4099	0.0901
0.91	0.3186	0.1814	1.35	0.4115	0.0885
0.92	0.3212	0.1788	1.36	0.4131	0.0869

z	Area between the Mean and z	Area beyond z	z	Area between the Mean and z	Area beyond z
	Area in Exhibit A	Area in Exhibit B		Area in Exhibit A	Area in Exhibit B
1.37	0.4147	0.0853	1.81	0.4649	0.0351
1.38	0.4162	0.0838	1.82	0.4656	0.0344
1.39	0.4177	0.0823	1.83	0.4664	0.0336
1.40	0.4192	0.0808	1.84	0.4671	0.0329
			1.85	0.4678	0.0322
1.41	0.4207	0.0793	1.86	0.4686	0.0314
1.42	0.4222	0.0778	1.87	0.4693	0.0307
1.43	0.4236	0.0764	1.88	0.4699	0.0301
1.44	0.4251	0.0749	1.89	0.4706	0.0294
1.45	0.4265	0.0735	1.90	0.4713	0.0287
1.46	0.4279	0.0721			
1.47	0.4292	0.0708	1.91	0.4719	0.0281
1.48	0.4306	0.0694	1.92	0.4726	0.0274
1.49	0.4319	0.0681	1.93	0.4732	0.0268
1.50	0.4332	0.0668	1.94	0.4738	0.0262
			1.95	0.4744	0.0256
1.51	0.4345	0.0655	1.96	0.4750	0.0250
1.52	0.4357	0.0643	1.97	0.4756	0.0244
1.53	0.4370	0.0630	1.98	0.4761	0.0239
1.54	0.4382	0.0618	1.99	0.4767	0.0233
1.55	0.4394	0.0606	2.00	0.4772	0.0228
1.56	0.4406	0.0594			
1.57	0.4418	0.0582	2.01	0.4778	0.0222
1.58	0.4429	0.0571	2.02	0.4783	0.0217
1.59	0.4441	0.0559	2.03	0.4788	0.0212
1.60	0.4452	0.0548	2.04	0.4793	0.0207
			2.05	0.4798	0.0202
1.61	0.4463	0.0537	2.06	0.4803	0.0197
1.62	0.4474	0.0526	2.07	0.4808	0.0192
1.63	0.4484	0.0516	2.08	0.4812	0.0188
1.64	0.4495	0.0505	2.09	0.4817	0.0183
1.65	0.4505	0.0495	2.10	0.4821	0.0179
1.66	0.4515	0.0485			
1.67	0.4525	0.0475	2.11	0.4826	0.0174
1.68	0.4535	0.0465	2.12	0.4830	0.0170
1.69	0.4545	0.0455	2.13	0.4834	0.0166
1.70	0.4554	0.0446	2.14	0.4838	0.0162
			2.15	0.4842	0.0158
1.71	0.4564	0.0436	2.16	0.4846	0.0154
1.72	0.4573	0.0427	2.17	0.4850	0.0150
1.73	0.4582	0.0418	2.18	0.4854	0.0146
1.74	0.4591	0.0409	2.19	0.4857	0.0143
1.75	0.4599	0.0401	2.20	0.4861	0.0139
1.76	0.4608	0.0392			
1.77	0.4616	0.0384	2.21	0.4864	0.0136
1.78	0.4625	0.0375	2.22	0.4868	0.0132
1.79	0.4633	0.0367	2.23	0.4871	0.0129
1.80	0.4641	0.0359	2.24	0.4875	0.0125

z	Area between the Mean and z Area in Exhibit A	Area beyond z Area in Exhibit B	z	Area between the Mean and z Area in Exhibit A	Area beyond z Area in Exhibit B
2.25	0.4878	0.0122	2.69	0.4964	0.0036
2.26	0.4881	0.0119	2.70	0.4965	0.0035
2.27	0.4884	0.0116			
2.28	0.4887	0.0113	2.71	0.4966	0.0034
2.29	0.4890	0.0110	2.72	0.4967	0.0033
2.30	0.4893	0.0107	2.73	0.4968	0.0032
			2.74	0.4969	0.0031
2.31	0.4896	0.0104	2.75	0.4970	0.0030
2.32	0.4898	0.0102	2.76	0.4971	0.0029
2.33	0.4901	0.0099	2.77	0.4972	0.0028
2.34	0.4904	0.0096	2.78	0.4973	0.0027
2.35	0.4906	0.0094	2.79	0.4974	0.0026
2.36	0.4909	0.0091	2.80	0.4974	0.0026
2.37	0.4911	0.0089			
2.38	0.4913	0.0087	2.81	0.4975	0.0025
2.39	0.4916	0.0084	2.82	0.4976	0.0024
2.40	0.4918	0.0082	2.83	0.4977	0.0023
			2.84	0.4977	0.0023
2.41	0.4920	0.0080	2.85	0.4978	0.0022
2.42	0.4922	0.0078	2.86	0.4979	0.0021
2.43	0.4925	0.0075	2.87	0.4979	0.0021
2.44	0.4927	0.0073	2.88	0.4980	0.0020
2.45	0.4929	0.0071	2.89	0.4981	0.0019
2.46	0.4931	0.0069	2.90	0.4981	0.0019
2.47	0.4932	0.0068			
2.48	0.4934	0.0066	2.91	0.4982	0.0018
2.49	0.4936	0.0064	2.92	0.4982	0.0018
2.50	0.4938	0.0062	2.93	0.4983	0.0017
			2.94	0.4984	0.0016
2.51	0.4940	0.0060	2.95	0.4984	0.0016
2.52	0.4941	0.0059	2.96	0.4985	0.0015
2.53	0.4943	0.0057	2.97	0.4985	0.0015
2.54	0.4945	0.0055	2.98	0.4986	0.0014
2.55	0.4946	0.0054	2.99	0.4986	0.0014
2.56	0.4948	0.0052	3.00	0.4987	0.0013
2.57	0.4949	0.0051			
2.58	0.4950	0.0050	3.01	0.4987	0.0013
2.59	0.4952	0.0048	3.02	0.4987	0.0013
2.60	0.4953	0.0047	3.03	0.4988	0.0012
			3.04	0.4988	0.0012
2.61	0.4955	0.0045	3.05	0.4989	0.0011
2.62	0.4956	0.0044	3.06	0.4989	0.0011
2.63	0.4957	0.0043	3.07	0.4989	0.0011
2.64	0.4959	0.0041	3.08	0.4990	0.0010
2.65	0.4960	0.0040	3.09	0.4990	0.0010
2.66	0.4961	0.0039	3.10	0.4990	0.0010
2.67	0.4962	0.0038			
2.68	0.4963	0.0037	3.11	0.4991	0.0009

z	Area between the Mean and z	Area beyond z	z	Area between the Mean and z	Area beyond z
	Area in Exhibit A	Area in Exhibit B		Area in Exhibit A	Area in Exhibit B
3.12	0.4991	0.0009	3.37	0.4996	0.0004
3.13	0.4991	0.0009	3.38	0.4996	0.0004
3.14	0.4992	0.0008	3.39	0.4997	0.0003
3.15	0.4992	0.0008	3.40	0.4997	0.0003
3.16	0.4992	0.0008			
3.17	0.4992	0.0008	3.41	0.4997	0.0003
3.18	0.4993	0.0007	3.42	0.4997	0.0003
3.19	0.4993	0.0007	3.43	0.4997	0.0003
3.20	0.4993	0.0007	3.44	0.4997	0.0003
			3.45	0.4997	0.0003
3.21	0.4993	0.0007	3.46	0.4997	0.0003
3.22	0.4994	0.0006	3.47	0.4997	0.0003
3.23	0.4994	0.0006	3.48	0.4997	0.0003
3.24	0.4994	0.0006	3.49	0.4998	0.0002
3.25	0.4994	0.0006	3.50	0.4998	0.0002
3.26	0.4994	0.0006			
3.27	0.4995	0.0005	3.51	0.4998	0.0002
3.28	0.4995	0.0005	3.52	0.4998	0.0002
3.29	0.4995	0.0005	3.53	0.4998	0.0002
3.30	0.4995	0.0005	3.54	0.4998	0.0002
			3.55	0.4998	0.0002
3.31	0.4995	0.0005	3.56	0.4998	0.0002
3.32	0.4995	0.0005	3.57	0.4998	0.0002
3.33	0.4996	0.0004	3.58	0.4998	0.0002
3.34	0.4996	0.0004	3.59	0.4998	0.0002
3.35	0.4996	0.0004	3.60	0.4998	0.0002
3.36	0.4996	0.0004			

Distribution of Chi Square

						Significance								
DF	0.99	0.98	0.95	0.9	0.8	0.7	0.5	0.3	0.2	0.1	0.05	0.02	0.01	0.001
1	0.000	0.001	0.004	0.016	0.064	0.148	0.455	1.074	1.642	2.706	3.841	5.412	6.635	10.828
2	0.020	0.040	0.103	0.211	0.446	0.713	1.386	2.408	3.219	4.605	5.991	7.824	9.210	13.816
3	0.115	0.185	0.352	0.584	1.005	1.424	2.366	3.665	4.642	6.251	7.815	9.837	11.345	16.266
4	0.297	0.429	0.711	1.064	1.649	2.195	3.357	4.878	5.989	7.779	9.488	11.668	13.277	18.467
5	0.554	0.752	1.145	1.610	2.343	3.000	4.351	6.064	7.289	9.236	11.070	13.388	15.086	20.515
6	0.872	1.134	1.635	2.204	3.070	3.828	5.348	7.231	8.558	10.645	12.592	15.033	16.812	22.458
7	1.239	1.564	2.167	2.833	3.822	4.671	6.346	8.383	9.803	12.017	14.067	16.622	18.475	24.322
8	1.646	2.032	2.733	3.490	4.594	5.527	7.344	9.524	11.030	13.362	15.507	18.168	20.090	26.124
9	2.088	2.532	3.325	4.168	5.380	6.393	8.343	10.656	12.242	14.684	16.919	19.679	21.666	27.877
10	2.558	3.059	3.940	4.865	6.179	7.267	9.342	11.781	13.442	15.987	18.307	21.161	23.209	29.588
11	3.053	3.609	4.575	5.578	6.989	8.148	10.341	12.899	14.631	17.275	19.675	22.618	24.725	31.264
12	3.571	4.178	5.226	6.304	7.807	9.034	11.340	14.011	15.812	18.549	21.026	24.054	26.217	32.909
13	4.107	4.765	5.892	7.042	8.634	9.926	12.340	15.119	16.985	19.812	22.362	25.472	27.688	34.528
14	4.660	5.368	6.571	7.790	9.467	10.821	13.339	16.222	18.151	21.064	23.685	26.873	29.141	36.123
15	5.229	5.985	7.261	8.547	10.307	11.721	14.339	17.322	19.311	22.307	24.996	28.259	30.578	37.697
16	5.812	6.614	7.962	9.312	11.152	12.624	15.338	18.418	20.465	23.542	26.296	29.633	32.000	39.252
17	6.408	7.255	8.672	10.085	12.002	13.531	16.338	19.511	21.615	24.769	27.587	30.995	33.409	40.790
18	7.015	7.906	9.390	10.865	12.857	14.440	17.338	20.601	22.760	25.989	28.869	32.346	34.805	42.312
19	7.633	8.567	10.117	11.651	13.716	15.352	18.338	21.689	23.900	27.204	30.144	33.687	36.191	43.82
20	8.260	9.237	10.851	12.443	14.578	16.266	19.337	22.775	25.038	28.412	31.410	35.020	37.566	45.315
21	8.897	9.915	11.591	13.240	15.445	17.182	20.337	23.858	26.171	29.615	32.671	36.343	38.932	46.797
22	9.542	10.600	12.338	14.041	16.314	18.101	21.337	24.939	27.301	30.813	33.924	37.659	40.289	48.268
23	10.196	11.293	13.091	14.848	17.187	19.021	22.337	26.018	28.429	32.007	35.172	38.968	41.638	49.728
24	10.856	11.992	13.848	15.659	18.062	19.943	23.337	27.096	29.553	33.196	36.415	40.270	42.980	51.179
25	11.524	12.697	14.611	16.473	18.940	20.867	24.337	28.172	30.675	34.382	37.652	41.566	44.314	52.620
26	12.198	13.409	15.379	17.292	19.820	21.792	25.336	29.246	31.795	35.563	38.885	42.856	45.642	54.052
27	12.879	14.125	16.151	18.114	20.703	22.719	26.336	30.319	32.912	36.741	40.113	44.140	46.963	55.476
28	13.565	14.847	16.928	18.939	21.588	23.647	27.336	31.391	34.027	37.916	41.337	45.419	48.278	56.892
29	14.256	15.574	17.708	19.768	22.475	24.577	28.336	32.461	35.139	39.087	42.557	46.693	49.588	58.301
30	14.953	16.306	18.493	20.599	23.364	25.508	29.336	33.530	36.250	40.256	43.773	47.962	50.892	59.703

Distribution of *t*

DF	Level of significance for a one-tailed test						
	0.1	0.05	0.025	0.01	0.005	0.001	0.0005
	Level of significance for a two-tailed test						
	0.2	0.1	0.05	0.02	0.01	0.05	0.001
1	3.078	6.314	12.706	31.821	63.657	318.309	636.619
2	1.886	2.920	4.303	6.965	9.925	22.327	31.599
3	1.638	2.353	3.182	4.541	5.841	10.215	12.924
4	1.533	2.132	2.776	3.747	4.604	7.173	8.610
5	1.476	2.015	2.571	3.365	4.032	5.893	6.869
6	1.440	1.943	2.447	3.143	3.707	5.208	5.959
7	1.415	1.895	2.365	2.998	3.499	4.785	5.408
8	1.397	1.860	2.306	2.896	3.355	4.501	5.041
9	1.383	1.833	2.262	2.821	3.250	4.297	4.781
10	1.372	1.812	2.228	2.764	3.169	4.144	4.587
11	1.363	1.796	2.201	2.718	3.106	4.025	4.437
12	1.356	1.782	2.179	2.681	3.055	3.930	4.318
13	1.350	1.771	2.160	2.650	3.012	3.852	4.221
14	1.345	1.761	2.145	2.624	2.977	3.787	4.140
15	1.341	1.753	2.131	2.602	2.947	3.733	4.073
16	1.337	1.746	2.120	2.583	2.921	3.686	4.015
17	1.333	1.740	2.110	2.567	2.898	3.646	3.965
18	1.330	1.734	2.101	2.552	2.878	3.610	3.922
19	1.328	1.729	2.093	2.539	2.861	3.579	3.883
20	1.325	1.725	2.086	2.528	2.845	3.552	3.850
21	1.323	1.721	2.080	2.518	2.831	3.527	3.819
22	1.321	1.717	2.074	2.508	2.819	3.505	3.792
23	1.319	1.714	2.069	2.500	2.807	3.485	3.768
24	1.318	1.711	2.064	2.492	2.797	3.467	3.745
25	1.316	1.708	2.060	2.485	2.787	3.450	3.725
26	1.315	1.706	2.056	2.479	2.779	3.435	3.707
27	1.314	1.703	2.052	2.473	2.771	3.421	3.690
28	1.313	1.701	2.048	2.467	2.763	3.408	3.674
29	1.311	1.699	2.045	2.462	2.756	3.396	3.659
30	1.310	1.697	2.042	2.457	2.750	3.385	3.646
50	1.299	1.676	2.009	2.403	2.678	3.261	3.496
40	1.303	1.684	2.021	2.423	2.704	3.307	3.551
60	1.296	1.671	2.000	2.390	2.660	3.232	3.460
80	1.292	1.664	1.990	2.374	2.639	3.195	3.416
120	1.289	1.658	1.980	2.358	2.617	3.160	3.373
∞	1.282	1.645	1.960	2.326	2.576	3.091	3.291

Glossary

alphanumeric or string variables (Chapter 2) Alphanumeric variables are variables whose values may be stored as letters, digits or other characters or a combination of them. Alphanumeric variables are also known as string variables and are not available for arithmetic operations in **SPSS**.

antecedent (Chapter 9) An antecedent variable is one that has a causal influence on another variable.

association (Chapter 9) A relationship between two categorical variables. Two variables are associated when the proportion in each category of one variable differs according to the categories of the other.

asymmetric (Chapter 9) A characteristic of a measure of association. A measure is asymmetric when the value it takes depends on which variable is considered to be the **independent** and which the **dependent** variable.

backward elimination (Chapter 12) A procedure for exploratory analysis that successively deletes variables from the **regression equation** until there is a significant reduction in the **variance** explained.

bar chart (Chapter 4) A graphical method appropriate for **nominal** and **ordinal** variables where the proportion in each category of a variable is represented as a vertical or horizontal bar.

bivariate analysis (Chapter 8) Statistical analysis involving two variables.

bivariate relationship (Chapter 1) A statistical relationship between two variables.

boxplot (Chapter 6) An exploratory data analytic method to display the distribution of a single variable, where the box is defined by the **upper** and **lower quartiles** and the 'whiskers' extend to the highest (or lowest) values that are not **outliers**. Sometimes known as a box and whisker plot.

categorical variable (Chapter 1) Both **nominal** and **ordinal** variables are categorical variables whose attributes have simply been categorized. For instance sex is a categorical variable where respondents have been classified or categorized as either male or female.

cell (Chapter 9) The 'box' into which a number (a frequency, proportion or percentage) is put when constructing a table.

census (Chapter 10) A survey of every case in a population.

central limit theorem (Chapter 10) The theorem states that the distribution of the **means** of numerous samples all taken from the same distribution tends to the **normal curve** (the greater the number of samples included, the better the approximation to a normal curve). The theorem holds regardless of the form of the distribution from which the samples are taken.

chi square (Chapter 11) A test statistic used when the data consist of **counts**.

cluster analysis (Chapter 12) A form of analysis that groups variables (or cases) into clusters according to their similarity (the **correlations** between variables, or common patterns of values for cases).

codebook (Chapter 3) A document that lists the dictionary information about all the variables in a data file. This usually includes the original question text, the

SPSS variable names if appropriate, and the **value labels** for each coded response. A codebook may also contain information about **derived variables** and notes given to interviewers or coders when preparing the data file.

coding (Chapter 2) The process by which numbers are ascribed to responses to a survey questionnaire in preparation for computer analysis. For example, to the question 'Are you male or female?', male may be coded with the number 1 and female with the number 2.

coefficient of determination (Chapter 8) See **R square**.

column percentage (Chapter 9) A percentage calculated by finding the count in a cell compared with the total count for the column (the column **marginal** count). For example, if there are 530 unemployed women in a sample including 1192 women in all, the column percentage of unemployed women is $(530/1192)\times 100\%$, or 44%.

concordant (Chapter 9) If there are two cases, A and B, and case A has a higher value on one variable than case B, and case A also has a higher value on another variable than case B, the two cases are concordant for the two variables.

confidence interval (Chapter 10) The range within which it can be inferred that a population **mean** lies with some specified degree of confidence. For example, the 95 per cent confidence interval is the range within which we can be confident that the population mean can be found. It is equal to the sample mean plus or minus 1.96 **standard errors**.

confidence level (Chapter 10) The probability that a population **mean** lies within an interval. For example, at the 95 per cent confidence level, the population mean lies within plus or minus 1.96 **standard errors** of the sample mean (see confidence interval).

confirmatory analysis (Chapter 12) A

statistical analysis that aims to test a pre-specified **hypothesis** or **model**.

contingency table (Chapter 9) A table of two or more variables cross-classified, consisting of **cells** showing the number of cases in each combination of categories from the variables. Also called a cross-tabulation.

continuous variables (Chapter 1) A continuous variable is one which can be measured at any point on a continuous scale. For instance, age may seem to be a **discrete variable** because it is usually measured to the nearest whole year. However, since time is a continuum, age can in principle be measured down to a fraction of a second.

control variable (Chapter 9) A variable that specifies which are the **partial** tables in a tabulation of three variables.

Cook's distance (Chapter 12) A measure of the extent to which an **outlier** has an influence on a regression models' coefficients.

correlation coefficient (Chapter 8) A measure of association for continuous variables obtained by dividing the **covariance** by the product of the **standard deviations** of the two variables. (So for variables X and Y, the product of the standard deviations is s_x times s_y.)

count (Chapter 9) The number of times a case with a particular combination of attributes occurs in a data set. For example, the count of unemployed men within a data set might equal 421.

covariance (Chapter 8) A measure which indicates how the values of two continuous variables vary together, obtained by dividing the sum of the **cross-products** by one less than the number of cases.

Cramér's V (Chapter 9) A measure of **association** appropriate for measuring the strength of a relationship between two variables, one or both of which have more than two categories.

critical region (Chapter 11)   The region of the **sampling distribution** between the **critical value** and positive or negative infinity, depending on how the test is formulated (or between the positive critical value and positive infinity, plus the region between the negative critical value and negative infinity, for a two-tailed test – see Exhibit 11.6).

critical value (Chapter 11)   The value (a number of standard deviations) that defines the boundary of the **critical region**. If the test statistic falls within this region, the **null hypothesis** is assumed to be false.

cross-product (Chapter 8)   Obtained by multiplying the deviations from the **means** of pairs of values of two variables. The cross-products are obtained as a first step in the calculation of the **covariance**.

crosstabulation (Chapter 4)   A table of the joint **frequency distributions** of two **nominal** or **ordinal variables**. Also called a contingency table.

data matrix (Chapter 1)   The name given to the column-by-row organization of numerical responses which results from coding survey questionnaires. The rows correspond to the cases and the columns contain the responses to each variable.

deduction (Chapter 1)   A method of analysis that proceeds by formulating a theory and testing it with data. See **induction** for an alternative approach.

degrees of freedom (Chapter 11)   The number of values free to vary in the calculation of a statistic. For example, if we have a 2×2 table and we know the **marginal** frequencies, we would need to know at least one value in order for the other three values to be completely determined. Such a 2×2 table has one degree of freedom.

dependent variable (Chapter 6)   A dependent variable is a variable whose values are predicted by another variable or variables, the **independent variable**(s).

The dependent variable is usually the subject of primary interest in a study.

derived variable (Chapter 3)   A derived variable is one that has been created out of the responses from the original variables in the data file. Thus one may derive the variable age group from data collected about age.

dichotomous (Chapter 9)   A variable with only two categories, such as male and female, is called dichotomous.

discordant (Chapter 9)   If there are two cases, A and B, and case A has a higher value on one variable than case B, and case A has a lower value on another variable than case B, the two cases are discordant for the two variables. They are also discordant if case A has a lower value on one variable while case B has a higher value on the other.

discrete variable (Chapter 1)   A discrete variable is one which can only be counted in whole numbers. For instance, number of people in a family; number of cars in a household. For comparison, see **continuous variable**.

dummy variables (Chapter 12)   A **dichotomous** variable used in a **regression equation**. **Categorical** variables with more than two categories need to be converted into a set of equivalent dummy variables (with one less dummy variable than there are categories) in order to include them in the regression model.

elaboration (Chapter 9)   A method for exploring and testing ideas about causal relationships between three or more variables It involves examining tables of two variables, **controlling** for a third.

expected counts (Chapter 9)   For a table of two variables, the **count** which would be obtained if there were no **association** between the two variables.

explanation (Chapter 1)   An **independent** variable explains a **dependent** variable if knowledge of the value of the independent variable provides good predictions of the value of the dependent variable for all cases.

exploratory analysis (Chapter 12)   A statistical analysis that aims to discover theoretically interesting hypotheses or models describing the data.

factor analysis (Chapter 12)   A form of statistical analysis that is built on the assumption that the data were generated by some small number of unmeasured latent variables that in combination created the measured variables. The analysis re-creates the latent variables as 'factors'.

falsification (Chapter 11)   The idea that while it is impossible to prove that a hypothesis is true, it is possible to show that a hypothesis is false (since only one piece of evidence that is counter to the hypothesis is sufficient to show that it is false). Acceptance of a theory only means that we have not yet disproved it.

fitted values (Chapter 8)   Fitted or expected values are obtained by substituting values for the independent variables into a regression equation. For example, if the regression equation is $Y = 1 + 3X$, substituting a value of 2 for X will give a fitted value for Y of 7 (i.e. $1 + 3 \times 2$). Denoted as $\hat{y}$, pronounced 'y hat'.

forward selection (Chapter 12)   A procedure for exploratory analysis that successively adds more variables to the regression equation until there is no further significant improvement in the **variance** explained.

frequency distribution (Chapter 3)   A frequency distribution is a table of frequencies of occurrence of each value of a variable. In **SPSS** 9.0 a frequency distribution is obtained by selecting **Analyze| Descriptive statistics ▶|Frequencies** ... and usually includes a percentage calculation for each value.

frequency polygon (Chapter 4)   The graphical representation of the distribution of an interval or ratio variable where the upper class limit of each interval is represented by a marker which is then joined by a line to the next upper class limit marker.

gamma (Chapter 9)   A measure of **association** appropriate to variables where one or both are measured at the **ordinal** level of measurement.

Goodman and Kruskal's tau (Chapter 9)   An **asymmetric** measure of **association** between two variables appropriate when one variable is considered to be the cause and the other the effect.

grouped data (Chapter 5)   Data which have been **recoded** or grouped into fewer categories than when originally collected. For instance, age, measured on an **interval** scale, could be grouped into age groups in order to create a histogram.

histogram (Chapter 4)   The graphical representation of the distribution of an interval or ratio variable where the frequency of occurrence of each interval is represented by the height of a bar and the width of the bar is proportional to the real class interval.

independent variable (Chapter 6)   An independent variable is one that predicts the values of another variable, the **dependent** variable. Sometimes called a predictor variable.

indicator (Chapter 1)   A method intended to measure a concept. For instance, a common indicator of the concept of social class is a person's occupation. Since class is not something we can measure directly, an indicator has to be used. See **reliability** and **validity**.

induction (Chapter 1)   A method of analysis that derives theories by generalizing from evidence, usually from a large number of cases. See **deduction** for an alternative approach.

inner fence (Chapter 6)   In a **boxplot**, the inner fences are the boundaries of the main body of the data beyond which lie the **outliers**. It is positioned at 1.5 times the **IQR** above or below the **upper** and **lower quartiles** respectively.

interquartile range (Chapter 5) The value of the **upper quartile** minus the value of the **lower quartile**. Denoted by IQR.

interaction (Chapter 9) See **specification**.

interval variable (Chapter 1) An interval variable is one in which categories may be ranked or ordered and the distance between the categories is precisely defined, e.g. salary, age. See **level of measurement**.

intervening (Chapter 9) A variable is intervening if another variable has an effect on it and it in turn affects a third variable.

kurtosis (Chapter 5) A property of a distribution which reflects the 'peakedness' of the plotted curve. A tall, peaked distribution is called leptokurtic while a flat, plateau-like shaped distribution is called platykurtic. A symmetrical curve is called mesokurtic.

level of significance (Chapter 11) The probability that the research outcome could have happened by chance.

level of measurement (Chapter 1) The name given to the classification scheme which distinguishes the relationships between the categories or attributes of a variable. See **nominal, ordinal, interval** and **ratio variables**.

leverage (Chapter 12) A measure of the extent to which an **outlier** is both distant from the **regression line** and has a large value on an **independent** variable.

logistic regression (Chapter 12) A type of **regression** used when the dependent variable is **categorical**.

longitudinal data (Chapter 9) Data collected from the same people over a period of time.

lower quartile (Chapter 5) The cate-gory or value which defines the upper boundary of the bottom 25 per cent of cases when they are arranged in rank order. Denoted by Q_1.

marginal (Chapter 9) The sum of the **counts** for a particular category of a variable. These sums are often placed in the right-most column or bottom row of a table and are therefore in the margins of the table.

mean (Chapter 5) A **measure of central tendency** appropriate for interval and ratio variables. It is the arithmetic average of the values of a distribution, and is denoted by $\bar{x}$ (sample mean) or μ (population mean). It is required along with the **standard deviation** or **variance** to summarize the distribution of a variable.

measure of central tendency (Chapter 5) A statistic which describes the value of a random variable which is the 'most probable' in some sense. See **mean, median** and **mode**.

measure of association (Chapter 8) A statistic which measures the degree of association or relationship between two variables. Examples include **phi** for **nominal** variables and the **correlation coefficient** for **interval** variables.

measures of dispersion (Chapter 5) Statistics that describe the spread of a distribution or how the values of a distribution are scattered around the mean. The simplest is the **range**, but see also **variance** and **standard deviation**.

median (Chapter 5) A **measure of central tendency,** most appropriate for **ordinal** variables. It is the category or value that occurs in the middle of a ranked distribution. Also known as the 50th **percentile**.

missing value (Chapter 3) Values are declared as missing when the researcher wishes to exclude them from statistical analysis. For instance, some respondents may have refused to answer a question about their age. Every response must be given a code, so you may decide to code this 'no response' with the number 999. However, you would want to ensure that this code is not treated as a valid age response. If it was, the average age for the sample would be incorrect.

mode (Chapter 5)   A **measure of central tendency**, most appropriate for nominal variables. It is the value or label of the most frequently occurring category.

model (Chapter 12)   A theory that proposes relationships between two or more variables.

multidimensional scaling (Chapter 12) A form of analysis that positions points (representing variables and cases) according to their similarity, with the most similar being nearest to each other.

multivariate analysis (Chapter 8)   Statistical analysis involving three or more variables.

multiple regression analysis (Chapter 8)   Statistical methods concerned with explaining or predicting the variability of a **continuous dependent** variable using information from two or more continuous **independent** variables.

nominal variable (Chapter 1)   The categories of a nominal variable bear no relationship to one another, other than that they are different. For example, marital status is a nominal variable with the categories, married, single, divorced etc. Nominal variables are measured at the lowest **level of measurement.**

normal distribution (Chapter 7)   A theoretical, continuous probability distribution where the horizontal axis plots all possible values of the variable and the vertical axis is the frequency of occurrence of each value.

normal curve (Chapter 7)   A symmetric, bell-shaped curve describing a **normal distribution**.

null hypothesis (Chapter 11)   The con-

verse of a **working hypothesis**: if the null hypothesis is found to be false, this can be taken as indirect support for the working hypothesis.

observed counts (Chapter 11)   The **counts** obtained from the data.

one-sample test (Chapter 11)   A test comparing a sample statistic with a **population** parameter.

one-tailed test (Chapter 11)   An inferential test in which the null hypothesis will be rejected if the **test statistic** lies in the **critical region**.

ordinal variable (Chapter 1)   The categories of an ordinal variable can be ordered or ranked but the distance between the categories is unknown. For instance, educational level is an ordinal variable ranging from none through higher. How close one category is to another is unknown. See **nominal** and **interval levels of measurement.**

ordinary least squares (Chapter 8)   The statistical procedure used in **regression** analysis to arrive at the 'best-fitting' regression line. It is a mathematical method that ensures that the squares of the deviations from the **regression line** are minimized.

outer fences (Chapter 6)   In a **boxplot**, the outer fences define the boundary beyond which lie the extreme **outliers** at 3.0 times the **IQR** above and below the **upper** and **lower quartiles.**

outlier (Chapter 6)   A case with an extremely high or extremely low value compared with the rest of a distribution. An outlier has a value more than 1.5 times the **IQR** above the **upper quartile** or 1.5 times the IQR below the **lower quartile**.

partial correlation coefficient (Chapter 12)   The **correlation coefficient** between two variables when other variables have been controlled.

partial regression coefficient (Chapter 12)   A **regression coefficient** describing the relationship between a **dependent** and an **independent** variable obtained when **controlling** for one or more other independent variables.

partial table (Chapter 9) A table that displays counts for part of a data set, for example, just for the men.

percentile (Chapter 5) The Nth percentile is the category or value which defines the upper boundary of the bottom N per cent of cases when they are arranged in rank order. The 25th percentile is called the **lower quartile**, the 50th percentile is the **median**, and the 75th percentile is the **upper quartile**.

phi (Chapter 9) A measure of **association** appropriate for measuring the strength of a relationship between two **dichotomous** variables.

pie chart (Chapter 4) A graphical method appropriate for nominal and ordinal variables where the proportion in each category of a variable is represented as a segment of a circle.

pooled variance t test (Chapter 11) A t test for two samples that uses the variance estimated from all the cases in both samples. A pooled variance t test is appropriate when both samples are drawn from the same **population**.

population (Chapter 11) The set of all those to whom the **research hypothesis** is assumed to apply (a synonym for **universe**).

pre-coded (Chapter 1) A question in a survey questionnaire is pre-coded when a number has been assigned to every possible response in advance of the survey. See **coding**.

prediction (Chapter 1) On discovering an **association** or relationship between two or more variables in a **sample**, a prediction may be made about how other cases in the population, that were not measured, may behave under the same conditions.

primary analysis (Chapter 1) Analysis of data collected by the researcher. See **secondary analysis**.

proportional reduction in error (Chapter 9) The increased accuracy (i.e. reduction in error) in predicting the characteristics of a sample on one variable that one obtains if the values of a second variable are known, compared with not knowing the second variable. For example, three-quarters of all those in work, work full-time (see Exhibit 9.11). Knowing only this, one can predict that there is a 3 in 4 chance that any person in the sample is a full-timer. The chances of error in the predication are reduced if one also knows that a person is female, because we know that, for women, 55 per cent are in full-time work. The proportional reduction of error is related to the **association** between the two variables.

pseudo-random number (Chapter 10) A number generated from a complex formula designed for the purpose, usually by computer, which has the properties of a random number.

quartiles (Chapter 5) The categories or values of a ranked distribution which divide it into four equal parts each containing 25 per cent of the cases. See **lower** and **upper quartiles**.

R square (Chapter 8) A measure that describes how well a regression line fits the scatter of data points. It describes the proportion of **variance** of the **dependent variable** that is 'explained' by the **independent variable**. In **simple regression**, it is the square of the **correlation coefficient**, r. Also known as the **coefficient of determination**.

random number seed (Chapter 10) The starting value for a generator of **pseudo-random numbers**. The stream of pseudo-random numbers from the generator is always the same for the same starting seed.

random sample (Chapter 10) A **sample**

in which the cases are selected from the **population** at random and in which every case has a chance of being selected.

range (Chapter 5)   The difference between the lowest and highest values of a distribution.

ratio variable (Chapter 1)   A ratio variable is one that can be measured on an **interval** scale and also has a meaningful zero. For instance, income is a ratio variable because it is possible to have a zero income. See **level of measurement.**

real class intervals (Chapter 3)   When grouping data into more convenient categories, it is usual to declare real class intervals that are one level of precision greater than the original data. This ensures that every possible value can be accounted for in the new coding scheme. For example, if age data have been collected to the nearest whole year, the real class intervals would be reported to one decimal place. For example, the stated interval of 10 to 19 years would be expressed as a real class interval of 9.5 to 19.5.

real class limits (Chapter 3)   Real class limits are the upper and lower values that contain a real class interval.

recoding (Chapter 2)   Recoding in **SPSS** is the procedure used to change or regroup the numeric codes of a variable. For example, if age is coded using respondents' ages in years and you wish to group individuals into those above and below the age of 40, you could recode age so that codes from 0 through 40 are changed to code 1 and all other codes are changed to code 2.

regression equation (Chapter 8)   An equation that describes the relationship between a **dependent variable** (Y) and one or more **independent variables** (X). In its simplest form, it is written $Y = a + bX$, where a and b are the **regression coefficients**.

regression line (Chapter 8)   The regres-

sion line is a graphical representation of the **regression equation**. It summarizes the relationship between a **continuous dependent variable** and one **independent variable** using the **ordinary least squares** criterion to obtain the best-fitting line. The regression line may be obtained by substituting two values of X into the regression equation, thus obtaining two pairs of X, Y coordinates.

regression coefficient (Chapter 8)   Part of the **regression equation** which describes the extent of the relationship between the **dependent** and an **independent** variable. In the regression equation $Y = a + bX$, a, the constant, is the intercept on the Y axis and b is a measure of the slope. The **standardized** b coefficient is called the beta coefficient.

regression plane (Chapter 12)   The analogue of a regression line when there are two **independent** variables. The plane plots in three-dimensional space the expected values of the **dependent** variable for all values of the two independent variables.

reliability (Chapter 1)   Reliability is concerned with whether the **indicator** we use to measure a concept gives the same answer each time it is used. See **validity**.

representative sample (Chapter 10)   A **sample** in which cases are included in proportion to the number in the **population** that resemble them.

research hypothesis (Chapter 11)   A proposition to be investigated that can be assessed as either true or false, expressed in terms of theoretical concepts.

residual (Chapter 8)   In regression, residuals are obtained by subtracting the **fitted values** from the data values. The residuals are also called deviations from the fitted values.

resistant measure (Chapter 5)   A statistic that is less likely to be affected by a few extreme high or low values (outliers) in a distribution. The **median** is a resistant measure which is not affected by extreme values. The **mean** is not a resistant measure.

rounding (Chapter 3)   A method of simplifying numbers to fewer significant figures. There are several ways to round numbers but the most common is as follows. When rounding a number to N decimal places, look at the $(N + 1)$th decimal place. If it is between 1 and 4 then round down, and if it is between 5 and 9 then round up. For example, 41.4 rounds down to 41 and 41.5 rounds up to 42.

row percentages (Chapter 9)   A percentage calculated by finding the count in a cell compared with the total count for the row (the row **marginal** count). For example, if there are 530 unemployed women in a sample including 648 unemployed people in all, the row percentage of unemployed women is 530/648%, or 82%.

sample (Chapter 1)   A set of people selected from a **population**, usually with a random method that ensures that everyone has an equal chance of selection.

sample distribution (Chapter 10)   The frequency distribution of an empirical sample. Not to be confused with **sampling distributions.**

sampling distribution (Chapter 10)   A theoretical frequency distribution of any statistic calculated for a sample. For example, the sampling distribution of the mean could be generated by collecting an infinite number of similar size samples and calculating the means for each. These means would then form a distribution which could be plotted and would form a **normal curve**. Sampling distributions are the basis of inferential statistics.

sampling error (Chapter 10)   The difference between an estimate derived from a **sample** and the true value measured in the **population**.

saturated (Chapter 12)   A model that includes all possible effects.

secondary analysis (Chapter 1)   Reanalysis of data collected by another researcher or organization that may originally have been collected for other purposes. See **primary analysis.**

separate variance t test (Chapter 11)   A t test for two **samples** that uses the **variance** estimated from the cases in each sample separately. A separate variance t test is appropriate when the samples are drawn from the different **populations**.

simple regression analysis (Chapter 8)   Statistical methods concerned with explaining or predicting the variability of a **continuous dependent** variable using information from one continuous **independent** variable.

skewed distribution (Chapter 5)   A distribution which has either predominately low values and a few extreme high values (positively skewed) or one where there are predominately high values and a few extreme low values (negatively skewed). When plotted, such a distribution produces a non-symmetric curve where the **mean, mode** and **median** do not coincide.

specification (Chapter 9)   If the strength of the **association** between two variables differs according the level of a third variable, the third variable specifies the relationship. Also called interaction.

SPSS (Chapter 2)   A computer program used for the management and analysis of social science data.

spurious (Chapter 9)   A relationship between two variables is spurious if it disappears when a third variable is controlled.

standard deviation (Chapter 5)   The square root of the **variance**. Denoted by s or SD.

standard deviation (SD) line (Chapter 8)   The line obtained by plotting the **means** and **standard deviations** of two **continuous** variables.

standard error of the mean (Chapter

10) The **standard deviation** of the distribution of sample means.

standard error of the difference (Chapter 11) The standard error of a test statistic obtained from comparing two samples.

Standard normal curve (Chapter 7) A **normal curve** after standardization to z **scores**.

standardization (Chapter 7) The procedure to create standard scores (z **scores**) in order to compare variables measured in different units.

stem and leaf diagram (Chapter 6) An exploratory data analytic method to show the distribution of a **continuous** variable.

stepwise selection (Chapter 12) A procedure for exploratory analysis that alternates between using **forward selection** and **backward elimination** in order to find the most satisfactory set of variables to use in a regression equation.

stub (Chapter 9) The left-hand column of a table, in which the labels describing each row are placed.

subsample (Chapter 2) A subsample is a selection of cases from a **sample**. For example, if you remove all the males from a sample of both males and females, you are left with a subsample of females.

test statistic (Chapter 11) The statistic used to test a **null hypothesis**. The test statistic must be one whose distribution is known; common test statistics are the z score, the t statistic, chi square and the F statistic.

transformation (Chapter 7) A mathematical procedure employed to change the scale of a variable from one set of values into another set of values, without changing their relative order. This procedure is often employed in order to produce a more linear relationship between two continuous variables. Examples include transforming proportions into percentages by multiplying each value by

100 and, in regression analysis, transforming raw scores into logarithmic scores.

two-sample test (Chapter 11) A test comparing two statistics derived from the characteristics of different samples.

two-tailed test (Chapter 11) An inferential test in which the **null hypothesis** will be rejected if it falls into either the **critical region** above the mean value, or the critical region below the mean value (see Exhibit 11.6).

type I error (Chapter 11) The probability that a **null hypothesis** will be rejected although it is actually true.

type II error (Chapter 11) The probability that a **null hypothesis** will be accepted although it is in fact false.

unexplained variance (Chapter 8) In **regression**, unexplained **variance** is the variance after the variance 'explained' by the regression is subtracted from the total variance of the dependent variable. Often called the variance of the **residuals**.

univariate statistics (Chapter 3) Univariate statistics are statistics that describe the characteristics of a single variable.

universe (Chapter 11) The set of all those to whom the **research hypothesis** is assumed to apply (a synonym for **population**).

upper quartile (Chapter 5) The category or value which defines the lower boundary of the top 25 per cent of cases when they are arranged in rank order. Denoted by Q_3.

validity (Chapter 1) Validity concerns how well an indicator measures the concept it is designed to measure. For instance, if we wanted to measure height and all we had was a set of bathroom scales, we would not have a valid indicator since the scales measure weight. However, the scales are a very reliable measure since we get the same weight each time. However, if we used an elastic tape measure to measure height, we may get a different height each time we use it – it is very unreliable but it *is* a valid indicator since it does measure height. See **reliability**.

value label (Chapter 2)   Value labels in **SPSS** are an optional way of explaining the numeric codes ascribed to each response of a variable. For example, code 1, indicating those respondents who are married, may be given the value label 'married'.

variable name (Chapter 2)   Required by **SPSS** to identify each variable. Variable names may be up to 8 characters long and must be unique in any one data file. For example, marital status may be given the variable name MARSTAT.

variable label (Chapter 2)   A label that may be created in **SPSS** to describe each variable. Variable labels, with a limit of 255 characters, allow you to expand on the 8-character variable name. The variable label for the variable MARSTAT could be 'Respondent's marital status'.

variable-centred (Chapter 1)   A type of data analysis concerned with exploring relationships between variables, rather than exploring relationships between cases.

variance (Chapter 5)   A measure of dispersion which is calculated from the average of the sum of the squared difference of each value from the mean value. It is required along with the **mean** to summarize the distribution of a variable. A distribution with a low variance has most values clustered around the **mean**; a distribution with a high variance has a wide spread of values around the mean. Denoted by s^2 (sample variance) or σ^2 (population variance).

working hypothesis (Chapter 11)   A reformulation of a **research hypothesis** in terms of indicators rather than concepts.

X **variable** (Chapter 8)   An **independent variable** in a regression analysis.

Y **variable** (Chapter 8)   The **dependent variable** in a regression analysis.

z **score** (Chapter 7)   Standardization of a value by subtracting the variable's **mean** from the value and dividing by the variable's **standard deviation**. A distribution of z scores always has a mean of 0 and a standard deviation of 1.

REFERENCES

Abell, P. (1987) *The Syntax of Social Life: The Theory and Method of Comparative Narratives*. Oxford: Clarendon.

Arber, S. and Gilbert, N. (1992) 'Re-assessing women's working lives', in S. Arber and N. Gilbert (eds), *Women and Working Lives: Divisions and Change*. London: Macmillan, pp. 1–16.

Bowling A. (1991) *Measuring Health: A Review of Quality of Life Measurement Scales* (2nd edition). Milton Keynes: Open University Press.

Burgess, R. (1984) *In the Field: An Introduction to Field Research*. London: Routledge.

Charles, N. (1993) *Gender Divisions and Social Change*. Hemel Hempstead: Harvester Wheatsheaf.

CTI (1997) *SocInfo Software Catalogue*, Edition 4. Stirling: CTI Centre for Sociology, Politics and Social Policy, University of Stirling.

De Vaus, D.A. (1996) *Surveys in Social Research*. London: UCL Press.

Fielding, N. and Lee, R. (1993) *Using Computers in Qualitative Research*. London: Sage.

Fisher, R.A. and Yates, F. (1974) *Statistical Tables for Biological, Agriculture and Medical Research* (6th edition). London: Longman.

Gilbert, N. (ed.) (1993a) *Researching Social Life*. London: Sage.

Gilbert, N. (1993b) *Analyzing Tabular Data*. London: UCL Press.

Gilbert, N. and Troitzsch, K.G. (1999) *Simulation for the Social Scientist*. Milton Keynes: Open University Press.

Goldthorpe, J.H. (1980) *Social Mobility and Class Structure*. Oxford: Clarendon Press.

Kish, L. (1965) *Survey Sampling*. New York: Wiley.

Knight, I. (1984) *The Height and Weight of Adults in Great Britain*. London: HMSO.

Marsh, C. (1988) *Exploring Data*. Cambridge: Polity Press.

Marshall, G., Rose, D., Newby, H. and Vogler, C. (1988) *Social Class in Modern Britain*. London: Unwin Hyman.

Mason, J. (1996) *Qualitative Researching*. London: Sage.

Moser, C.A. and Kalton, G. (1971) *Survey Methods in Social Investigation* (2nd edition). London: Heinemann.

Office for National Statistics (1995) *Living in Britain: Results from the 1995 General Household Survey*. London: The Stationery Office.

Office of Population Censuses and Surveys (1993) *General Household Survey, 1991*. London: HMSO.

Parsons, T. and Bales, R.F. (1956) *Family, Socialisation and Interaction Process*. London: Routledge.

Robson, C. (1993) *Real World Research*. Oxford: Blackwell.

Skidmore, W. (1979) *Theoretical Thinking in Sociology* (2nd edition). Cambridge: Cambridge University Press.

Social and Community Planning Research (1993) *British Social Attitudes Survey, 1993*. London: SCPR.

SPSS (1998) *SPSS Base 8.0 User's Guide*. Chicago: SPSS Inc.

Twigger, C. (1995) Report on Community Surveys for the Policy Instruments for Environmental Regulation project. Unpublished report to the European Commission, Department of Sociology, University of Surrey.

World Bank (1992) *Social Indicators of Development 1991–2*. Baltimore, MD: Johns Hopkins University Press.

Index